North Carolina During the Great Depression

# North Carolina During the Great Depression

*A Documentary Portrait of a Decade*

COMPILED BY ANITA PRICE DAVIS

McFarland & Company, Inc., Publishers
*Jefferson, North Carolina, and London*

Library of Congress Cataloguing-in-Publication Data

North Carolina during the Great Depression : a documentary
portrait of a decade / compiled by Anita Price Davis.
p.    cm.
Includes bibliographical references and index.

ISBN-13: 978-0-7864-1315-7
(softcover : 50# alkaline paper) ∞

1. North Carolina — History — 20th century.   2. North Carolina —
History — 20th century — Pictorial works.   3. Depressions — 1929 —
North Carolina.   4. New Deal, 1933–1939 — North Carolina.
5. North Carolina — Biography.   6. Interviews — North Carolina.
I. Davis, Anita Price.
F259.N883   2003       975.67'042 — dc21       2002152270

British Library cataloguing data are available

©2003 Anita Price Davis. All rights reserved

*No part of this book may be reproduced or transmitted in any form
or by any means, electronic or mechanical, including photocopying
or recording, or by any information storage and retrieval system,
without permission in writing from the publisher.*

*Cover Photograph: The Titus Oakley family stripping, tying, and
grading tobacco in their bedroom in Granville County, November 1939.
Photograph by Marion Post Wolcott, Farm Security Administration.*

Manufactured in the United States of America

*McFarland & Company, Inc., Publishers
Box 611, Jefferson, North Carolina 28640
www.mcfarlandpub.com*

*My mother, Mrs. Nell Burns*

*North Carolina During the Great Depression* is dedicated with love and gratitude to my mother, Nell Burns (1923–1998), who gave me her love, a desire to learn, and an appreciation for those who survived the Great Depression. Like many others of the time, she met the 1930s with hard work, satisfaction in a job well-done, and dignity. When World War II came, she sacrificed a husband (my father) to German battlefields. A single mother at 21, she demonstrated pride, a will to live, a radiant beauty, and an inner strength.

# *Acknowledgments*

Financial help from the Archie K. Davis Fellowship from the University of North Carolina enabled me to do the research for this book. Dr. H. G. Jones, Chapel Hill, encouraged and advised. Financial help to secure the federal photographs and validation for the project itself came from the Converse College Administration and from the Faculty Research and Development Fund.

Carolyn Barbee, Mack Jolly, and Lisa Gosnell supplied photographs and information. Reba Hamrick, Jessie Gibbs, Donnis Curtis, Norma and Kenneth Kelley, Carolyn Wellmon, Mae Blanton, Virginia Rucker, John Brooks, T. W. Martin, T. W. Jones, Ed Price, Falls Price, Lucille Carpenter, Martha Freeman, Dan and Annette Martin, Jo Ann Martin, Susan McGee, Rev. Wayne Blackwood, Dorothy Greene, Helen Collins, Nancy Skelton, Thomas Parramore, Sarah Jones, and Tracy Davis supplied help and confidence. Jimmy Walker provided images, enthusiasm, facts and figures, and friendship.

My new friend Mrs. Walda Carpenter gave me her love, support, photographs, and vast knowledge. Special thanks go to Mr. W. H. McArthur, who has provided images from glass negatives to me and has shared ideas through emails, telephone calls, and chats; he and his wife always received me graciously into their home. Dr. Jeff Willis, Dr. Joe Dunn, and especially Dr. Melissa Walker have offered interest, assistance, and encouragement. Sarah Yarborough provided expertise as she helped me with the photographs for "book talks." Staff members at Spartanburg Photographic Center (Bill Moody and Jennifer Caddell) and photographer Robert Watkins have expressed interest, answered questions, provided quality work, and demonstrated professionalism.

Dr. Thomas R. McDaniel, my "boss" and colleague of more than 30 years, has been with me on this trip to the past for more almost 10 years. Without his urging, I might never have submitted the work for consideration because I believed non-acceptance of the work would be a rejection of my culture, my past, my family, and my work. He expressed faith in my work and in me. I can never thank him enough for reading, for editing — and encouraging.

I extend gratitude to the president of Converse College; to Tabatha Huskey and Darla Cudd; to Dena Gomez; and to the staff of the Mickel Library, particularly Wade Woodward, Mark Collier, Becky Dalton, Becky Poole, Ingrid Myrick, Trudy Cox, and especially Dr. Jim Harrison, who graciously stored my photographs in the Converse Archives. Staci Sigrist, Curtis Hinkle, and Cathy Terrell at the Spartanburg Public Library shared their expertise as did Sue Toms at the Mooneyham Public Library. Warm thanks to the TVA, the National Park Service, the Grove Park Inn, Betty Hinson, Lois

Moore Yandle, *Progressive Farmer* magazine, John Deere Company, University of Wisconsin, Duke Power, Simplicity Patterns, Dwight Moody, the Briarhoppers, the Charlotte Public Library, the staff at the libraries of UNC–Asheville and UNC–Chapel Hill, Russ Busby at the Billy Graham Evangelistic Association, and especially Alicia McCourry, who helped supply interest, support, and organization to the project. Special thanks go to Steve Massengill with the North Carolina Department of Cultural Resources for his wealth of knowledge and suggestions.

Thanks also go to Pitt Davis, Chris and Kay Wright, Jim Geddings, Dennis Lawson, Jeff Pierce, and (particularly) to Imogene Dillon.

My deep love and appreciation to my dear son and daughter-in-law, to Joanne Jolly, and to my church — especially Louise, who listened, cut, and pasted — and to Evan.

Lastly, my love and continued commitment to my dear husband. Your constancy is the bulwark of my life.

# Table of Contents

| | |
|---|---:|
| *Acknowledgments* | vii |
| *Preface* | 1 |
| *Introduction* | 3 |
| ONE: Water, Soil, and Industries Based on Natural Resources | 15 |
| TWO: Population | 76 |
| THREE: Education | 124 |
| FOUR: Health | 140 |
| FIVE: Housing | 161 |
| SIX: Labor | 174 |
| SEVEN: Popular Entertainment | 187 |
| APPENDIX I: *Important Federal Photographers in North Carolina During the Great Depression* | 225 |
| APPENDIX II: *Roy Stryker (1903–1975) and His Work with the Federal Government* | 237 |
| *Bibliography* | 242 |
| *Index* | 249 |

# *Preface*

North Carolina suffered intensely from the hardships of the Great Depression. Attesting to this fact are hundreds of federal photographs capturing both the settings and the people of North Carolina in that era.

The production of these images was part of a federal effort employing photographers to capture images of the Depression throughout the United States. From this project came some 107,000 photographs comprising a permanent record of both despair and pride among young and old, rich and poor, urban and rural, landed and landless, employed and unemployed.

Eight federal photographers recorded more than 2,000 images in the state of North Carolina. *North Carolina During the Great Depression: A Documentary Portrait of a Decade* selects from those photographs and others to present a complete picture of the people, problems, and strengths of an earlier time. It is an album of rich pictorial images of North Carolinians.

But the story of North Carolina in those difficult times needs to be spoken as well — and so the book is also a collection of words. These words remain in newsreels of the time; in the music and recordings of the era; in books like *These Are Our Lives*, a series of interviews recorded by participants of the Federal Writer's Project of the Works Progress Administration; and in interviews I conducted with people who remember the state in the 1930s. Though human memory sometimes fails, the fact that events of the Great Depression coincided with significant milestones and circumstances in these people's lives kept memories vivid and accurate.

As I carried out these interviews, former tenant farmers like Mrs. Getty Davis proudly showed me the dates on the deeds to land purchased with federal assistance and pulled the "receipts" for foods prepared and preserved during the 1930s. Mrs. Nell Burns, a Depression-era student, shared class photographs, medals earned in elocution, and a high school ring purchased with money earned from the National Youth Administration. Others displayed yellowed, brittle newspaper clippings marking significant events—like President Roosevelt's caravan through a neighboring town. Letters and diaries provided a written record of intimate thoughts and ideas. Historians like Professor H. G. Jones were able to tie personal feelings and memories to dates and events of the decade they had not only studied but also remembered from first-hand experience. Along with their stories, the people I interviewed offered booklets, journals, photographs, and other artifacts, some of which have been incorporated into this book along with the federal photographs.

In compiling this volume, I first had trouble finding the right way to organize the text and photographs. A chronological account at first seemed logical, but I soon found that the collected photographs and the events of the decade did not always lend themselves to a sequential, month-by-month, year-by-year approach. I struggled for some time with this problem until it occurred to me to borrow the structure of another remarkable project of the federal government.

During his administrations, President Franklin Delano Roosevelt had often expressed concern about the South, its economy, its people, and its problems. Roosevelt viewed the South as "the Nation's No. 1 economic problem — the Nation's problem, not merely the South's" (Roosevelt's letter to the Members of the Conference on Economic Conditions in the South, National Emergency Council, p. 1). On June 22, 1938, Roosevelt requested a detailed report on the economic problems of the South from the National Emergency Council (NEC), a group he had appointed to explore problems and solutions. The twenty-two-member committee consisted of college presidents, publishers, a judge, bank officers, an attorney, a planter, a labor union member, a governor, and several heads of major companies. The representative from North Carolina was Frank Porter Graham, president of the University of North Carolina.

Roosevelt wrote directly to the members of the NEC on July 5, 1938, to instruct them to report directly to him on the economic conditions in the South. In this letter, Roosevelt did not discuss the history or causes of the problems in the nation and the South; he merely asked for a description of the conditions as they existed. The result was the *Report on Economic Conditions of the South*.

The NEC centered its report on several main topics, including health, housing, education, and the natural resources of the South. This structure became the skeleton of *North Carolina During the Great Depression: A Documentary Portrait of a Decade*. The chapter titles in this book reflect the main topics of the NEC report.

In addition, this book contains another chapter, titled "Popular Entertainment." Some relaxation was essential to helping Carolinians maintain their physical and emotional health. The federal photographers captured North Carolinians — the young and the old, the employed and the unemployed — at play as well as at work.

If the NEC report is the skeleton, the photographs made in North Carolina by eight of the best of the federal government's 16 photographers are the vital organs for this book. The memories of the people of the era, their spoken conversations, their recorded words and music, their newsreels, their legal documents, their newspaper accounts, and their personal papers and possessions are the "flesh" of the work — a living record of the time, the place, and the people. I offer this work to the people of North Carolina as a tribute to their heritage.

# Introduction

## The Great Depression

No one lived through the 1930s without being affected by the Great Depression. Stocks dropped, banks closed, and industries failed. Lenders foreclosed. Jobs decreased, and workloads increased even as salaries dropped. Droughts and floods ravaged the land. Disease and malnutrition escalated. Despair prevailed. Even the well-to-do knew of the pain and suffering about them. Hard times had come.

The Great Depression defined the nation and continues to shape current generations. The work ethics, the life styles, the values, and the traditions begun in the 1930s still remain constant in the lives of many of that generation and in the lives of their descendants. Even those who rebel against squeezing the last of the toothpaste from the tube and "putting back for hard times" remind us that the past is still with us.

The years before the decade of the thirties did not clearly indicate what was to come. The economy of most sections of the United States experienced only a brief slow-down after the end of World War I and after the peace negotiations in May of 1920. Proudly displaying their war trophies, American soldiers returned to the United States from French battlefields. They found awaiting them a new era: the "Roaring Twenties," the "Jazz Age."

Most of the nation experienced in the 1920s seven years of economic expansion unprecedented in American history. The rules of the decade for many parts of the country were personal extravagance, labor-saving devices, materialism, and unwise investments. New social codes were apparent in everything from motion pictures to a new craze for chewing gum. Prohibition caused many ex-soldiers to carry flasks of bootleg liquor instead of rifles.

A particular feature of the 1920s was the considerable increase in the number of automobiles. There was a jump from 548,000 registered cars in 1910 to 8,132,000 in 1920. This meant that in 1910 about 1 out of every 36.5 households owned an automobile; by 1920, 1 out of every 3.0 households had a car. The number of cars registered in the United States in 1928 was 21,362,000—almost triple the number in 1920; the new average was 1 car for every 1.4 households—a sizeable increase over the 1 for every 3.0 households of only eight years before (Kurian, 30, 267; Donovan, pp. 32, 158).

From 1908 until 1927 the Model T Ford dominated car sales in the United States. Model T automobile production was half the car industry's total output in 1918–1919 and from 1921 to 1925. Ford earned more than all other automakers combined for the years 1911–1915, 1918, and 1921. The Model T came in many different models, but all of these

*This exhibit train stopped at the Rutherfordton depot shortly after the end of World War I to display trophies from the war. Will McArthur made the photograph.*

body styles had the same engine and almost exactly "the same chassis: the Model T roadster, coupe, coupelet, runabout, roadster torpedo, town car, touring, and the fordor and tudor sedans" ("Model T Photographs"). The car had a possible speed of 45 mph, a gas mileage of 13 to 21 miles per gallon, and a 20-horsepower engine. A ceremony marked the end of the Model T line in May of 1927; Ford had produced more than 15 million Model T's ("A Short History of the Model T Automobile"). When its purchase price dropped from the nearly $1,000 of 1908 to under $300 in 1927, the car stopped being a toy for the affluent and became a necessary vehicle for the masses (Foner).

Music changed, as did clothing styles. Patterns for women's dresses in 1910 had required ten to twenty yards of materials. In 1920 only about two yards were necessary for a woman's dress; slacks required even less. Cotton textile mills would have done well to examine closely this aspect of society. This trend of less consumption coupled with only 7 percent exports helped to create a saturated national market for textiles.

Overproduction and poor marketing strategies increased problems for an already ailing textile industry. The prescriptions used in North Carolina for the textile industry were increased production, night shifts, merging of the mills, "layoffs," lower wages, and "stretch-outs" that forced employees to tend more machines in the factories at an even faster pace. The textile industry of North Carolina was beginning to concern its workers—but many ignored the symptoms (Bell, pp. 28–29).

When production far exceeded national demands, when the American government adjusted tariffs, when the foreign market for American manufactured goods and foodstuffs

*Will McArthur took this photograph in Forest City in the late 1920s or the early 1930s. Jim Womack of the Rutherford County Farm Museum made the identification.*

decreased, when foreign countries did not meet the deadlines for repayment of money borrowed from the United States, when some European countries began to recover and no longer needed aid from the United States, parts of the nation that had prospered in the past began to feel the first pinch of the Great Depression. Southern laborers, however, noticed "nothing new"; lean times had long been with them.

Investors began to take even greater chances. The stock market began to pulsate and tremble. The long, rolling downward slide gained momentum. On the morning of Thursday, October 24, 1929, a panic occurred. Traders exchanged more than 12 million shares in a single day. The crash of the stock market followed on October 29, 1929 — Black Tuesday; this was a sixteen-million-share day. Rapidly the loss became more than $30 billion. The Great Depression had begun.

Throughout the nation others, too, began to feel the effects of the Great Depression. Banks began to fail. The number of

*Ola Mae Adams Shockley (1902–1992) in a Chevrolet.*

*A rural scene at the turn of the century. The amount of cloth necessary for the dress styles of the 1920s and the 1930s was much less than is apparent here — a contributing factor to the cotton and fabric surplus and the low market prices. Elyas and Laura Whitesides raised their dogs for hunting and entertainment.*

households with vehicles began to decline, an indication of the economic problems (McElvaine, *Down and Out*, p. 20). With the Great Depression of 1929

> ...the nation [would gain] a thorough understanding of just how important the automobile had become ... they were a fixation, part of the body and soul of everyday life. No matter how poor and needy those in the depression became, they [often] would not give up their cars. If forced to choose between gasoline and beans, the average man may decide the gasoline was more important. Replacement parts were scavenged and repairs were improvised from whatever could be found. Will Rogers said that Americans would be the first people to go to the poor house in an automobile ["Automotive History"].

Even those with vehicles could not always afford to keep them in working condition or purchase the gasoline to keep them running; these impoverished owners often converted their cars and trucks to locomotion with the help of a mule or a horse. To create these "hacks," the owners themselves often became "shade tree mechanics." They jacked up the cars and removed both the entire power train to make the automobile lighter; next they attached a tongue to the front axle and hitched a horse or mule to the front. By attaching a doubletree to the tongue and attaching a singletree to each end of the doubletree, the owners could attach two horses or mules and double their power (T. W. Jones). Sometimes called "Hoover Carts" or "Hoover Wagons," these vehicles were more comfortable than the typical wooden cart and steered much better than a wagon,

Left: *Elizabeth "Babe" Cook in a "red devil dress," 1928.* Right: *Ola Mae Adams Shockley (1902–1992), taken in the mid–1930s. Pants for women were popular throughout the decade. The amount of material needed for either attire is much less than earlier.*

but they symbolized that the owners were experiencing financial hardships (T. W. Martin).

Throughout the nation laborers and the unemployed alike were finding their livelihoods and homes threatened from all sides. They responded in a variety of ways. Some despondent Americans resorted to suicide. Contrary to public opinion, most of these suicides did not occur with the crash of the stock market in 1929. The Metropolitan Life Insurance Company noted that more than 20,000 persons— 20.5 per 100,000 — took their lives in 1931 (Time-Life, *This Fabulous Century,* Volume IV, p. 25). In the year 1932, 17.4 per 200,000 — as compared to 14 per 100,000 in 1929 —committed suicide (McElvaine, *Down and Out,* p. 18).

Some Americans asked for government assistance; however, President Hoover opposed appropriations for direct federal relief. A Quaker, Hoover wanted communities to take care of the less fortunate; he encouraged "socially responsible individualists" to take charge. As president, Hoover urged voluntary charity, local aid, and state relief (McElvaine, *Down and Out,* p. 20). The President's Organization on Unemployment Relief (POUR) and the Committee on the Mobilization of Relief Resources placed an ad in the *Farm Journal* of December 1931:

CERTAINLY WE WILL LEND A HAND

Grandmother never waited! When a neighbor's wife was having a baby and the doctor couldn't get there, grandmother put on her bonnet and shawl!

Mother never waited! When the neighbor's house burned down in the night, mother opened her door. She said, "Come right in."

The instinct to help is *in your blood.*

A few valleys away may be folks who need your helping hand now.

By giving generously you will have your share in a great common achievement. America is marshaling her forces to deal a death blow to depression.

She is setting an example to the world. She is

laying the firm foundation for better days for all [*Farm Journal*, p. 15].

Two specific events accentuated the arrival of hard times. First, in the summer of 1932 eleven thousand men assembled in Washington, D.C., to demand additional government payments from Congress for ex-servicemen. Some of these men in the Bonus Expeditionary Force, as they called themselves, brought their families with them and moved into vacant buildings. Others set up shacks outside of Washington (Chitwood, p. 765). Observers called their squalid village made of foraged cardboard and scraps "Hooverville"; it was much like any other such village that countless homeless people set up in vacant lots across the country during this bleak period.

Congress did not pay additional funds to the Bonus Army, but Hoover was able to offer $100,000 to help the veterans with their return home. Six thousand of the troops accepted the money and left the capital city; the others refused to leave. President Hoover attempted to use troops to evict the men from the buildings and to usher them out of the city (Chitwood, p. 765).

On July 28, 1932, General Douglas MacArthur and Major Dwight Eisenhower marched with infantry, cavalry, and tanks up Pennsylvania Avenue. The troops attempted to rout the squatters from the buildings and to chase the campers from their shacks. One baby succumbed to the tear gas; two veterans died, and two others were seriously wounded. A storm of protest followed. Americans seemed to be losing faith rapidly in Washington — especially when MacArthur and Hoover attempted to defend their actions (Jennings, pp. 154–155).

The second event to proclaim further the arrival of hard times occurred on the morning of March 4, 1933. America and Herbert Hoover awoke to the collapse of the banking system. This final defeat brought Hoover's remark, "We are at the end of our string." Many Americans agreed.

T. W. Martin remembers vividly the closing of the bank in Mooresboro, North Carolina. In order to secure a high school education at Boiling Springs High School for his children, T. W.'s father had sold their farm, put the money in the bank, and moved with his family to Boiling Springs. With the unexpected closing of the bank, however, T. W.'s father lost everything he had in his account and was caught with only $18.00 in his pocket. Times were hard, but even leaner years lay ahead for many.

In 1933, after his election in 1932, Franklin Delano Roosevelt took the oath of office as President of the United States. Concerned with the problems of the nation and particularly with the problems of the farmers, he persuaded the federal government to create the Civilian Conservation Corps (CCC) and the Agricultural Adjustment Administration (AAA) in 1933.

Rexford Tugwell was a loyal member of President Roosevelt's advisers (his first "Brain Trust"). He came to Washington in 1933 as Assistant Secretary of Agriculture. To the nation's capital and to the AAA, Tugwell drew many Columbia students. One of these was Roy E. Stryker.

*Oil painting of Administrator Rexford Tugwell by Boris Deutsch, photographed between 1935 and 1942.*

*Roy E. Stryker, photograph chief of the Farm Security Administration, Washington, D.C., January 1942.*

As a part of his work with the AAA, the Resettlement Administration, and the Farm Security Administration, Stryker directed and organized a corps of federal photographers whose assignment was to record images of the United States during the Depression. Stryker's work at the federal level would later extend to the Office of War Information.

## North Carolina During the Great Depression

North Carolina is 503 miles from east to west, and 187 miles from north to south, so that leaves plenty of room for growth and change. Still, I am glad I know it as it is, and remember it as it was [Kuralt, p. 19].

In 1922 when times were good for much of the nation, Dr. Lucius B. Morse conceived the idea of building a summer resort at Chimney Rock, North Carolina. He and other North Carolinians incorporated Chimney Rock Mountains, the largest corporation at that time ever to receive a charter in the state of North Carolina. In 1925 bonds helped finance a contract for building a dam across the Rocky Broad River; the dam, which would help to generate power, would form a 1,500-acre mountain lake with shorelines of 27 miles. Plans called for the development of a pavilion, local lots, beaches, and an amusement center; progress proceeded rapidly (Griffin, *The History of Old Tryon and Rutherford Counties,* p. 498).

In 1926 construction work began on the $400,000 Lake Lure Inn. People were buying lots and home sites in the village of Lake Lure, near the fast-filling lake site, and close to Chimney Rock.

The events of 1929 and afterward began to take their toll. Even though Dr. Morse and his associates were able to complete their plans for building the pavilion, lake, and Lake Lure Inn, they could not continue with further development in the area. They had added $10,000,000 in taxable wealth to the county and built "for Rutherford County a resort unequaled elsewhere in the state ... unfortunately most of the men who had spent their money in the project realized but small return on their investment, due to the depression" (Griffin, *The History of Old Tryon and Rutherford Counties,* pp. 498–499).

Following World War I most Carolina textile workers, laborers, miners, and farmers had not felt the optimism and "good times" that helped to bring about the construction of Lake Lure. These Carolina workers could not attest personally to the economic expansion of much of the nation. In fact, a surplus of workers and products, low farm prices, and new labor-saving devices served only to increase the ranks of the unemployed. North Carolinians became acutely aware of a maldistribution of wealth — a leading cause of the Great Depression (McElvaine, *The Great Depression,* p. 38). When the nation as a whole began to feel the first pinch of hard times, many Carolinians noticed nothing new.

As the decade continued, North Carolinians took in their belts another notch. The farmer — who was already in dire straits — felt even more burdens. The price of farm goods kept falling despite all the Federal Farm

*This dam closed on September 20, 1926, and began to impound the water of Rocky Broad River. The 1,500 acre Lake Lure with its bathing beaches and 27 miles of shoreline would also generate electric power. Photograph by Will McArthur.*

Board could do. For example, in 1919 tobacco prices rose as high as 86 cents a pound in Spring Hope. By 1920 the price plummeted to 22 cents a pound. The farmers later felt a slight recovery, but prices fell again in 1929 and 1930 (Daniel, *Breaking the Land*, p. 35).

Cotton dropped in price also. From 1920 to 1925 the price for cotton per pound was 22.5 cents; by the period 1925 to 1928 the price had dropped to 17 cents per pound (Pendleton). By the year 1930, cotton prices averaged 10 cents a pound (Mills.) In Cleveland County later in the decade the cotton dropped to 5 cents a pound — the same price as a Big 5 pad of paper (T. W. Martin).

In 1930 alone, 88 banks in North Carolina closed; by comparison, only 98 banks closed in the state in the entire decade of the 1920s. In addition, 233 building and loan associations folded in 1930; in 1933, 209 other associations closed. Many people in Carolina were losing their homes, their farms, their businesses (Powell, p. 482).

Newspapers tried to ease the panic. For example, on February 6, 1930, in the same article reporting the closing of six banks in one week in the county, *The Forest City Courier* used very positive phrasing on its front page to note that some area banks were still solvent:

> Standing like the rock of Gibraltar amid the stress of the financial storm Tuesday was the Industrial Loan and Investment Banks, Forest City, the First Industrial Bank, Rutherfordton, the Haynes Banks, Cliffside and Avondale; the Bostic Bank and the Ellenboro bank.
>
> Locally, thousands of dollars have been deposited in the Industrial Banks since the financial debacle of Tuesday.
>
> Officials of the Farmers Bank have a statement on this page, a perusal of which will aid greatly to restore confidence and allay the fear of loss by depositors.
>
> The *Courier* wishes to urge any of those distressed over the local banking situation to take stock, calm your alarms and allay your fears....
>
> Go ahead with your business, don't get discouraged and within a short time Forest City

Top: *The Lake Lure Inn before the lake began to fill. Will McArthur was the photographer.* Bottom: *The Inn, begun in 1926, cost $400,000 to build. Lake Lure was still filling at the time Will McArthur took this photograph.*

## CAROLINA PAPERS REPORT THE PANIC AND CRASH OF 1929 AND THE BANK CLOSINGS OF 1930

*These articles from the* Forest City Courier *and the* Rutherford County News *detail business prior to the Wall Street Crash, predictions that "the stock depression … is not likely to have any profound effects upon the general business life of the country," and the closing of some Carolina banks.*

will be moving ahead and business stronger and better under the restore confidence and new banking relations.

As the writer heard a physician illustrate: Our financial situation is to be compared to a boil. It has now erupted, the source of infection has been expelled and now all we have to do is to wait the healing process.

Unfortunately, the healing process was not complete. Some of the "Gibraltar banks" would collapse. Carolinians who mined, farmed, worked in industry, and labored would recognize that they had long been "at the end of their strings." The closings of the banks hit these ordinary persons particularly hard. In Rutherford County, for example:

[O]n February 4th [1930] the Rutherford County Bank and Trust Company, at Rutherfordton, and its branches at Union Mills and Spindale, closed. On the same day the Farmers Bank and Trust Company, at Forest City, and the branch at Caroleen, suspended business. The next day the Chimney Rock Trust Company at Chimney Rock, closed. The resources of these banks were in excess of three and one-half million dollars.... The psychological effect of these banks closing was sufficient to paralyze business and industry, had they not been touched otherwise. The life savings of many citizens were wiped out. Reserves held for operating expenses in many lines of business were indefinitely tied up, and most of the funds eventually lost....

The year 1932 is notable as being one of the leanest of the depression period. Economic development was stopped, salaries and wages dropped to a low scale, unemployment increased by leaps, banks and business establishments were closing daily; farm produce and other marketable goods could not be sold for a reasonable price....

The year 1933 entered upon a despondent scene. The depression was at its peak. Bank failures and bankruptcy of business institutions crowded the news columns daily. The ranks of the unemployed grew by leaps and bounds.... Despondency and defeat pervaded the air of the Old North State when the General Assembly convened on January 4th.... In his inaugural address he [Governor J. C. B. Ehringhaus] called attention to the unsettled condition of the state and nation.... "Confronting us at this hour are problems of such magnitude as the state has not faced since Reconstruction days," he said [Griffin, *The History of Old Tryon and Rutherford Counties,* pp. 517, 520, 521].

Farmers borrowed on their insurance, and they — along with other unemployed Carolinians searching for jobs — felt fear. Many Carolina factories were unable either to collect the debts owed to them or to sell the goods on hand; the result was that even more workers lost their jobs.

Nature and the people themselves further compounded the already severe economic problems of the 1930s. The decade began with a severe drought followed by two hurricanes hitting the Carolina coast in August and September of 1933. Uninformed or careless Carolinians continued denuding the forests, harnessing streams inappropriately, and ignoring important soil conservation techniques. The results of their thoughtlessness included advanced erosion and amplified economic decline.

Hard times touched every area of the daily life in North Carolina and deeply affected natural resources, industries, education, health, entertainment, housing and labor in the state. In recalling the 1930s through the words and the images in this book, the reader learns just how the decade of the Great Depression shaped the story of the state, the region, and the nation.

CHAPTER ONE

# Water, Soil, and Industries Based on Natural Resources

North Carolina in the 1930s was rich in many natural resources, including its water, soil, and forests. During the Great Depression water, soil, and industries related to the resources were of particular importance to the economic health and to the people of the nation and the state.

## I. Water

The ultimate source of all water is, of course, precipitation. Typically, available water combined with the rich Carolina soil to ensure distinguished agricultural products. Before the 1930s, North Carolina usually fared well with 49 inches of average precipitation per year; regional or yearly departures from that amount were usually slight (Hobbs, p. 22). The years of the 1930s, however, were exceptions.

**Drought.** The decade began with a drought for the state and much of the nation. The least annual precipitation for Carolina since 1899 occurred in Mount Airy, North Carolina, in 1930; the 22.69 inches of rainfall that Mount Airy received that year was less than half of the normal annual precipitation for the state. Other states also were experiencing a decreased annual precipitation; West Virginia, for instance, had only 9.5 inches; Maryland, 17.8; and Washington, 2.6. Improper conservation methods coupled with the severe drought conditions caused immense problems—including erosion and a drop in farm production. These troubles of the individual states impacted, in turn, the nation (Ludlum, pp. 282–286).

Droughts continued. The federal government attempted to alleviate the situation for the farmer and nation through various programs. The Civilian Conservation Corps—the CCC—helped with conservation. In May of 1933, the government established by law the Agricultural Adjustment Administration (AAA) to aid the nation's beleaguered farmers and ultimately the nation. This organization helped to educate the farmer, to encourage effective agricultural techniques, to assist particularly both the small and the tenant farmer, to control the market, and to make benefit payments to those employing soil conservation measures and limiting certain crops. This was the beginning of the "alphabet soup" of programs to follow as a result of the New Deal legislation.

Roy E. Stryker, who served with the Assistant Secretary of Agriculture Rexford Tugwell, organized and directed a group of federal photographers who captured the images of the drought, the flooding, the settings, and the people of the nation after 1933. These

*Landscape with a bad gully in a field of young tobacco before a rain, Shoofly, Granville County, May 1940. Photograph by Jack Delano, Farm Security Administration.*

photographs showing drought conditions and destitution helped to document the need for federal assistance to farmers across the nation. Other programs to aid the less fortunate would be forthcoming; Stryker's work directing the photographing of America would continue for more than a decade.

**The fall line.** The Blue Ridge Mountains of North Carolina form a divide: rivers to the west drain into the Mississippi River, and rivers to the east drain into the Atlantic. Rapids are a usual feature where rivers cross the fall line. Those who fish for sport, for a livelihood, and for food and those who seek to navigate the rivers and shoot the rapids for recreation still find the fresh water at the North Carolina fall line a challenge.

In the 1800s and after, factories flourished in the Piedmont area; industrialists could use the Carolinians as a cheap, plentiful labor source. The rapidly flowing water for hydroelectric power made the area even more attractive.

North Carolina's first textile plant was the Schenck-Warlick Textile Mill. Powered by water, the mill was located in Lincolnton in 1813. North Carolina began additional manufacturing industries. Mills sprang up, particularly in the Piedmont. The Cliffside Mill was the leading producer of gingham in the 1930s. Some of the other Carolina plants included the manufacture of paper, paper products, furniture, clothing, wood products, and foodstuffs (corn meal, flour, and others). In the 1930s North Carolina industrialists still harnessed natural water power for mills and plants.

Millers often placed their businesses near water and used its power to turn the wheels of the gristmills.

> The water-powered corn mills, with their picturesque wooden water wheels standing sentinel

*The spillway of Cliffside Mill. R. R. Haynes and Dr. T. B. Lovelace began the mill in 1899.*

over huge clapboard buildings are yet to be found on the creeks and in the coves of Western North Carolina, but in steadily diminishing numbers.... [T]he old type water mill required in nearly every instance an entire building of two or more stories, an impounding dam across some creek, a mill race and other appurtenances necessitating constant care and maintenance.... [Water] furnished the only practical solution of the power problem in grinding corn.... In fact, water was also extensively used as motive power in sawmill operations until the turn of the century....

All of these old-fashioned grist or corn mills were built along astonishingly similar lines. The huge wooden wheel, 60 to 75 feet in circumference, stood at the end of the mill where the water from the mill race poured over it, furnishing the motivating power. This big wheel was geared to the simple machinery inside, all of which was wood, except the two large millstones, which crushed the corn into meal. The plants usually consisted of one large building, about two stories in height. On the inside, on a high platform, erected over the wooden machinery operated by the water wheel, was the mill. On the floor level was the long box into which the warm, pleasant-odored meal poured. Usually at one end of the big room was a large fireplace. Other fixtures of the typical mill room usually consisted of a corn sheller, a pair of scales or steelyards, a few wooden barrels into which toll corn was poured, some re-bottomed home-made chairs and a mountainous pile of corncobs [Griffin, *Essays*, pp. 1 3].

The Carolina rapids normally are not a source of great flooding even during heavy rains and do not usually pose a great hazard to local residents. Flooding is more frequent in the mountains and Piedmont areas immediate to the streams.

In 1940, for example, the French Broad River spilled into the low-lying areas when heavy rains flooded many communities in western North Carolina. Spectators in Asheville, North Carolina, stood on the Asheville-Biltmore Bridge to watch the swollen Swannanoa River push against its banks and the bridge. Heavy losses of lives and property resulted from this destructive 1940 flood, which helped to pilot in a new decade just as the drought of 1930 had helped

*A mill in Fuquay Springs in September 1935. Photograph by Arthur Rothstein, Farm Security Administration.*

to usher in the decade of the Great Depression (Jones, *North Carolina Illustrated*, p. 343).

**Rivers.** North Carolina has many important rivers. The Cape Fear River is a principal one. Other important rivers of the state include the Catawba, the Neuse, the Haw, and the Roanoke. These rivers are vital sources of food, power, travel, and leisure-time activities to Carolina residents and tourists from other areas. The mark of the rivers is apparent throughout the state.

**Waters of the Coastal Plain and the Atlantic Seaboard.** The rivers of North Carolina become more sluggish near the Coastal Plain. The Plain waters sometimes cause major flood damage — particularly during the autumn hurricane and the spring flood seasons. The Coastal Plain houses the few natural lakes of the state, numerous flood plains, and river swamps of the state. The best-known of the swamps is the Dismal Swamp at the Virginia–North Carolina line (Orr, *Merit Students Encyclopedia*, Vol. 13, pp. 458–466). By the 1930s the rivers and the beaches along the Carolina coast had been sites of travel and leisure-time activities for many years.

**Fishing.** The warm waters of the Atlantic wash the long shoreline of North Carolina, a state that ranks high among the South Atlantic states in commercial fishing (Hobbs, p. 25). Shrimp, flounder, trout, spot, and fish for industrial use come from the waters off the coast. Fish from the fresh waters, too, are an important source of tourism, food, and income (Orr, *Merit Students Encyclopedia*, Vol. 13, pp. 458–466). In fact, in 1930 North Carolina ranked 16th among the 29 commercial

83-637. NORTH CAROLINA COLLECTION, UNIVERSITY OF NORTH CAROLINA LIBRARY AT CHAPEL HILL

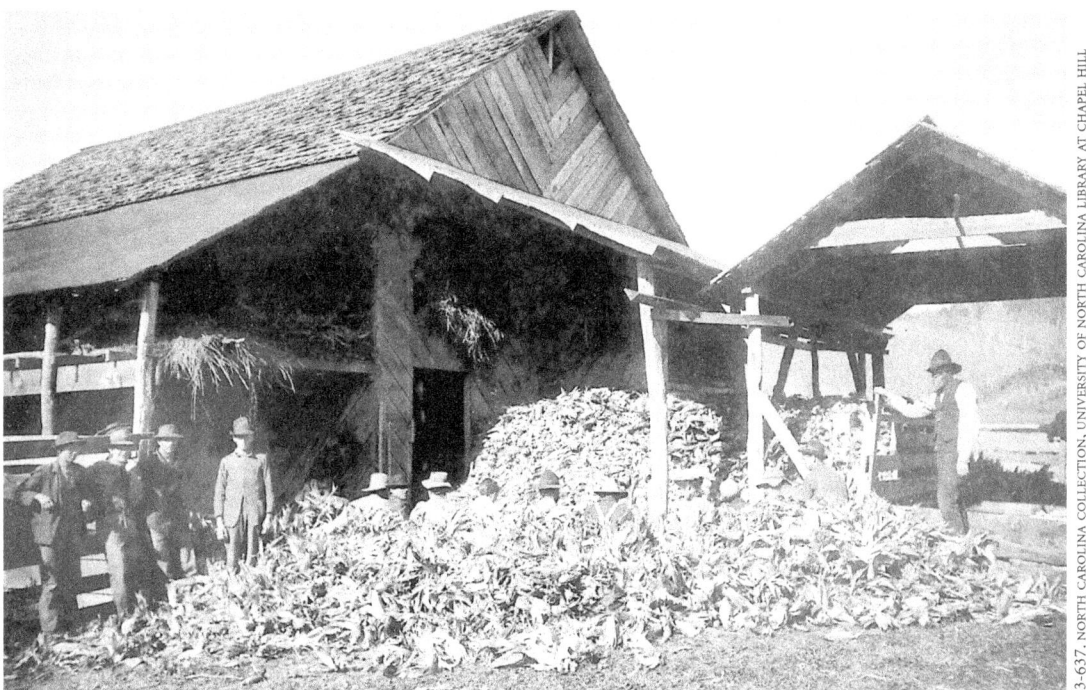

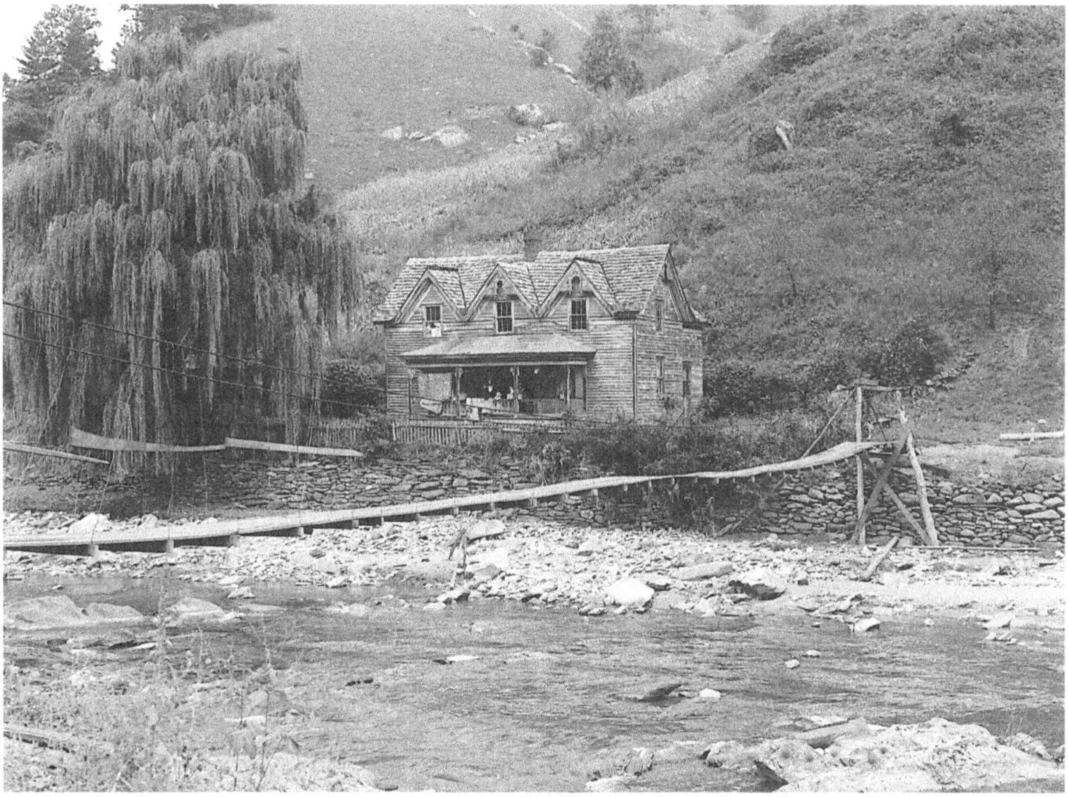

LC-USF-34-55978-D. LIBRARY OF CONGRESS, PRINTS AND PHOTOGRAPHS DIVISION, FSA-OWI COLLECTION

Top: *Corn shucking in Burke County.* Bottom: *A farm house along a creek bed in a recently flooded area in Asheville, September 1940. Photograph by Marion Post Wolcott, Farm Security Administration.*

Top: *Haw River in Pittsboro, Chatham County, in September 1939. Photograph by Marion Post Wolcott, Farm Security Administration.* Bottom: *A rain-soaked tobacco field in Shoofly, Granville, May 1940. Photograph by Jack Delano, Farm Security Administration.*

*Dismal Swamp of eastern North Carolina.*

fishing states—including Alaska—in the value of its fishery products. By 1940 its position was number 14 (Hobbs, p. 38).

Inside the barrier reef along the entire length of North Carolina are 3,000 square miles of fishing waters, both salt and fresh. The Atlantic Ocean lies just outside the reef. More than 25 species of finfish, shrimp, clams, scallops, and crabs are available for the taking in these waters (Federal Writer's Project, *North Carolina: A Guide to the Old North State*, p. 23).

The Pamlico Sound and the shallow water from the Bogue Sound to the South Carolina state line are capable of producing oysters. However, only 12,000 of the possible million acres of oyster grounds were used in the early 1930s.

To stimulate the culturing of oysters, the State Department of Conservation and Development sponsored the project of the federal government and the Works Progress Administration to plant several million bushes of oysters and shells. In 1935, through federal aid, a cooperative was formed; advanced money financed the establishment and the initial expenses of three branches and a main plant at Morehead City.

The fertilizer and oil industry use menhaden, found around Beaufort and Southport. The catch of the fish had declined, however, after its peak in 1918 (Federal Writer's Project, *North Carolina: A Guide to the Old North State*, pp. 23–24).

Directly dependent on the fisheries were 15,000 Carolinians. The total value in 1934 of the 163,462,000 pounds of caught fish was $1,672,200. Marketing and maintaining the sources of the industry were important priorities. Federal hatcheries in the Great Smoky Mountains National Park and the Sandhills supplemented the six hatcheries that the State Department of Conservation and Development established for the propagation of freshwater game fish. To protect the game fish, the state instituted certain closed fishing seasons and set aside certain grounds for spawning (Federal Writer's Project, *North Carolina: A Guide to the Old North State*, p. 24).

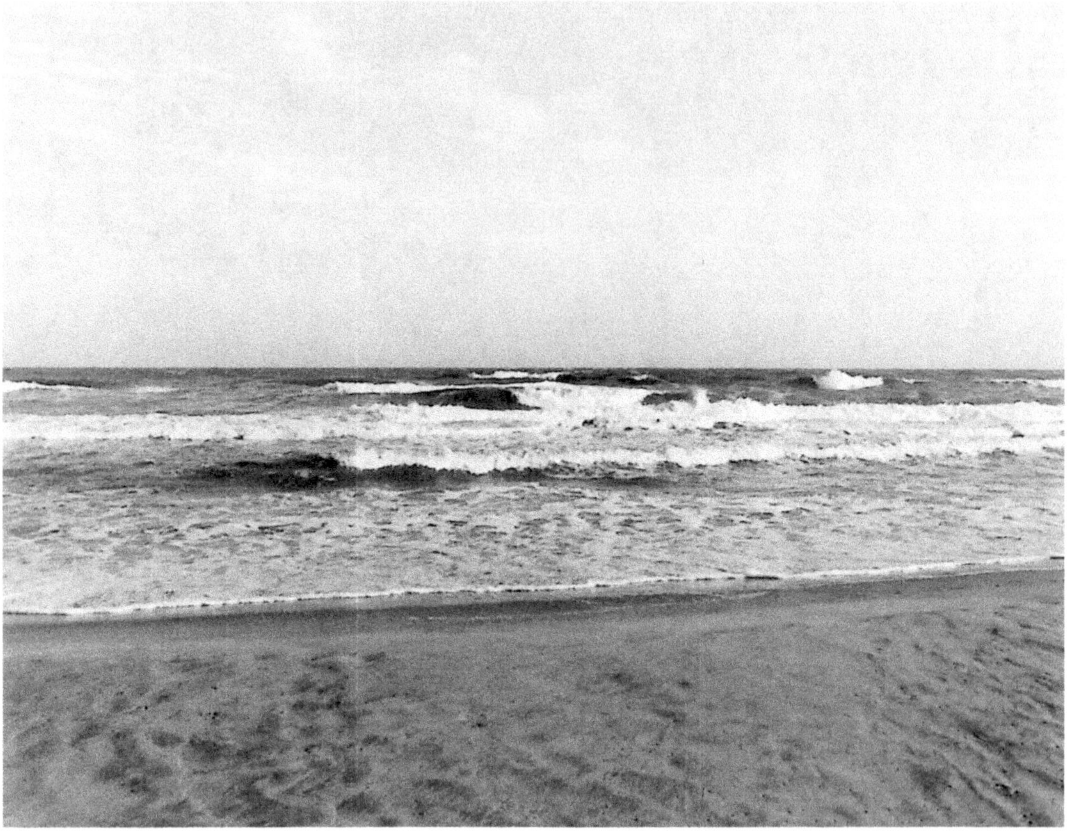

COURTESY MACK JOLLY

COURTESY NORTH CAROLINA DIVISION OF ARCHIVES AND HISTORY

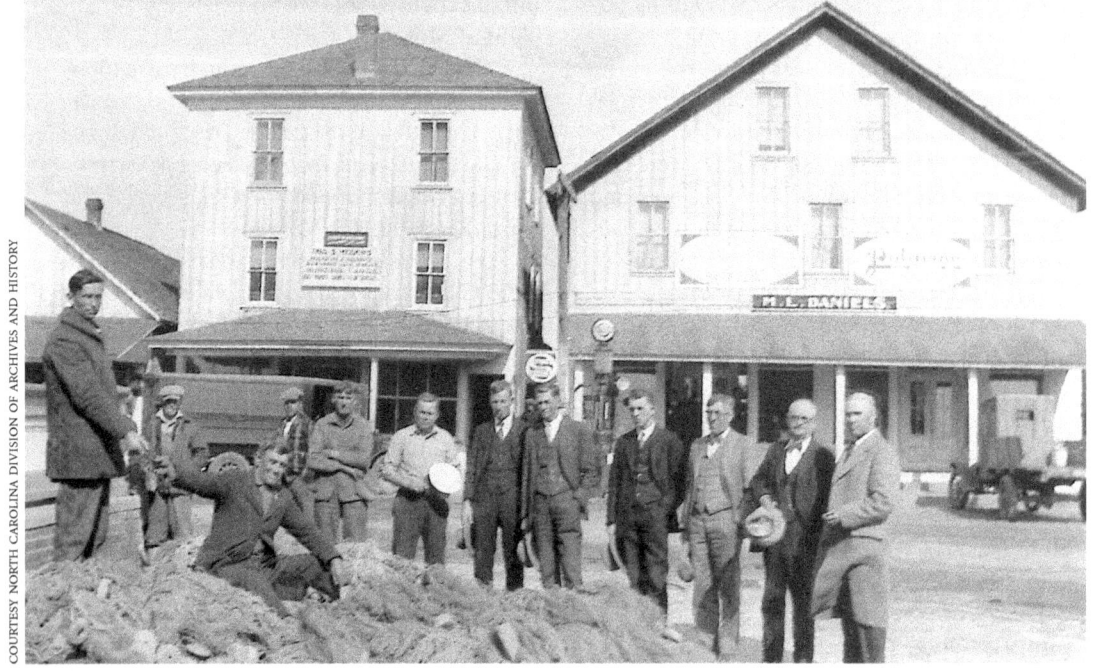

Top: *The shores of North Carolina.* Bottom: *Fish net sale at Manteo, circa 1930.*

**Water transportation.** Water transportation was important to tourism and Carolina's development. Federal and state programs helped to improve much of the Carolina water transportation system. Real work on a coastal route between Chesapeake Bay and Charleston, South Carolina, had begun in 1911. In 1932, at a cost of over $14 million, the long waterway between Norfolk, Virginia, and Wilmington, North Carolina, was at last complete (Hobbs, p. 152).

The Army Corps of Engineers initiated its project to improve waterways for navigation in 1928. Federal aid helped to develop these routes even further. The Inland Waterway entered North Carolina from Virginia by

Right: *Etol Dorn poses with fish caught on the coast during the late 1930s.* Below: *John Davis fishes on the coast of North Carolina.*

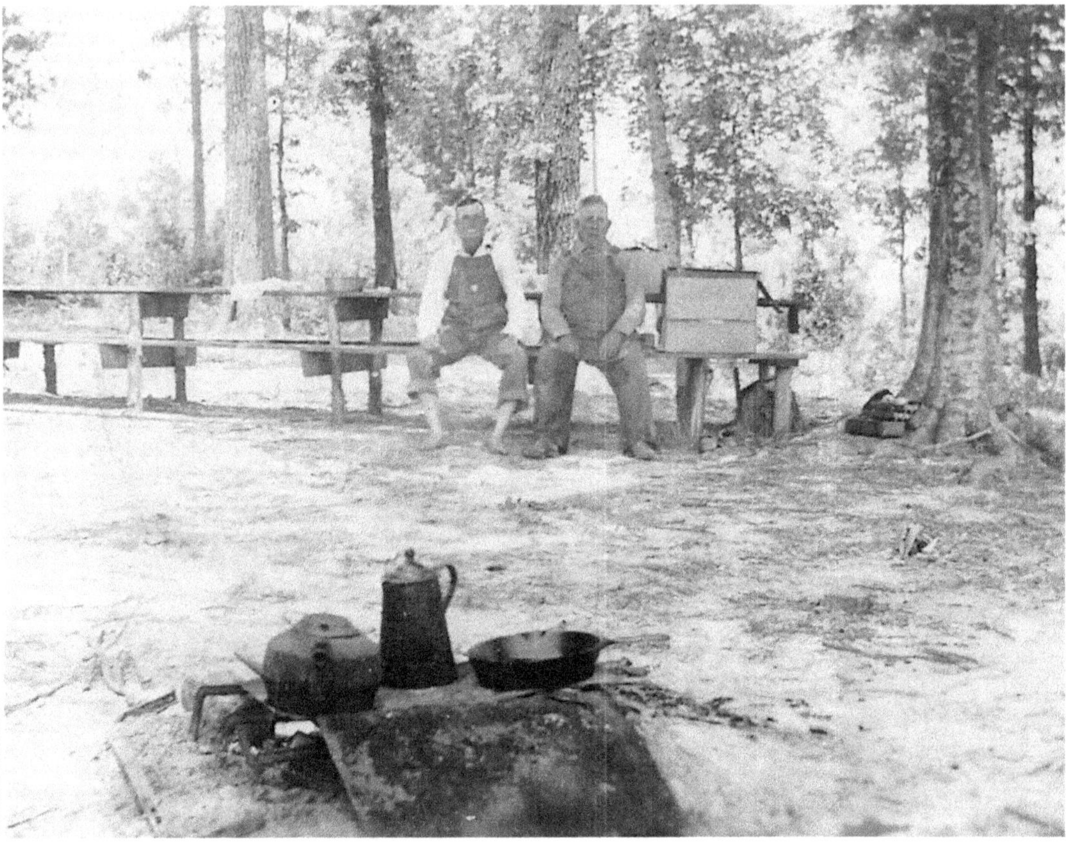

COURTESY PITT DAVIS

30.4.84. COURTESY NORTH CAROLINA DIVISION OF ARCHIVES AND HISTORY

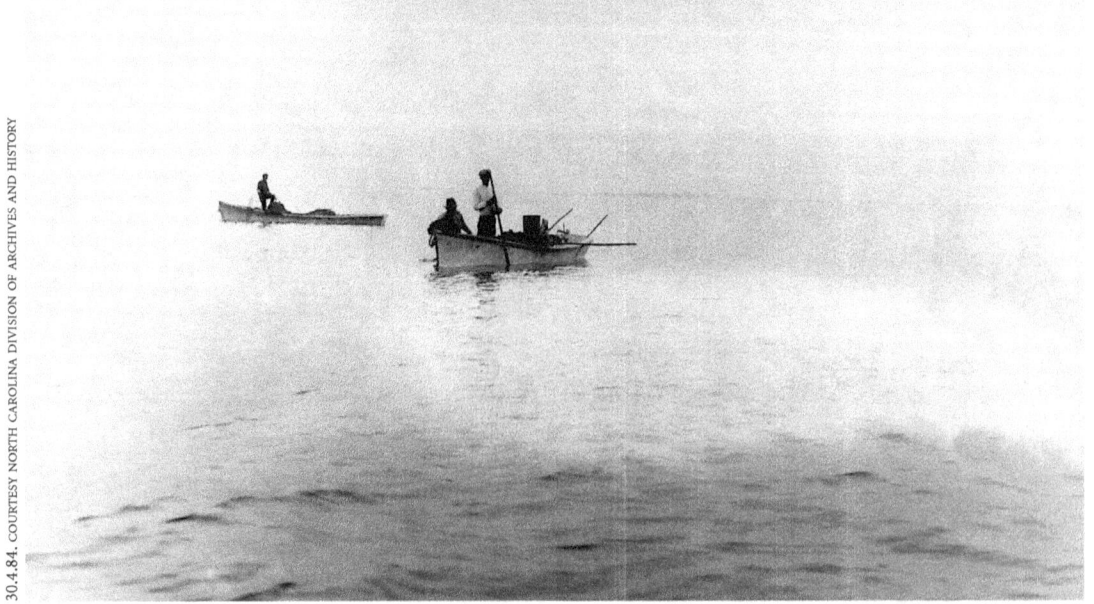

Top: *John Davis at a picnic site near a river in North Carolina.* Bottom: *Oyster boats, hand tonging oysters, circa 1935.*

*Oyster planting in Broad Creek, North Carolina.*

two distinct routes: the Dismal Swamp Canal Route (surveyed by George Washington) and the Albemarle and Chesapeake Canal Route. A third alternate route branched from the sound through Core Sound and from there to Beaufort, North Carolina. There were several waterways for shallow-draft vessels and several channels classified as connecting bodies of water. (Hobbs, pp. 152, 154)

**Coastal problems.** Despite the many improvements, two problems along the Atlantic Coast of North Carolina in the 1930s were the shifting of the sand dunes and the washing away of the sand near the Atlantic Coast with the rising and the receding of the waters. In many areas the land had eroded so badly that only bald beaches remained. Where the waters had cut the shores severely, the sea threatened even the Cape Hatteras Lighthouse.

In the Elizabeth City *Independent* for July 21, 1933, banker Frank Stick outlined a program for a coastal park for North Carolina. After the reclamation of the eroded areas would come a national seashore park project that would provide work and income to residents and would preserve the area in its natural state. Last would come the construction of a modern coastal highway from Nags Head to Beaufort to encourage visitors.

The need for the highway and the control of erosion became particularly evident when a major hurricane hit the area in August; another followed in September. The Civil Works Administration made available funds in excess of one million dollars to help with the project. The State of North Carolina purchased bridges at Roanoke Sound and Currituck Sound. The North Carolina State Highway Commission, the Director of the

*Cape Hatteras Lighthouse, March 1939.*

North Carolina Department of Conservation and Development, the State Geologist, the National Park Service, local citizens, and the State Forester supported the plans. The program expanded to include mosquito control, the restoration of the "Cittie of Ralegh" on Roanoke Island, and improvements at the Wright Brothers Memorial.

The North Carolina Historical Commission, the Federal Theater Project, and other agencies of the Works Progress Administration had several visions for the coastal area of North Carolina. First, they developed a natural amphitheater seating 3,000. This would provide culture to the citizens of the state and would increase tourism to the coast (Stick, pp. 248–249).

A historical program to be approved for presentation at the Roanoke Island Amphitheatre and the actual presentation of the program were next on the agenda. Carolina resident Paul Green wrote the drama. (More about Green is in Chapter Seven, "Popular Entertainment.") The production of Paul Green's *The Lost Colony* was such a success in 1937 that it has ever since been a regular feature of the months July through August—except during the war years (Stick, pp. 248–249).

The North Carolina Erosion Control Project began on October 11, 1934, with the establishment of the Civilian Conservation Corps Camp in Manteo. The workers built a fence for about 125 miles from the Hatteras Inlet to the Virginia state line. Although the workers tried various types of fences (brush, slab, burlap), they found that brush was most effective. They also planted native grasses, shrubs, and trees as the beach built up around the fences. On April 15, 1936, the U.S. Biological Survey took charge of the camp and the project (Report of J. S. Holmes, State Official for CCC, as cited by Merrill, pp. 157–158).

By July of 1940, A. C. Stratton and James R. Hollowell of the National Park Service declared:

> Southward from the Virginia State Line extending to Hatteras Inlet a great barrier dune has been built for the protection of the Banks from the ocean. In some places it is as much as twenty-five feet high with a base of nearly three

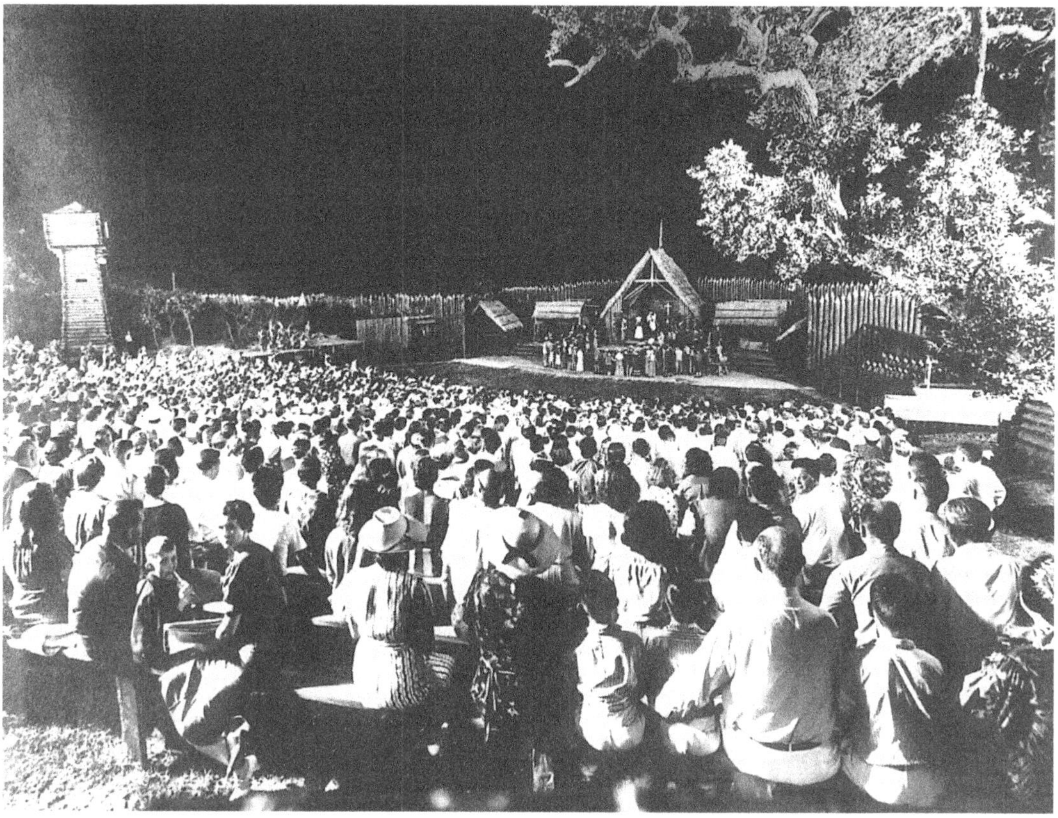

81.6.7. COURTESY NORTH CAROLINA DIVISION OF ARCHIVES AND HISTORY

C AND D 6995-C. COURTESY NORTH CAROLINA DIVISION OF ARCHIVES AND HISTORY

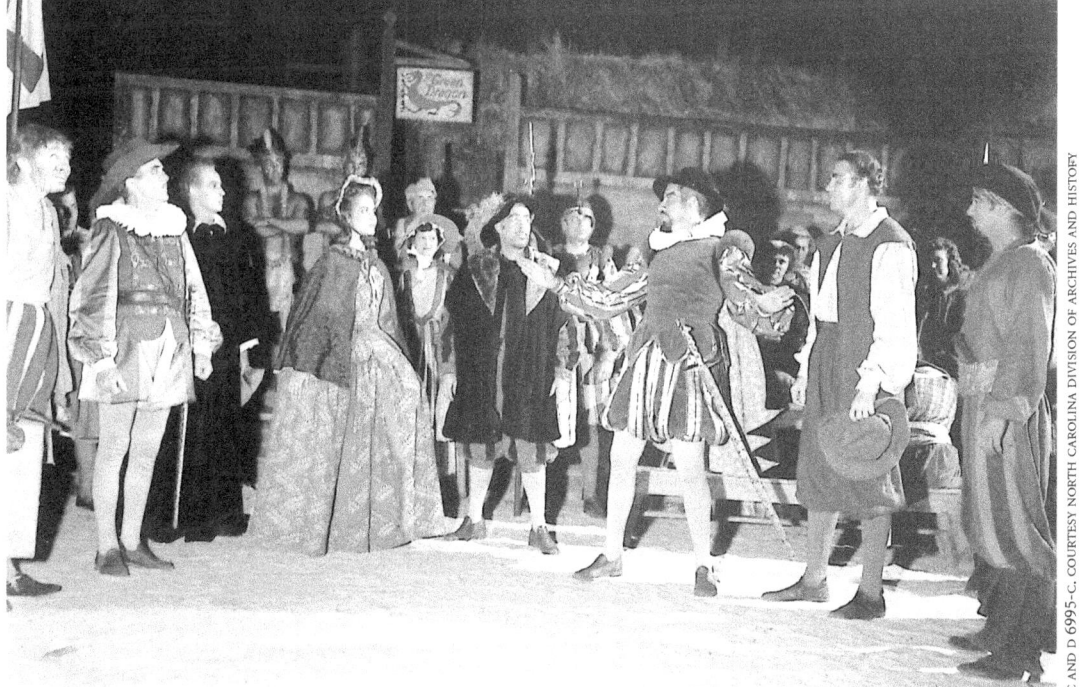

Top: *Amphitheater for* The Lost Colony, *Manteo, circa 1930–1940.* Bottom: *A scene from* The Lost Colony.

hundred feet.... In addition to this a barrier dune was built up on the shoreline of Ocracoke Island for about half of the distance of the island.... In all, one hundred and fifteen miles of barrier dune has been constructed. Over six hundred miles of fencing was used.... A total of 141,841,821 square feet of grassing has been planted ... 2,552,339 seedlings and shrubs were set out [Stick, p. 250].

**The Tennessee Valley Authority.** On April 10, 1933, President Franklin Roosevelt sent to Congress "A Suggestion for Legislation to Create the Tennessee Valley Authority." He suggested that this corporation

> ...be charged with the power of the Government but possessed of the flexibility and initiative of a private enterprise. It should be charged with the broadest duty of planning for the proper use, conservation, and development of the national resources of the Tennessee River drainage basin and its adjoining territory for the general social and economic welfare of the nation [*The Public Papers and Addresses of Franklin D. Roosevelt*, pp. 122–123].

This project was to develop the North Carolina–Tennessee area, provide flood control, increase navigation, and furnish power; both North Carolina and Tennessee would directly benefit. Congress approved the "Tennessee Valley Authority Act of 1933" on May 18, 1933. Controversy surrounded many of the Tennessee Valley Authority projects—particularly that in the Hiwassee River area of North Carolina.

The Hiwassee River rises not far from Clay County in southwestern North Carolina. Its high altitude contributes to the 60 inches of annual rain in the area. The homes and industries of the area have always faced the potential danger from flooding, an increased threat with the construction of an improperly built dam. Residents protested relocation, the prices they received for their land, the loss of family property, and the "new look."

The plans for the Hiwassee Dam recommended a height of 307 feet — about the same as a 20-story building. The TVA engineers specified that such a dam built on the Hiwassee River must be able to discharge 150,000 cubic feet per second — three times the record discharge of 1920. This proposed construction would back the water 22 miles toward Murphy and would necessitate the purchase of 6,500 acres; the plans also called

*The TVA began construction of a dam on the Hiwassee River in western North Carolina that was completed in 1940.*

for the acquisition of 18,500 additional acres as a forest preserve.

In Cherokee County alone many families found it necessary to move because they were dependent on the lumber of the area for their livelihood. The TVA had to relocate 261 families (Billings, pp. 110–121). This relocation

> ...required all the wisdom and tact that the TVA could muster out of its former experience ... these mountain people had spent their whole lives in the coves and valleys bordering the Hiwassee, and except for an occasional trip to Murphy had never been more than 10 miles from home [Billings, p. 120].

The Hiwassee Dam was primarily for power, flood control, and storage — not for navigation. Although its capacity was only one-sixth of the Chickamauga Dam, the Hiwassee Dam — because of its great height — was able to generate even more units of power than the Chickamauga Dam. The turbines could convert 85 percent of the energy of the falling water into power (Billings, pp. 121–125).

## II. Soil

On June 22, 1938, President Franklin Delano Roosevelt requested that the National Emergency Council — a group he had appointed and which included the North Carolinian Frank Porter Graham, the president of the University of North Carolina — present to him a detailed report on the economic problems of the South and possible solutions to the problems. On a positive note, the National Emergency Council reported emphatically that "Nature gave the South good soil." (National Emergency Council, pp. 3, 9)

**The four types of Carolina soil.** North Carolina has four distinct types of "good soil." Gray-brown soils are characteristic of the mountain area of the state. The Atlantic Coastal Plain has light-colored, sandy soils. The Piedmont soil is clay and clay loam in texture. The well-drained soils of the state are primarily red-yellow in color (Orr, p. 40).

These rich Carolina soils encouraged agriculture and a variety of crops within the state. Corn had always been a leading food

*A weather board house with chinaberry and badly eroded soil in the foreground in Person County, July 1939. Photograph by Dorothea Lange, Farm Security Administration.*

*A country road in the coastal area, July 1939. Photograph by Dorothea Lange, Farm Security Administration.*

and livestock crop for North Carolina; tobacco, peanuts, and cotton had also been important to the state.

**North Carolina farms.** In the 1930s North Carolina was a state of small farms. While the average size of a Southern farm (71 acres) was the smallest average in the nation (National Emergency Council, p. 9), the average size of a North Carolina farm in 1930 was even smaller — only 64.5 acres. By 1940 the average size of a North Carolina farm had risen — but only to 67.7 acres, still below the average of the South as a whole (Dodd, *Historical Statistics of the South*, p. 41).

These small farms meant that the per capita income of Carolina farmers might be less than the income of farmers on larger tracts. The Carolina farmer was also more inclined to use family as laborers than were owners of larger farms. In fact, the small farms in Western North Carolina were "almost completely owner operated" (Van Noppens, p. 283).

Buren Davis comments on farming in his family:

My family in most years did all the work on the farm. In some years we might hire some help, but in other years the family alone was totally responsible for the planting, cultivating, and harvesting.

All of our work was always done with mules. My family did not invest in a tractor until the 1950s. From the 1920s until the end of my family's farming days in the 1960s, tending the farm was primarily a family enterprise.

Top: *J. A. Johnson and family are sharecroppers in Statesville; they work about 10 acres. They receive half the cotton and must pay for half the fertilizer, October 1939. Photograph by Marion Post Wolcott, Farm Security Administration.* Bottom: *A dirt road, July 1939. Photograph by Dorothea Lange, Farm Security Administration.*

*A country scene in the Rutherford–Lake Lure area. The photograph was in the collection of Beulah Pruett.*

Nell Burns also reports on her family's farm during the 1930s:

> Our family did all the work on the farm. Once when the fields were white with cotton, I rushed into the kitchen and reported, "Papa has planted the whole world in cotton!" Papa heard me from the next room, and I never commented on his decisions after that!

Reba Hamrick remembers work on her family's farm during the 1930s.

> I remember how hard the boys and girls in our family worked. I have often wondered if today's young men and women would work as hard as my family did—willingly and without complaint. We survived the Great Depression through our hard work. [Daniel on page 298 in *Breaking the Land* refers to these ethics as "a vigorous work culture" that he believes has "withered."]
>
> There was never any question of seeing if our family qualified for any government aid. Our family did not believe in "handouts."
>
> We never had a tractor on our farm in the 1930s. In fact most people in our area did not have tractors. Instead the plowing was done with mules. The boys were the only ones to work with the mules. The girls did not have to plow, cut cane, or shock the corn; my father considered those chores men's work.
>
> The animals on our farm were important economically, but the family loved the animals. Once one of the older mules dropped dead in the fields. The family regretted the death of the animal as much as the financial hardship its death caused.

Tractors were indeed slow in coming to North Carolina and the South. In 1930 only 3.9 percent of the Southern farmers owned tractors; the percent for the nation as a whole was 13.5 percent. By 1940 only 9.3 percent of the Southern farmers owned tractors; it was 1945 before the South achieved the 13.5 percent that the nation as a whole had achieved in 1930. The South was 15 years behind. North

Top: *Fay Toney with mule. The photograph was in the collection of Mrs. Betty Toney Davis.* Bottom: *Joseph Bernie Harper (1908–1981) with his mule.*

Carolina was one of the slowest states in changing from mules to tractors; one reason, besides cost, was the small size of the farms (Daniel, *Breaking the Land*, pp. 175–176). Another reason was that cheap farm labor was readily available in the form of sharecroppers, tenant farmers, and the family of the farm owner; when World War II came and many laborers went into service, tractors became more important. Along with the tractor came other labor-saving machinery, such as combines, hay balers, and forage harvesters (Weathers, Henry L., p. 252).

**Laborers, sharecroppers, and tenant**

farmers. All the people who tilled the good soil of the state, however, did not have title to the land they farmed. Many North Carolina dirt farmers owned no land; they worked as laborers, as sharecroppers, or as tenant farmers during the Great Depression.

African Americans who remained in the South and owned no land often served as a source of cheap labor. These workers seldom profited much from their toil. In the rural areas, African Americans and others, too, worked as day laborers. Rural life for them was often an endless cycle of work and debt (Tarrow). Of the African American farmers, most were tenant farmers. In 1920 the percent was 71 percent; this grew to 74 percent in 1930. In 1935 the percent was 71 percent, and in 1940 it was 70 percent (Lefler, 1963, pp. 613–614).

Working as a tenant was never strictly a racial matter in North Carolina during the Great Depression. Both whites and African Americans worked as tenant farmers. In 1920 about 54 percent of the tenants were white, but that percent increased in the 1930s. The percent rose to 58.5 percent in 1930, to 65.5 percent in 1935, and to 66 percent in 1940 (Lefler, 1963, pp. 613–614).

Throughout the decade of the thirties the number of white tenants in North Carolina was greater than the number of African American tenants. In 1920 there were 63,542 white tenants and 53,917 African American tenants; by 1935 the number of white tenants had increased to 93,173, and the number of African American tenants had dropped to 49,985. By 1940 the numbers of both white and African American tenants had decreased: the whites to 81,842 and the African Americans to 41,994 (Lefler, 1963, pp. 613–614).

*FSA (Farm Security Administration) borrower's family (tenants) on porch of their home in Caswell, North Carolina. Photograph by Marion Post Wolcott.*

Tenant farmers who no longer had jobs often lost a place to live also; coupled with the fact that many mills no longer provided housing, a place to live became a problem for many residents across the nation. Daniel notes that the 1930s seemed to have "evicted the tenants" and to have cut off the traditional shelter of both the tenant farmers and the mill workers (Daniel, *Breaking the Land*, p. 292).

Landowners paid the laborers by the day or by the week. The distinction between sharecroppers and the tenants, unfortunately, was not always clear. Raper and Reid define *sharecropper* in this way:

> For the real meaning of the term "sharecropper" look to such matters as low wages, insecurity, and lack of opportunity for self-direction and responsible participation in community affairs. A sharecropper shares in the risk without sharing in the control. The enforced sales, bankruptcies, foreclosures, and mergers of rural and urban plantations themselves suggest that they, too, do not escape the cost of the sharecropper system [Raper, p. vi].

This labor system for the rural areas became "codified in the statute books." Coercion to continue the system of sharecropping, day laboring, and tenant farming came from the contract, from violence, from illiteracy on the part of the worker, and from the laws themselves (Daniel, *Breaking the Land*, p. 5).

Sharecroppers might furnish the mule, farm animals, or some of the farm equipment; they often had certain fields for which they were responsible to the farm owners. The landowners gave the sharecropper "his due" (portion of money or crop, as previously agreed upon) at harvest time for a year of working the land. Sharecroppers might live in a house belonging to the landowner. Others lived miles away from the land they tilled (Mrs. Getty Davis; Kirby, p. 140).

The "interchangeability of the two statuses [sharecropping and tenant farming] is evident in nearly every surviving farm and plantation ledger before the New Deal and the age of evictions." Tenant farmers often had the use of a place to live and "legal rights" to their crops. Many landowners in the northeastern coastal plains of North Carolina

*Tenant farmer John Davis. Mrs. Getty Davis permitted making a copy of her personal photograph of him.*

furnished cash to the tenants before the harvest, but the practice did not persist elsewhere. Tenants often had to buy their necessities "on time" until they harvested the crops. (Mrs. Getty Davis; Kirby, pp. 55, 66) The crop lien system locked many into an endless cycle of poverty and debt (Walker, *Southern Women*, p. 2).

Mrs. Getty Davis and her husband John were North Carolina tenant farmers from 1926 until 1941. She told of another variable: the purchase of fertilizer for the crops.

> John and I were tenant farmers. We farmed on the halves. We received one-half of the amount the cotton crop brought. We planted and tended the crop and paid one-half of the cost of fertilizer. Mr. Joe, the landowner, had a "seed house" where he stored the cotton seed after ginning. We did not, therefore, have to share in the cost of the seed because the seeds were not a major expense for Mr. Joe each year.
>
> Mr. Joe owned 900 acres of land in North Carolina and South Carolina. We lived in a house on his land from our marriage (1926) until 1941. The land where we lived was in North Carolina, but our hog pen was in South Carolina.
>
> Mr. Joe promised that we could buy some land

from him, but he never got around to allowing us to purchase even a small part of his 900 acres. We were very disappointed that he never set terms for us to buy, but it seemed to work out for the best for all of us anyway — as life frequently does.

**Cash crops and land misuse.** Because the average North Carolina farm was small, each year most landowners tried to use every foot of land for the same cash crops. These landowners encouraged tenant farmers to plant crops all the way to the door of the tenant house each season. This ruling often limited the land available for the tenant families to use for garden plots and increased their cost of living.

Dr. Joseph Goldberger, who researched the cause of pellagra in the 1920s and before, was quite concerned about this use of the land. The *Spartanburg* (S.C.) *Herald-Journal* reported, many years later:

> Cotton, grown to supply the textile mills, was "king" in the South when Goldberger came to [the South].... What disturbed him was seeing cotton rows planted up to the porches of sharecropper shacks, with no room left to grow the foods needed to stop the pellagra epidemic ... (Henderson, p. A-6).

Mrs. Getty Davis also commented on being asked to plant crops all the way to the door:

*A sharecropper with his wife and child in their tobacco field, which is planted all the way up to the porch, July 1939. Photograph by Dorothea Lange, Farm Security Administration.*

*Badly eroded and gullied land in Wadesboro, December 1939. Photograph by Marion Post Wolcott, Farm Security Administration.*

Mr. Joe did not at first permit us to use much of the land near the house we lived in for a garden plot. After several years Mr. Joe allowed us to plant some wheat for our own personal use in a field. He allowed us to do this even though we would be putting land usually devoted to the cotton cash crop into wheat for our personal use; Mr. Joe would receive no portion of our wheat. Being able to plant wheat was a help to our family. We had enough wheat ground into flour for our family for the entire year. We had flour for biscuits, pies, cakes, gravy, and other foods.

North Carolina farmers before the 1930s and even in the early years of that decade did not always plant cover crops or use terracing even when it was advisable. Farmers did not rotate the crops, a practice that would have made the soil more productive. Erosion was common.

**Help for farmers.** Ever since it had created the Department of Agriculture in 1862, the federal government had participated in the scientific study of agriculture and the dissemination of information. The local farm bureaus, the American Farm Bureau Federation, state departments of agriculture, and private agencies had also tried to improve farming and the status of those who tilled the soil. The Morrill Act of 1862 subsidized in almost every state a college of agriculture, which gave direct instructions, set up experimental stations, and maintained extension divisions (Saloutos, p. 28). To answer questions and help acquaint farmers with new farming methods and soil conserving techniques like terracing, rotating crops, and the planting of cover crops, most rural residents of the 1930s relied on the advice of family and friends, the county farm agent, the state, the federal government, and the *Progressive Farmer*.

The purpose of the county agent was to assist farmers with their problems, to bring about a higher standard of living on the farm, to raise the status of the farm family, and to increase the productivity of the land. By the time of the Great Depression, this service had been around for some time in the state. For example, in 1912, J. N. Jones, the first Agriculture Extension Agent for Rutherford County, took office; more help, however, was needed. When President Roosevelt realized the problems with conservation and agriculture, he became intent upon offering increased federal assistance to rural areas and to the nation.

**The Civilian Conservation Corps.** One federal agency that Roosevelt directed particularly to help conserve the soil was the Civilian Conservation Corps (CCC). At his third press conference (March 15, 1933), President Franklin Delano Roosevelt discussed the idea for a federal agency to help with conservation.

> The idea is to put people to work in the national forests and on other Government and State properties on work which would not otherwise be done; in other words, work that does not conflict with existing so-called public works.... [*The Public Papers and Addresses of Franklin D. Roosevelt*, II, pp. 68–70].

On March 21, 1933, Roosevelt described to Congress his idea for a civilian conservation corps as

> ...simple work, not interfering with normal employment, and confining itself to forestry, the prevention of soil erosion, flood control and similar projects.... [T]his type of work is of definite, practical value, not only through the prevention of great present financial loss, but also as a means of creating future national wealth.... More important, however, than the material gains will be the moral and spiritual value of such work. The overwhelming majority of unemployed Americans ... would prefer to work. We can take a vast army of these unemployed out into healthful surroundings. We can eliminate to some extent at least the threat that enforced idleness brings to spiritual and moral stability ... it is an essential step in this emergency. I ask its adoption [*The Public Papers and Addresses of Franklin D. Roosevelt*, II, pp. 80–81].

By executive order no. 6101, President Roosevelt started the CCC on April 5, 1933. The act brought about the largest and most rapid mobilization of men in history. Within three months 300,000 men had enrolled and had settled in the 1,468 camps (*The Public Papers and Addresses of Franklin D. Roosevelt*, II, pp. 107, 110).

**The CCC and North Carolina.** Every state — including North Carolina — had some of these CCC camps. The CCC members dug ponds, built firebreaks, cleaned the beaches of North Carolina and installed fences to prevent erosion of the dunes, built fire towers, restored historic areas, planted seedlings to hold the soil and prevent erosion, and cut trees for timber (Time-Life, *This Fabulous Century, 1930–1940*, p. 131).

More than 27,000 Carolina men participated in the sixty-one CCC camps in the state. The participants had to be single, between the ages of seventeen and twenty-five, primarily from families on relief, live in the camps, wear uniforms, and work in companies of about 200 men (Lefler, 1963 edition, pp. 580–581; Powell, p. 400).

Even the most vehement opponents of the New Deal had little to say against the CCC. The efforts of this agency paid the young men monthly about $30; the workers had to send some of their pay — usually $25 — home to their families. The 200 million trees, which CCC members planted across the nation, would be ready for harvest in the years to come. In addition, these trees would help to hold the soil and prevent the prevalent erosion.

*Opposite: The June 1–14, 1932, issue of* Progressive Farmer *magazine, bought by Clarence Poe about 1903, was a cultural force in the community; it became the second largest circulated farm magazine in the nation.*

All Set for Steady Cutting the Next Day

June 1-14, 1932     **Kentucky-Tennessee Edition**

*Clarence Hamilton Poe (1881–1964), editor and owner of the Raleigh-based magazine* Progressive Farmer *for 57 years. He became editor of the publication at 18 and was owner by the age of 22. He was a member of the State Board of Agriculture, leader in education, forestry, medical care, health, social welfare, and rural life advancement. He educated himself and received five honorary degrees. His awards included the World Peace Medal of the American Freedom Association.*

CCC workers also fought diseases of trees, installed drainage ditches, and built firebreaks. One observer said that a young man who had a job with the CCC would know how to work (Time-Life, *This Fabulous Century, 1930–1940*, p. 131).

Walda Carpenter, in her work with the Welfare Department in Rutherford County, had as one of her duties the interviewing of young men for work with the Civilian Conservation Corps (CCC):

> In order to secure employment with the CCC, workers had to meet certain criteria. In my job, I helped to certify those who were eligible for work with the Civilian Conservation Corps. Frequently it was I who actually transported them to the Civilian Conservation Camp in Rutherford County where they would stay and work for their salary.

**The CCC, the Great Smoky Mountains National Park, and President Franklin D. Roosevelt.** In 1933, President Franklin D. Roosevelt had signed a bill to provide $1.5 million to develop the Great Smoky Mountains National Park. At the peak of the CCC program (1934 and 1935) in the Great Smoky Mountains National Park, there were 16 camps and 4,350 men at work building trails, fire control roads, fire towers, walls, and other constructions. Smaller numbers of camps operated in the area both before and after that period (Campbell, pp. 125, 126).

President Roosevelt toured the Great

MP 237-248, SECTION 2C. COURTESY BLUE RIDGE PARKWAY, NATIONAL PARK SERVICE, UNITED STATES DEPARTMENT OF THE INTERIOR

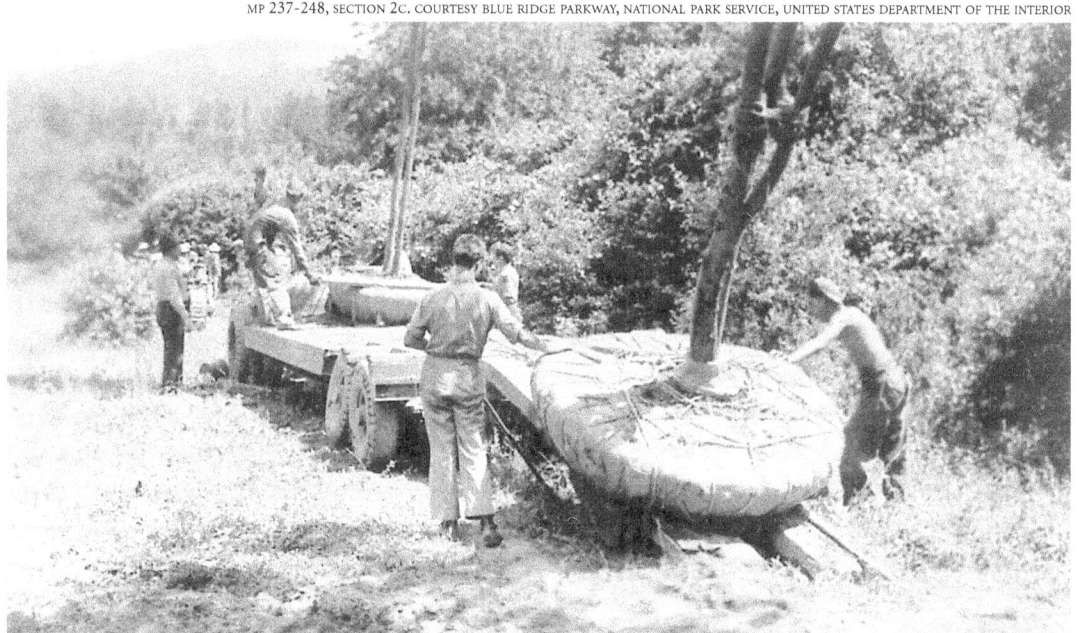

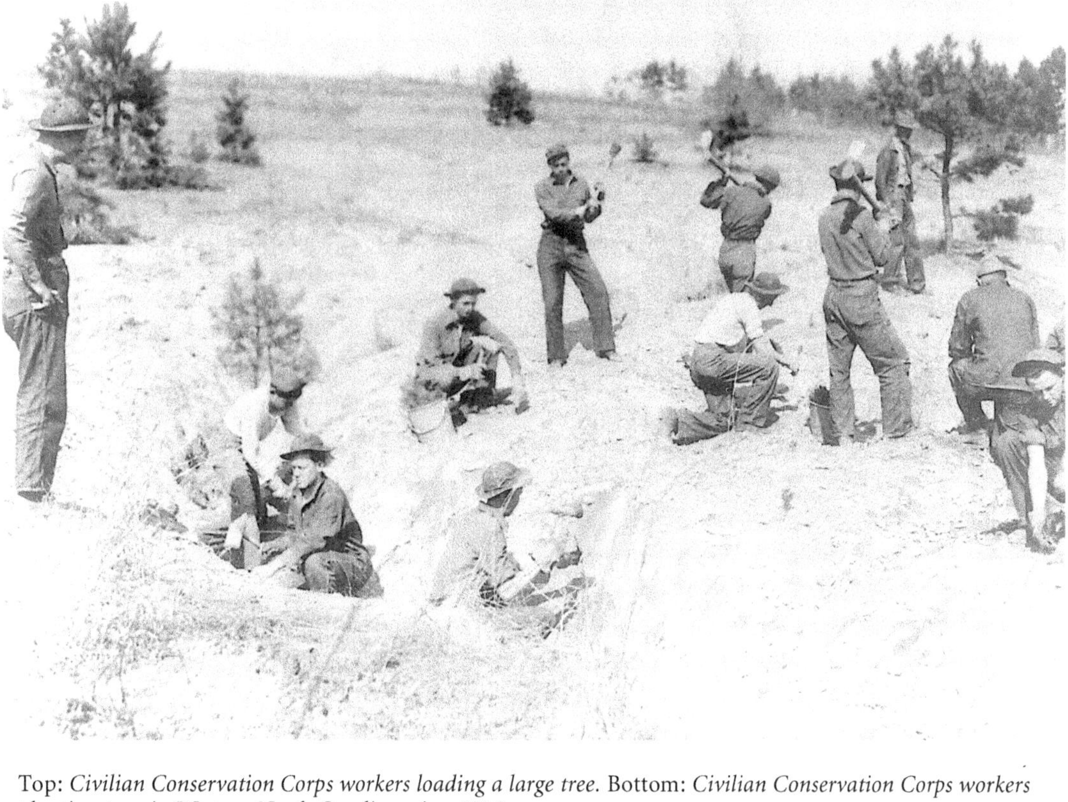

84-6-40. COURTESY NORTH CAROLINA DIVISION OF ARCHIVES AND HISTORY

Top: *Civilian Conservation Corps workers loading a large tree.* Bottom: *Civilian Conservation Corps workers planting trees in Western North Carolina, circa 1936.*

Smokies in September of 1936. He spent the night of September 9, 1936, in Asheville at the Grove Park Inn. The Grove Park was unique. Advertisements billed it as "The finest Resort Hotel in the world" (Johnson, Bruce, p. 53).

Most stores and businesses closed on September 10; people hoped to get a glimpse of the President of the United States. In the immediate area about fifty thousand people—including children from the Asheville schools—lined the streets to catch a glimpse of their President. President Roosevelt gave an "extemporaneous" address at midday. Twenty thousand people in that city were able to get close enough to say that they had participated in the event (Johnson, Bruce, p. 53). Roosevelt said in his speech that he was "tremendously impressed with what we are doing in opening up the Smokies through this great national park" ("Informal Extemporaneous Remarks at Asheville, N. C., September 10, 1936," *The Public Papers and Addresses of Franklin D. Roosevelt*, V, p. 121).

The same day as his Asheville speech, President Roosevelt and his party motored from Asheville to Charlotte to address the Green Pastures Rally. Thousands of people lined the roadways from Asheville to Charlotte to watch for President Roosevelt's car. Griffin states that en route to Charlotte and the Green Pastures Rally, President Roosevelt passed through Rutherford County. The President had

> ...lunch at Lake Lure. He was given a tremendous ovation along almost every foot of the highway from Asheville to Charlotte. Thousands of people lined the sidewalks of Rutherford County towns and villages to catch a glimpse of the President. A sudden, heavy downpour of rain failed to dampen their ardor. Those fortunate enough to possess a good vantage point along the road or street held their places, despite the soaking rain. Between ten and twelve thousand people gathered in Forest City alone to greet the chief magistrate [Griffin, *The History of Old Tryon and Rutherford Counties*, pp. 533–534].

School buses transported school children to the main roads so that they might see the President and his party. Nell Burns told often her childhood remembrances of this event:

> I remember the day well. I was thirteen. A school bus took the students from Hollis School to Highway 74 in Ellenboro, North Carolina. The day was rainy, but when President Roosevelt passed through Ellenboro, he had not put the top up on his car. I could see him clearly.
> I was standing on the side of the road and was waving and calling to him. I felt that his eyes made contact with mine and that he waved directly to me. I was happy to have seen the President of the United States. I felt his greeting was personal.

Children and adults in Shelby, North Carolina, were not so fortunate. The motorcade took a turn the police did not expect and many of the onlookers waited in vain. I would have never forgotten the disappointment of not seeing the President—just as I have never forgotten his personal gaze.

Lee Weathers wrote of this "tragic disaster" in Shelby, North Carolina.

> What might also be classed as a tragic disaster occurred on September 15, 1936 [Lee Weathers gives the date as September 15, 1936; *The Public Papers and Addresses of Franklin D. Roosevelt*, V, p. 343 and Griffin's *The History of Old Tryon and Rutherford Counties*, pp. 533–534 give the date as September 10, 1936], when President Franklin D. Roosevelt, the first President ever to visit Shelby, "passed on the wrong street." Thousands had gathered early in the morning to see him motor through on his way from the Smoky Mountain National Park to Charlotte, where he was to deliver an address at the Green Pastures Democratic Rally. Secret Service men had routed him over Warren Street, where banners of welcome had been displayed and thousands lined the street for miles, filling the windows of store buildings and perched in trees. For hours they waited in the boiling sun. [Other accounts mention that the day was overcast and that a downpour occurred.]
> The President's party was delayed, however, and, whereas he had been expected to stop for a few minutes, the caravan rushed through on Marion Street. The thousands who had lined Warren Street for hours scampered through yards and over fences to get a glimpse of the beloved President.
> The cause of this route change, which disappointed the massed gathering, has never been explained to the public. Max Gardner told me that upon seeing the President in Washington shortly thereafter, he explained. The President, as we all know, was a polio victim and a cripple, so he had notified the pace-setting patrolmen that he needed to void his kidneys in a bottle that he always carried in the car. Seeing a patch

# The finest Resort Hotel in the world has been built at Sunset Mountain, Asheville, N. C.

*Open all the year*
*Absolutely Fireproof*

Mr. E. W. Grove, of St. Louis, Mo., has built at Asheville, N. C., the finest resort hotel in the world — Grove Park Inn. Built by hand of the great boulders of Sunset Mountain, it is full of rest and comfort and wholesomeness. The front lawn is the hundred-acre eighteen-hole golf links of the Asheville Country Club, and with it sixty acres belonging to the hotel.

The purest water obtainable is piped seventeen miles from the slopes of Mount Mitchell, over 6,000 feet altitude.

Biltmore milk and cream exclusively, supplied from 200 registered Jerseys on the estate of Mr. Geo. W. Vanderbilt. It is doubtful if this famous dairy is equaled in the world.

Four hundred one-piece rugs were made at Aubusson, France. Seven hundred pieces of furniture and over 600 lighting fixtures of solid copper made by hand by the Roycrofters.

Five hundred feet of porche at Grove Park Inn

The plumbing material is the finest that has ever been placed in any hotel in the world. Bath-tubs and fixtures all solid porcelain. No pipes visible anywhere. No radiators to be seen — all placed in recesses under windows. No electric bulbs visible.

The "Big Room," or what some call the lobby, is 80 by 120 feet, and is probably the most unique public room in the country. Two great fireplaces in it will burn twelve-foot logs.

For the golfers there are lockers and shower-bath rooms with a forty-foot swimming pool not excelled by the finest clubs in existence, and the players are less than 100 yards distant on the links.

Situated amid the most inspiring mountain scenery, Grove Park Inn offers the finest combination of climate, comfort, and happiness that we believe has ever been made possible.

Especially available for northern guests in the spring, Fall, and Winter, going and returning from farther southern resorts, or for an all Winter resort. Persons with any form of tubercular trouble will not be received at the Inn.

Rates — American Plan $5.00 a day upward. Reached by the Southern Railway.

## GROVE PARK INN

Sunset Mountain        Asheville, N. C.

New York Booking Office, 1180 Broadway

"Mention the Geographic — It identifies you."

*Advertisement for the Grove Park Inn, Asheville, North Carolina.*

*FDR in the Asheville crowd of 20,000 at midday on September 10, 1936.*

of woods on West Marion Street as they approached the city from the west, the patrolmen routed the official car over a street one block from where the people had gathered and the banners of welcome had been displayed [Lee Weathers, p. 60].

Before continuing to Salisbury and Greensboro, the President spoke to the Carolinians gathered in Charlotte.

I have seen the denuding of your forest; I have seen the washing away of your topsoil; I have slid into the ditch from your red clay highways. I have taken part in your splendid efforts to save your forests, to terrace your lands, to harness your streams and to push hard-surfaced roads into every county in every State ["Your Life and Mine, Though We Work in the Mill, the Office or the Store, Can Still Be a Life in Green Pastures and beside Still Waters," Address at the Green Pastures Rally, Charlotte, N. C., September 10, 1936," *The Public Papers and Addresses of Franklin D. Roosevelt*, V, p. 343].

**Chestnut trees in North Carolina.** In addition to the denuding of the forests, the washing away of the topsoil, the erosion, the unharnessed streams, and the poor roads, North Carolinians suffered yet another problem. Because of a blight caused by the fungus *Endothia parasitica*, chestnut trees became a rare sight in North Carolina. The chestnut itself is a food for roasting whole or for use in various recipes. Furniture, tannin for tanning leather, railroad ties, and fence posts came from chestnut trees. Robert Davis recalls:

One of the stories that my great-grandfather P. R. Price [2/22/1887–11/5/1976] frequently told was of eating chestnuts as a child and of the beauty of the chestnut trees. When I was in daycare [1976], I remember seeing chestnuts for the first time in a grocery store; evidently they had been imported into the area. My mother and I thought of my grandfather and his stories of the chestnut tree. A pound of the chestnuts for him to roast in the fireplace formed my Christmas

*A chestnut tree.*

present for my great-grandfather who acted genuinely surprised and pleased to receive the unexpected treat and the wrought iron nutcracker in the shape of a dog that accompanied them.

**The Agricultural Adjustment Administration.** To help with the problems of the farmers, in particular, Roosevelt envisioned a second agency — the Agricultural Adjustment Administration (AAA) — in addition to the CCC. He mentioned it at his third press conference on March 15, 1933.

The other measure is not only a constructive measure but also an immediate one.... That is the effort to increase the value of farm products [*The Public Papers and Addresses of Franklin D. Roosevelt*, II, pp. 68–69].

The next day Roosevelt addressed Congress on a "New Means to Rescue Agriculture." He described a step that he deemed "of definite, constructive importance to our economic recovery." This second measure or agency

...relates to agriculture and seeks to increase the purchasing power of our farmers and the consumption of articles manufactured in our industrial communities, and at the same time greatly to relieve the pressure of farm mortgages and to increase the asset value of farm loans made by our banking institutions [*The Public Papers and Addresses of Franklin D. Roosevelt*, II, p. 74].

The Agricultural Adjustment Administration discouraged foreclosures, encouraged the refinancing of farm debts, discouraged planting the same crop every year, helped to develop market agreements, provided benefit payments for certain agricultural commodities, provided compensation to farmers who limited production of certain crops and who practiced soil conservation — including terracing. (Appendix II describes in detail federal legislation and actions related to the AAA. Other federal legislation during the 1930s is also contained in this Appendix.)

Indeed price increases for cotton were needed. Whereas the state of North Carolina received $62.4 million for its cotton crop in 1929, it received only $19.5 million for its 1932 crop. Many farmers received less for the crops than they had spent to produce them. Foreclosed mortgages, sold property for tax nonpayment, and increasing bills accompanied these low prices (Powell, p. 486).

**Cotton acreage reduction.** On June 24, 1933, John Christoph Blucher Ehringhaus (North Carolina Governor from 1933 until 1937) proclaimed and set "apart the week of June 26 as Cotton Acreage Reduction Week." He called upon North Carolinians for cooperation. On August 31, 1933, and December 19, 1933, Ehringhaus issued proclamations of voluntary tobacco marketing holidays. On September 7, 1933, he called upon growers to sign the tentative governmental contracts so North Carolina could report complete cooperation to Washington. (Corbitt, *Ehringhaus*, pp. 69, 71, 72–73).

**Tobacco in 1932–1933.** Like cotton farmers, tobacco farmers were also in serious trouble in the state. In 1928 the average tobacco cropper received $313 for a share of the cotton crop and $593 for a share of the tobacco crop; after expenses the cropper and family would have $766 for a year of work. Four years later (1932) the cropper would receive $350 for a year's work — if the family were lucky enough to have kept a job. Some other surveys estimate $134 for the year of 1932 (Badger, p. 11).

Four factors contributed to the low prices for tobacco growers. First, the tobacco crop was a highly perishable one; growers could not hold their leaves until the price was right. Second, there were primarily only three companies — American Tobacco, R. J. Reynolds, and Liggett and Myers — which bought the top quality tobacco; the lack of competition in companies limited the options. Third, the grading system that the companies used for the tobacco leaves was a secret; the growers were not sure what made a superior leaf and this made it difficult to command the desired prices. Fourth, the companies could carry over finished products and delay purchases if necessary; this fact worked to the detriment of the tobacco growers. Fifth, the auction warehouse system limited the points at which tobacco growers could sell their harvest (Badger, pp. 25–37).

Before the time of the New Deal, tobacco growers had been unsuccessful in their own four main attempts at improving their marketing position. The first, the Tri-State Growers' Cooperative, failed because of contention from the warehouses and manufacturers. The second, a cooperative under the auspices of the Federal Farm Board, had not been successful because the farmers found that they could neither achieve monopoly power through the cooperative nor set prices. Creditors pressed farmers to desert the cooperative,

One: Water, Soil, and Industries Based on Natural Resources    47

Top: *Linnie Bailey, his son, and his son-in-law Mr. Mann treat their three small farms as one unit. Graham, Alamance County, September 1939. Photograph by Marion Post Wolcott, Farm Security Administration.* Bottom: *Robertson's cotton gin.*

*A tobacco auction in North Carolina.*

the warehouse operators refused to lease their buildings to the cooperatives for sales, locals paid higher prices to nonmembers of the cooperatives, and there was a wait period for cooperatives to pay the growers. The third attempt was an effort to restrict production by interstate agreement or individual state legislation; because no one could guarantee that all participants would adhere to the conditions, this attempt failed. The fourth attempt was Governor O. Max Gardner's "Live at Home" program; this endeavor encouraged farmers who were growing cash crops to devote some land to growing feed for their livestock and food for their family; when his term expired, however, his emphasis began to fade (Badger, pp. 25–37).

Some agricultural departments modeled Gardner's program. A. B. Bushong, teacher at Ellenboro, set the pace. The front page of the February 6, 1930, issue of *The Forest City Courier* reports:

> The first hatch of baby chicks was taken from the Ellenboro School Hatchery last Thursday, the day on which the hatch comes off each week. All of the chicks were sold to a local poultryman who is growing them out for broilers.
>
> The Ellenboro School hatchery with a capacity of 7,000 eggs is owned and operated by the agricultural department of the school to stimulate more poultry in the community for a better live-at-home program and for another cash crop.

Appeals to tobacco growers to reduce their tobacco acreage had failed; tobacco growers would not voluntarily cut back on their acreage unless they had assurance that others would do so. Although some did reduce their acreage in 1932 when they could not afford a larger crop, they still produced as large an acreage as usual in 1933: "[T]he tobacco growers of North Carolina had little option but to wait for Washington and Franklin Roosevelt's New Deal" (Badger, p. 37). The struggle for compulsory control had brought unity to the tobacco growers and their governmental representatives. This unity had not always been the case (Badger, p. 97).

*Booth of E. O. Foster, Farm Security Administration Borrower, the first prize winner at the Caswell County Fair in Yanceyville, October 1940. Photograph by Marion Post Wolcott.*

**Non-support of the Bankhead Act.** When the New Deal "plow up" of 20 percent to 33 percent of the cotton, tobacco, and corn crops came, some landlords chose the fields of the tenant farmer for destruction in the summer of 1933. It seemed to many that the tenant farmers, day laborers, and sharecroppers—"the little folks"—suffered from the actions of the AAA. Even the mules seemed to protest. Mules, which had been trained for years to walk between the rows of crops, refused to pull the plows that destroyed the crops (Taylor, p. 240). Farmers finally devised a plan of hitching two mules together and placing the plow between the two animals; the mules, which had heretofore refused to walk on the rows, now destroyed the crops by walking in their proper place: between the rows (Biles, p. 40).

Another problem with the federal plan was that unscrupulous landowners sometimes kept all the benefit payments instead of sharing with the tenant farmer or the sharecropper.

> The structure of Agricultural Adjustment Administration crop reduction programs allowed landowners to avoid sharing cash payments with tenants. Landlords, themselves strapped by the economic depression, often used the government payments to mechanize their farms and evicted now-unneeded sharecroppers [Walker, p. 4].

Several states identified seven other problems with the type of help the federal government administered. First, many of the states viewed the regulation of agriculture as a local activity reserved to them — not the federal government. Second, the AAA provided "benefit payments" to farmers who limited their production of cotton, tobacco, wheat, and certain other crops and who practiced soil conservation. These actions often reduced production of crops and raised prices; if one's farm was small, however, the increased prices did not always compensate for planting less. Third, some states viewed the raising of money for the payments to farmers as an improper use of the taxing power (Powell, p. 616; Lefler, 1954 edition, p. 582). Fourth, many deserving people did not receive the payments, which were supposed to help the poor. Fifth, some other occupations were having problems also and had little or no financial help. Sixth, it seemed to many that the tenant farmers, the day laborers, the sharecroppers, and other laborers—"the little people "—suffered from the actions of the AAA (Taylor, pp. 238, 240). For instance, the slaughter of 6 million piglets and 200,000 sows to prevent a glut was, to ordinary Americans, an insanity that they complained about bitterly. In actuality, the Surplus Relief Corporation canned the meat and dispensed it to those in need (McElvaine, *Down and Out*, pp. 27–28). Seventh, some areas seemed affected more than others; whereas other states reported a loss of one-fourth of the cotton, tobacco, and corn crops, Rutherford County reported one-third of its cotton crops destroyed (Griffin, *The History of Old Tryon and Rutherford Counties*, p. 526; McElvaine, *Down and Out*, p. 27).

**Support of the Bankhead Act.** In some cases the farmers had a vote for or against federal control of the tobacco and cotton crops in the state. One of the first examples of this opportunity of the farmers of the state of North Carolina to decide policies came on December 14, 1934, when they voted on the retention or disbandment of the Bankhead Cotton Act of the AAA. The previous summer they had plowed up about 30 percent of their cotton and received payment for the acreage by the government.

A Gallup poll of January 5, 1936, showed that 59 percent of the nation's voters opposed the AAA. In the South, however, 57 percent supported the plan (Tindall, pp. 403–404). The Supreme Court on January 6, 1936, the day after the Gallup poll appeared, struck down the processors' tax which funded the AAA and, in effect, struck down the AAA also. ("Roosevelt's New Deal," p. 2).

**Soil Conservation and Domestic Allotment Act.** President Roosevelt seemed committed to improving the soil and agriculture of the nation. On March 1, 1936, he signed the Soil Conservation and Domestic Act. The new law provided benefits to farmers who improved the fertility of their farms and checked erosion. Congress provided $470 million for this program ("A Presidential Statement on Signing the Soil Conservation and Domestic Allotment Act, March 1, 1936," *The Public Papers and Addresses of Franklin D. Roosevelt*, V, pp. 95, 100). The Carolina farmers received more than $99 million between 1933 and 1940 for conservation; certain areas of North Carolina especially needed these conservation measures (Lefler, 1963, p. 582).

**Resettlement Administration.** The government's temporary replacement for the Agricultural Adjustment Administration was the already existing Resettlement Administration (RA), which both Stryker and Tugwell joined; this agency continued the federal photographic endeavors begun earlier under the direction of Tugwell and Stryker. Other offices, such as the Farm Security Administration and the Office of War Information, would later assume full responsibility for the already begun photographic collection (Griffin, *The History of Old Tryon and Rutherford Counties*, p. 525). The federal government tried through the RA to provide needed assistance. Its work in meeting the housing needs in North Carolina is a part of Chapter Five, "Housing."

**Bankhead-Jones Act of 1937.** President Roosevelt was concerned with the problem of farm tenancy. Secretary of Agriculture Henry A. Wallace reported to him on November 17, 1936, that farm tenancy had increased each year since 1880 ("White House Statement and Letter on the Appointment of a Special Committee on Farm Tenancy, November 17, 1936," *The Public Papers and Addresses of Franklin D. Roosevelt*, V, pp. 590–591).

On February 16, 1937, Roosevelt spoke

to Congress. His message addressed the problems of tenancy and the decline in living standards; immediately after his speech the legislature passed the Bankhead-Jones Act to aid tenant farmers by extending loans to purchase land (Note added to "White House Statement and Letter on the Appointment of a Special Committee on Farm Tenancy, November 17, 1936," *The Public Papers and Addresses of Franklin D. Roosevelt*, V, pp. 590–593). Chapter Five, "Housing," explores federal aid to housing in more detail.

**Farm Security Administration.** When the Department of Agriculture assumed responsibility for the RA, the federal government created the Farm Security Administration (FSA) in 1937 to provide assistance to the rural poor and the migrant agricultural workers. The FSA continued to produce the documentary photographs, and Stryker continued to supervise and organize the work of the photographers. He directed the work of federal photographers Arthur Rothstein, Dorothea Lange, Walker Evans, Marion Post Wolcott, John Vachon, and Ben Shahn—some of the best photographers of the time and all of whom captured images in North Carolina.

It was through the Farm Security Administration (1937) that the federal government extended financial aid to a selected number of tenants so that they might become land owners (Lefler, 1963 edition, p. 582).

## III. Industries

In the 1920s North Carolina was the leading industrial state in the Southeast and the nation's largest producer of textiles, of tobacco products, and of forest products. Despite the impact of the Great Depression, the Tar Heel State retained much of this supremacy. In the decade of the 1930s manufacturing tended to concentrate in the Piedmont and — to a somewhat lesser degree — in the mountain region of North Carolina. Cheap labor and hydroelectric power accounted for this centralization.

**"Cheap" labor.** The number of workers increased in North Carolina from 226,425 in 1929 to 293,358 in 1939. This was in part because of an aging population and in part because many workers moved to the Tar Heel State for employment. In fact by 1939 North Carolina had jumped from having 2.34 percent of the nation's employed (1929) to having 3.08 percent. The number of establishments in the state, however, declined during the era. In 1920, for instance, there were 5,999 institutions; by 1930 the number had fallen to 3,797; by 1940 there were only 3,225 (Dodd and Dodd, *South*, pp. 40–41, 70). The regulation of child labor and the limitations placed on the number of hours that employees could work meant, in many cases, the hiring of additional workers for those establishments that survived the 1930s.

**The textile industry.** The major industry in North Carolina was textile manufacturing. In 1930 about 125,000 residents worked in textile mills; by 1940 the number had increased to 175,000. Many of those employed in these mills were women. The chief textile products of North Carolina were, of course, cotton goods. The state had more mills than any other state, employed more workers, and housed one-fourth of all the spindles of the entire industry (Lefler, 1954 edition, pp. 596–599).

**Power companies and North Carolina industries.** Tobacco tycoon James B. Duke's concept to improve North Carolina was his "mill-a-mile" idea. Directed toward the textile industries, Duke's plan was to increase efficiency and production through the use of inexpensive, dependable electric power. His plan would hopefully

> ...pull the South out of the economic doldrums and into the mainstream of American progress. That was the reason he became involved in the production of power in the first place [Maynor, p. 67].

(Chapter Five further details electric power in the state.)

**Prohibition and the liquor industry of North Carolina.** The use of alcoholic beverages had long troubled North Carolina. In 1715 many Carolinians were involved in the movement to remove from the state the

Top: *Colfax gin, in Ellenboro, was a typical cotton gin in operation during the Great Depression.* Left: *Winding yarn on cones is one process for packaging, 1938.*

"odious and loathsome Sin of Drunkenness." Neither making alcohol more difficult to obtain by raising the prices, increasing the cost of a liquor license, nor punishing those who were drunk seemed to prevent the use of alcohol (Powell, p. 451).

In 1852 supporters of Prohibition presented a petition to the General Assembly of North Carolina. The petition listed violence, murder, fights, domestic violence, loss of family income, and political bribes as some of the evils of whiskey. The legislature, however, paid little attention either to the document or to the subsequent appeals—probably because none of the 20,000 signers of the petition

Top: *Cliffside Mill, built by Raleigh Rutherford Haynes and others between 1899 and 1905, was the nation's leading producer of gingham during the 1930s.* Bottom: *The Queen Ann Mill in Ellenboro was typical of many of the textile mills in North Carolina during the 1930s.*

were prominent in ruling circles (Powell, p. 451).

Shortly before the Civil War, the temperance movement burgeoned. Separate branches in the state included the Sons of Temperance for men, Daughters of Temperance for women, and Cadets of Temperance for children. With the focus changing to the Civil War, however, the temperance momentum was lost. The War did bring about the prohibition of using grain to distill liquor because troops needed the food.

After the Civil War the legislature banned the sale or the manufacture of liquor near schools or churches. If a town approved, however, a "dispensary" could sell liquor under the supervision of the commissioners that the town appointed. The National Prohibition Party offered a gubernatorial candidate to the North Carolina election shortly after the Civil War. A ban on alcohol existed throughout rural North Carolina by 1905 unless the municipality, saloon, or dispensary was legal through local vote.

In 1908 legislators yielded to public pressure and called for a referendum on the question of prohibition of alcoholic beverages. In 1909 North Carolina became "the first state in the Union to banish the liquor traffic by popular vote" (Powell, p. 452).

It was December of 1917 before Congress passed the Prohibition Amendment; on January 16, 1919, Nebraska completed the ratification of the amendment making Prohibition the rule across the nation. The Eighteenth Amendment (later repealed by the Twenty-first Amendment) states:

> Section 1. After one year from the ratification of this article the manufacture, sale, or transportation of intoxicating liquors within, the importation thereof into, or the exportation thereof from the United States and all territory subject to the jurisdiction thereof for beverage purposes is hereby prohibited.
> Section 2. The Congress and the several states shall have concurrent power to enforce this article by appropriate legislation.
> Section 3. This article shall be inoperative unless it shall have been ratified as an amendment to the constitution by the legislatures of the several states, as provided in the Constitution, within seven years from the date of the submission hereof to the states by the Congress [*United States Constitution, Eighteenth Amendment*].

**Brewing.** Outer Banks historian David Stick reports that during Prohibition, many people of the Outer Banks developed a new "cottage industry": making liquor. East Lake, North Carolina, became the "corn likker" capital of the nation in the 1920s (Stick, p. 243).

To make the corn liquor, the worker needed a still with at least 3 basic parts: the cooker, where the corn mash is heated; a copper arm that is attached to the cooker and that tapers off until it is as narrow as the copper tubing; and "the worm," or twenty feet of copper tubing that was coiled, attached to the arm, and run through a barrel of water. To coil the tubing, the producer of the still filled the pipe with sand to prevent kinking, stopped up both ends, and wrapped the pipe around a fencepost. Some people tried to use car radiators instead of tubing, but the result was often toxic (*Smoky Mountains Magazine*).

Apples, potatoes, rye, buckwheat, and other foods could be used to make the mash for the whiskey (grain alcohol), but the most common type of mash was corn. To turn the starch of the grain to sugar, the moonshiner placed the corn in a large container with a small hole in it. Added water kept the kernels warm and moist, but excess water drained out of the vat through the opening. Within three days the corn usually had sprouted. The worker dried the sprouted corn, ground the kernels into a meal, added about a half pound of yeast to 50 gallons of water and mash, and mixed it with sugar — the amount of which varied from recipe to recipe; the moonshiner tried to keep the mixture warm for the next few days. (Corn without yeast would ferment in about 10 to 12 days; at times brewers preferred to omit the yeast.) When the mash quit working, or bubbling, it was time to make the "run." At this stage

> ...it ain't good to drink at all, so don't even think about trying it out. It will make ya sicker than a dog. It is usually called warsh right at this stage, and it is sour enuf ta make your eyeballs cross a

*A still in Garner.*

couple of times if'n ya drinks it. Put yer mash in the still cooker and lights a fire under it ta get it to cooking proper (*Smoky Mountains Magazine*).

As the fermented mash cooked, steam went through the arm and into the worm. Because the worm was placed in a barrel of cool water, the steam "dewed" inside the worm; the 'shiner collected this condensation in a container. This collection had to be recycled at least once to get high quality whiskey. To test the strength of the drink, the whiskeymaker would usually throw about ⅛ cup of the liquid in the fire and note if the flames leaped. A connoisseur of whiskey could swirl it in a glass container to test for the proof.

> ...I seen them swirl the shine in the mason jar to watch the bubbles swirl. When they ain't much swirl to it, I mean when you cain't tell they's any water in that there mason jar, then they gits ta being real excited about it (*Smoky Mountains Magazine*).

**Locations.** Mountain residents, like Coastal and Piedmont residents, also engaged in the illegal "cottage" industry of distilling whiskey. The dense woods, the steep hills, and the valleys on the property of many mountain residents seemed perfect for camouflaging the paraphernalia needed for the production of the illegal *white lightning, mountain dew, brew,* or *moonshine*. Little initial investment was necessary to build the still or to secure the corn, jars, sugar, and yeast for the brew. The sparse population in the rural areas meant that few people knew one's business; secrets were easier to keep among the residents who knew and protected each other than in the urban areas where individuals came and went.

Many mountain fathers schooled their children in the intricacies of making moonshine, and the children often saw the work as the family business; intense family loyalties served to keep the recipe and the work secret in the family. Clannish communities saw the revenuer as an outsider pitted against each of them; they often kept mum about the whiskey production if they had any information. The rural poor viewed the federal prohibition law as a benefit to them; they did not consider themselves part of a criminal enterprise (Parramore, *Express Lanes,* pp. 15–16).

**Bootlegging.** In the vernacular, the sale of the illegal liquor was *bootlegging.* Some people purchased the contraband by going directly to the distilleries; others bought their drinks at illegal bars or "speakeasies." The place one bought one's alcoholic beverage reflected one's class—not the fact that one bought the liquor at all.

**Whiskey running.** Whiskey runners picked up their illicit cargo of alcohol from the distillers and sold it to the owners of bars or to "middle men."

> Back in the 1930s and 1940s, when the private manufacture of whiskey was a thriving industry, the farmers in the mountains ... had "liquor cars." These were modified sedans and roadsters with extra power and stiffer suspensions for delivering trunks full of white lightnin' to the cities. Naturally there were arguments about who the best drivers were, and whose car was the fastest. So they started racing the liquor cars at local fair grounds. The racing soon graduated to dirt tracks complete with grandstands [Parsons, p. 8].

Danger accompanied the manufacture, transport, and use of mountain dew. Jail sentences were typical for those caught by the revenuers. High speeds and curved roads brought danger to the runners. Violence between competitors and with revenuers was common. Poisoning from improperly made 'shine or from hazardous metals—like radiators—posed another hazard.

The end of national Prohibition in 1933 did not end the illegal production of alcoholic beverages. Residents of some counties that had voted to remain dry still had a need of the services of the moonshiner. This illegal industry continued to thrive in certain counties in the state.

**Destroying the illegal stills.** One of the jobs of the local sheriff was arresting those who broke the law—including the 'shiners who made, sold, or transported illegal whiskey. As a part of his duties, the law enforcement officer destroyed the still to prevent further illegal activity. Eugene Conrad was a sheriff during Prohibition and when whiskey was illegal in his district:

> I cut up 147 stills in four years. I was figurin' I was gonna get 50 a year, but I fell short a little. As time went on, you know, I cut up so many, it put a lot of 'em out of business. The first year I got fifty, and the last year I only got twenty-five. A lot of 'em went to the road [went to prison and worked on the gang on the roads]. I arrested, and there was eight convicted the four years I was in office for making liquor and selling it.
>
> A lot of 'em took pride in their work. In fact, it kindly runs in the family. I've even seen fathers take little kids five and six years old with 'em to the still. And they just growed up in it; they didn't think there was anything wrong with it. That was their family business.
>
> In fact, way back in the mountains, they practically had no other way to live except to make a little liquor like that, you see, and sell it.... You can see why—it'd just run in the family for years and years [Conrad in Ginns, p. 68].

**Government stills.** The government allowed some people to distill liquor even during Prohibition. The distiller, however, had to pay a tax for each gallon made. Reed Hawkins describes the government stills.

> Now, back when I was a boy, I knowed of two government stills.
>
> Old Man Boaz Riley had one. And he lived right at the edge of Madison County. Old Man Jess Pitt had one, and he lived on up on Turtle Creek.
>
> Government still—you had to have a revenue man there. A storekeeper and a gauger, they called 'em. And your government still—you're running a government still. All right, the government would hire *me* to stamp that liquor. Well, what liquor you run off, whether you run off two barrels or four barrels, the government got a dollar and ten cents a gallon back when I was a young'un.
>
> Now, back then, if you could get it, you could buy blockade liquor for eighty or ninety cents a gallon, but the revenue on it cost you more than the liquor cost you [Hawkins in Ginns, p. 67].

**The tobacco industry.** The tobacco industry in North Carolina continued to grow during the Great Depression; tobacco factories became major employers of African

*Destroying an illegal still in Garner.*

American women. Workers in the industry increased from 14,000 in 1920 to 16,500 in 1939 (Lefler, 1954 edition, pp. 549, 596). This increase reflects the growth in tobacco use and in its production during the 1930s. "King Tobacco" became so important in the state that some people began to call the State of North Carolina "Tobaccoland."

Because of the tobacco tax, Governor Clyde R. Hoey in 1938 was able to attest that the state of North Carolina was

> ...one of the largest and most stalwart supporting members of the family, contributing more to the government than any of the other 47 states, with the exception of New York, Pennsylvania, and Illinois ["Address Delivered before the North Carolina Society of Washington, D.C., Washington, D.C., December 16, 1938," p. 233].

Three cities in North Carolina contained the tobacco industry. Winston-Salem housed R. J. Reynolds, which made the very popular brand of Camels; Durham housed Liggett and Myers, which manufactured the important brand Chesterfield; and Durham and Reidsville housed American Tobacco Company, which produced Lucky Strikes.

The cigarette — as opposed to the cigar, pipe, snuff, and chewing tobacco — had become particularly important after 1913. An urban population began to use cigarettes partly because the pipe, cigar, snuff, and chewing tobacco were too "messy" for city life. Women and girls of the Jazz Age in the 1920s began to feel comfortable with cigarettes, which were more tidy, less expensive, and just as satisfying as the chewing tobacco, snuff, pipes, cigars, and roll-your-own of an earlier time.

Intense competition for the smoking market sprang up among the companies. Up until 1920 Camels had led all cigarettes in sales. Lucky Strike began to encourage Americans to reach for a "toasted" Lucky instead of something sweet; their advertisements featured skywriting "Lucky Strike" over the cities. In 1929 Lucky became the most popular brand of cigarette. In 1934 Chesterfield passed Lucky Strike—leaving Camels in last place in sales.

To counteract the advertising of competing brands, R. J. Reynolds placed 80 percent of its net revenue in advertising in 1934. It even placed an electric sign for Camels over Times Square. Camels in 1935 again became the leading cigarette and would remain at the top throughout the decade (Parramore, *Express Lanes,* pp. 27–28). The billboard outside the R. J. Reynolds Plant reminded passers-by that "I'd walk a mile for a Camel."

**Tobacco farming.** Much work preceded the actual manufacture of the products of the factories of Durham, Reidsville, and Winston-Salem. Tobacco farming was a job that could require eighteen hours or more a day. First, the entire family planted the tobacco seeds in a bed for two months; to keep the plants warm, the workers covered the seeds with cloth or with mulch.

After about two months, the workers proceeded to the second step: transplanting the plants into rows in the fields. The third step was keeping the soil loosened and weeded around the young plant. After the plants bloomed came the fourth step: removing the bloom to provide more nutrients to the leaves; this step was "topping." Next came removing the shoots that sprang up at the side of the plant; this fifth step was "suckering."

*Reynolds Plant, Greensboro.*

*Children help their father, a tobacco sharecropper, in the field, July 1939, Person County. Photograph by Dorothea Lange, Farm Security Administration.*

Removing the ripened leaves was the sixth step called "priming."

The fieldwork was complete, but other steps followed. Sleds helped to transport the leaves to the barn. In the barn — away from the rain and elements — workers strung the leaves into bunches and hung the bunches on racks to dry. In the foothills and eastward, where flue-cured tobacco grows, workers hung it in the tight barns with temperatures high enough to cure the leaves. Pipes circulated the hot air from the fires around the barn; the warm air yellowed the leaves, dried the stems so that the juice would not drip, and cured the leaves. To keep the fire all day and night for a week or more required careful monitoring and workers on various shifts. After the drying, there was still more work. The farmer had to sort, tie the leaves in bundles, and pack the bundles for the auction barn (Parramore, *Express Lanes,* p. 15).

All this work did not always yield enough

*In this barn in Johnston County the tobacco is "put in order" and a fire is built inside to make the tobacco moist and pliable, December 1936. Photograph by Arthur Rothstein.*

money for the tobacco farmer to "make ends meet." Tobacco farmers found the price they received for their tobacco declined from a high of 26 cents per pound in 1926 to just 9 cents per pound in 1932. A crop that might yield $88.6 million in 1929 dropped to $34.8 million in 1932 — less than half of the earlier year. Drought or flooding in an area could ruin a crop for a tobacco farmer and his workers (Powell, pp. 485–486).

Many farmers were receiving less for their crops than what it had cost them to produce the crops; they often could not pay their tax or their fertilizer bills. Mortgages foreclosed; the county sold property for nonpayment of taxes; and farmers sometimes just abandoned their land and moved hoping for a "break" somewhere else (Powell, pp. 485–486).

**Forests and the forest products industry.** Lumber, planing mill products, paper, and furniture became increasingly important for the state. By the 1930s North Carolina ranked tenth in the nation in lumber production. The nation's need for paper and cardboard increased. With this need, the pulp manufacturing in the state began increasing.

More than 699 industrial establishments in Carolina used wood as a basic element. In 1929 the total value of North Carolina furniture products was $54 million. By 1939 the value of furniture produced by the state reached $58.8 million. Although furniture production ranked only sixth in value for the state, North Carolina was the nation's leading producer of wooden furniture. High Point was the center of furniture manufacturing; Lenoir, Hickory, Newton, Conover, Thomasville, Lexington, Statesville, Morganton, Mount Airy, and Sanford were other important sites (Lefler, 1954 edition, p. 600; Federal Writers Project, *A Guide to the Old North State*, p. 20).

Although woodworking had started in New England, North Carolina was an excellent area for furniture-making. Its railroads, its forests, and its skilled, inexpensive laborers were three reasons for its appeal. Many workers came from the tenant farms and bought the furniture that the Carolina factories produced (Bamberger and Davidson, pp. 25–25).

**White's furniture line.** The oldest maker

*Rehabilitation client with his tobacco crop, Oxford, October 1936. Photograph by Arthur Rothstein, Farm Security Administration.*

of fine furniture in the South was White Furniture in Mebane, North Carolina. Will and Dave White founded the company in 1881— the same year as the incorporation of Mebane, a one-company town of 231 residents. The sons formed the company to pay their father's debts after he had declared bankruptcy (Bamberger and Davidson, pp. 23–24, 26).

White's declared a "line." It was perhaps the first furniture company in America to do so. Its trademark guaranteed satisfaction. The federal government even contracted in 1906 with White's for furniture for the officers at the Panama Canal. This was the first federal contract for furniture with a factory in the South (Bamberger and Davidson, pp. 27–28).

**White's furniture and the Grove Park Inn.** In 1921 Fred Seeley and Edwin Grove contracted with White Furniture to furnish the one hundred and fifty-six rooms of the Main Inn of the Grove Park (Bamberger and Davidson, p. 28; Johnson, p. 18). The Grove Park was an important resort to the state and nation; its reputation remained throughout the 1930s and beyond.

President Roosevelt stayed at the Grove Park Inn, used the White-made, North Carolina furniture, and spoke to the Asheville citizens on September 10, 1936, after his stay. President Roosevelt lodged there again when he spoke on September 2, 1940, at the dedication of the Great Smoky Mountains National Park. Eleanor Roosevelt was also a guest.

Many other presidents had stayed at this North Carolina resort and used the White furniture. The presidents before Roosevelt who had visited there included William Howard Taft (1909–1913), Woodrow Wilson

ROBERT WATKINS STUDIO

53.15.15.4618. COURTESY NORTH CAROLINA DIVISION OF ARCHIVES AND HISTORY

*White's Furniture in Mebane was the South's oldest maker of fine furniture and led to the incorporation of Mebane, a one-company town of 231 residents.*

(1913–1921), Calvin Coolidge (1923–1929), and Herbert Hoover (1929–1933) (Johnson, Thomas, p. 53).

Will White continued as President of White Furniture until his death in 1935. Paternalism marked his tenure. In 1923 when the factory burned, 67-year-old White gave the workers their Christmas bonuses, reinvested in the company, and made sure all employees had their jobs back. When he learned one worker was in Virginia, Will wired money for his return (Bamberger and Davidson, 29).

The company remained open during the Great Depression because workers at times accepted reduced wages to keep the factory open. At the death of Will White, Sam White became the new President of the White Furniture Company. His 70-year retirement pin was the first that the Balfour Pin Company had ever made for such a lengthy tenure (Bamberger and Davidson, p. 28).

After a hostile proxy battle, an increase in furniture imports, a decline in furniture sales, an emphasis on quantity for a factory that had always emphasized quality, and,

Opposite, top: *Hamrick's Lumber Yard in Ellenboro.* Bottom: *Lumber-pulp industry at Plymouth Box and Panel Company and McCann Erickson Company, 1937.*

according to some, a lack of profits, in 1993 the *Mebane Enterprise* announced the closing of White Furniture — a North Carolina institution for 112 years (Bamberger and Davidson, p. 40).

**National preserves, forests, purchase units, and parks.** The federal government purchased extensive forest areas in North Carolina for national preserves. These national forests served to protect the watersheds, to reforest denuded lands, to improve timber stands, to prevent and control fire and disease, to furnish water power licenses, to supply models for private landowners, and to furnish recreational areas (Federal Writer's Project, *A Guide to the Old North State*, p. 20).

In 1934 the federal government established in North Carolina two of its three National Forests and two purchase units: the Croatan National Forest and the Uwharrie purchase unit. President Franklin Delano Roosevelt was present at the dedication of the Great Smoky Mountains National Park on September 2, 1940.

Located in the western edge of North Carolina is the Cherokee Indian Reservation (Qualla Reservation). With the building and the opening of the Great Smoky Mountains National Park, this land became accessible to tourists who had not been able to visit the area easily in the past.

A Native American described the area — now a major tourist attraction — in this way:

> A series of mountains rise out of the great Appalachian Range in Graham County, North Carolina, southwest of the Great Smoky Mountains. For my people, the Eastern Band of Cherokees, it is an old, old landmark and they gave it the name Snowbird Mountains because it is said that long ago there once lived on the highest peak a giant white snowbird who was the grandfather of all the little snowbirds we see today.
>
> To me, this region is the top of the whole world — the land of the Sky People, it was said. The skyline is in all directions and close at hand. It is a land of cold, rushing rivers, small creeks, deep gorges, dark timber, and waterfalls. Great billowing clouds sail upon the mountains and in the early morning a blue-gray mist hangs just above the treetops [Tsisghwanai as quoted in Neely, p. 11].

*Pisgah National Forest, 1938.*

*One: Water, Soil, and Industries Based on Natural Resources* 65

*At the dedication of the Great Smoky Mountains National Park on September 2, 1940, President Franklin Delano Roosevelt spoke from a monument straddling the border of North Carolina and Tennessee.*

**Mining.** The most valuable of the seventy minerals that occur in North Carolina were those that industry and builders used. Seventy percent of the nation's mica and most of the nation's kaolin (used in coating paper and in making ceramics and porcelain) came from North Carolina (Lefler, 1954 edition, p. 551).

The farm of B. B. Brooks in North Carolina had two mica mines on the property. John Brooks, B. B. Brooks's son, recalls:

*President Roosevelt at the dedication of the Great Smoky Mountains National Park on September 2, 1940.*

In the 1930s a mica mining company came to our property and helped us get set up to remove the mica from the ground. Bulldozers removed some of the dirt so that we could more easily extract the mica from the soil.

Mica comes in crystals. To be suitable for use, we had to perform two steps. First, we had to dig the mica from the ground. Next, we had to trim the crystals to remove the dirt, rock, and imperfections. I have dug large mica crystals as clear as diamonds. Some mica can be split into layers and sheets.

My best friend Arthur Price and I worked during the week digging the mica and trimming it for sale. On Fridays or Saturdays we sold the mica in a neighboring town. I often took the week's worth of trimmed mica in a cigar box. The cigar box filled with cleaned mica crystals could sell for $20–$40. This was "good" pay for a week's work at this time in history.

Mica is resistant to heat. To demonstrate this resistance, I have even laid a mica crystal in a fire for 30 minutes and placed it directly on my tongue. The crystal was still cool and did not burn.

Mica was used as a viewing window for wood stoves and other fuel burning stoves. Mica is an excellent electric insulator and some forms of mica are used in roofing shingles. It made excellent insulation.

Mica was so valuable and so important to the war effort that after the beginning of World War II, I received a letter stating that because I was engaging in mica mining, I could be exempt from the draft. The lightweight mica insulation used in fighter planes in World War II was a vital commodity. Not wishing to be called "4-F's," Arthur and I both quit our jobs mining mica and both served our country in World War II.

Arthur was killed in Germany on December 28, 1944. I lost the best friend I would ever have in my life.

The state produced about half the national supply of feldspar, used in porcelain manufacture. The leading producing areas of feldspar included Spruce Pine and areas in Mitchell, Yancey, and Avery counties (Federal Writer's Project, *A Guide to the Old North State*, pp. 20–22). North Carolina brick, gold, talc, and granite were also very important to the state and the nation (Lefler, 1954 edition, p. 551).

**Other North Carolina manufacturing.** Although textiles, tobacco, and furniture comprised three-fourths of the value of manufacturing, other industries began to increase in importance in the state of North Carolina. Chemicals (cottonseed oil, medicines, and fertilizers) ranked number four. By 1939 foods (largely flour, butter, bread, and other foodstuffs) ranked third in total value (Lefler, 1954 edition, p. 596).

Nell Burns recalls the threshing of the wheat and cooking for the threshers.

> Wheat was vital to the life and health of Carolinians. The ripening of the wheat was an important event.
>
> Even before the wheat matured, the farmer had usually begun to contract with someone with equipment to cut the wheat and separate the chaff from the grain. Scheduling the threshers was crucial to a good yield, and the farmers often competed to secure the services of the machines—which, in the 1930s might be horse-drawn even though mechanized threshers were available.
>
> "Cooking for the threshers" was an important duty of the women and helped to determine which farm the threshers might schedule first. The harvesters would be more likely to come early in the day to a farm where the midday meal was good than to visit a farmer who provided a meager spread. Because cutting ripened grain before a heavy rain was crucial, "an extra edge" was often helpful.
>
> The farmer drove his truck loaded with sacks of grain to the local milling company where other vehicles and wagons filled with bags of wheat were in line for milling.
>
> The mills during harvest-time ran day and night because all the grain matured at the same time. The farmers found their place in line, left their wagon or their truck with the key still in the ignition, got an estimate as to the time to return, and went home until the approximate milling time. I have often wondered how many places today that one could leave a truck unlocked, loaded with a valuable commodity, and equipped with the key.
>
> A member of the company would move the trucks or wagons forward a "notch" at a time as the mill ground the wheat. Some farmers might have to return in the wee morning hours to watch their milling and receive the money for the crop.

Selma Philbeck Best grew up as the daughter of a dairy farmer in North Carolina. Good nutrition was a priority in her home, and she remembers her parents at work to ensure the health of their family and of their neighbors.

Trips to the local wheat milling companies were a part of her life as a child — as they were to many rural children and adults across the state.

> A favorite trip with my father was when we took some sacks of wheat to the Eagle Roller Mill in Shelby or the Yelton Milling Company in Spindale. We did not always wait for our own grain to be ground but instead exchanged our grain for already ground flour. When I went all the way to Spindale or Shelby on these trips, I felt that I had gone far! In reality the distance was probably 20 miles one way. My dad often bought me a special treat of candy or ice cream on these trips.

*North Carolina marble and granite quarries, circa 1930.*

Top: *Robert Ewart Burns, Ellenboro, in his wheat field where the wheat is up to his chest. This year the wheat production was largely stem.* Bottom: *Threshing wheat in Rutherford County, North Carolina. Photograph was in the collection of Beulah Pruett.*

*Yelton Milling Company in Spindale was built in 1915 and was still in operation at the turn of the century. This photograph shows the "wait line"—where the owner left the vehicle in line with the key in the ignition; an employee moved the vehicles forward as the company finished with the grinding of the wheat, and the employee called the owner at home when it was time to return to view the grinding process. This photograph was made by Glen James.*

Corn was an important part of our diet, but my mother made sure that we had a variety of foods to balance meals. A mill about ten miles from our home ground our corn. I would go with my daddy to the mill.

The corn we brought home was used for cornbread, hushpuppies, a flat cornmeal cake, and — my daddy's favorite — cornmeal mush. Cornmeal mush was particularly good on cold, wintry days. Mother would boil the cornmeal in water until it was thick and spoon it into our bowls. We would add milk, salt, and pepper and enjoy the hot cereal.

Our vegetable garden, dairy products, eggs, and poultry rounded out our diets.

Clarence Griffin in 1951 also remembered and wrote about the gristmills of an earlier time and the important services they rendered.

An ancient landmark of yesteryear, the old water-powered grist mill is fast going the way of the covered bridge and ox-drawn vehicle. Within a few more years the last remnants of this once prosperous industry will have disappeared....

Outside was the hitching rail for the farmers' horses, and in some instances a long feed rack ... the corn mill was to a large extent a community center in the rural areas. There the sheriff met the men of the neighborhood to collect taxes. It was a convenient spot for the taxlisters in the springtime. The farmers made frequent use of the mill for a variety of business, social and political purposes.

Indeed, the growth of North Carolina may be said to have been fostered and nourished around the early corn mills....

The operator of a corn mill, until recent years, was a privileged personage in his community. Under early state laws he was exempt from serving in the organized militia and could not be called to serve as juror. The latter law is still on the statute books. He enjoyed a number of privileges under state law not accorded to others, and was not subject to ordinary calls of the court except upon capias directed to him by the sheriff.

Memories of going to mill on a cold, frosty

Opposite, top: *Loading milk onto truck for selling.* Bottom: *The McKinney Mill in Rutherford County was built in 1860.*

One: Water, Soil, and Industries Based on Natural Resources  71

1845 B. COURTESY NORTH CAROLINA DIVISION OF ARCHIVES AND HISTORY

COURTESY JAMES M. WALKER

morning are yet vivid in the mind of this writer. The Ledbetter Mill ... was the gathering place of the men of the entire countryside. To the large fireplace in the big mill room came the farmers and local public officials to discuss crops, the affairs of the neighbors, politics ... public support of schools and roads, prohibition and multitudinous other topics, or, if in summer, the huge oaks and a lone beech tree afforded ample shade for a multitude, and the crowd availed themselves of a seat on the ground or on the benches along the massive porch, and occupied themselves whittling while weighty matters of state and personalities were discussed....

With the dawn of a new social and economic era following World War No. 1, the construction of good roads ... and other radical changes in the twenties, the community centers shifted.... [The gristmill] is now about to become a part of economic history [Griffin, *Essays,* pp. 1–3].

**Concerns of the National Emergency Council.** The National Emergency Council (NEC), which President Roosevelt appointed to prepare a detailed report on the economic problems of the South, noted that the "difference in freight rates creates a man-made wall to replace the natural barrier long since overcome by modern railroad engineering" (National Emergency Council, p. 59).

Governor Hoey, on December 16, 1938, reiterated this concern for fair freight rates:

North Carolina needs above other things fair freight rates. If there was ever a valid reason for the discrimination against the Southeastern states in this matter of freight rates, not a vestige of that reason now remains. We do not ask to take anything away from the other sections of the country, but we merely insist upon comparable freight rates for the same volume and mileage as accorded those states now arbitrarily placed in official territory. The Federal Government has passed the uniform hour and wage bill without any differentials in favor of the South,

*This train is coming up the Bostic Grade #1 in Bostic. This type of engine was in use from 1880 through the 1940s. This photograph was made circa 1930.*

*Norfolk Southern Depot at Wendell, 1931.*

then certainly by every rule of fair play and justice, the average of 39 per cent higher freight rate differential against the South should be promptly and wholly removed. In the recent hearings at Buffalo, the New England governors boldly admitted that New England now had this advantage over the South and they are determinedly resisting the effort to remove the handicap. Simple justice would demand that since we have uniform hours and wages in industry that we should likewise have uniform freight rates. Any other course would be viciously discriminatory [Corbitt, *Hoey*, "Address Delivered before the North Carolina Society of Washington, D.C., Washington, D.C., December 16, 1938," p. 233].

The NEC also noted the meager research facilities in the South, absentee ownership of Southern industries, the high cost of credit (National Emergency Council, p. 58), and the high tariff policy of the United States. The Council reported that this tariff had forced the South to sell its agricultural products in an unprotected market and to buy goods with high tariffs.

The result was that the South

...has been caught in a vise that has kept it from moving along with the main stream of American economic life. On the one hand, the freight rates have hampered its industry; on the other hand, our high tariff has subsidized industry in other sections of the country at the expense of the South. Penalized for being rural, and handicapped in its efforts to industrialize, the economic life of the South has been squeezed to a point where the purchasing power of the southern people does not provide an adequate market for its own industries nor an attractive market for those of the rest of the country.

Moreover, by curtailing imports, the tariff has reduced the ability of foreign countries to buy American cotton and other agricultural exports. America's trade restrictions, without sufficient expansion of our domestic markets for southern products, have hurt the South more than any other region [National Emergency Council, pp. 59–60].

*A tourist in the mountains near the end of the 1930s.*

**An agricultural leader in the state and nation.** Sharp minds with a desire to advance the State were hard at work. For instance, A. B. Bushong, agricultural teacher at Ellenboro High School, surveyed the community when he came to North Carolina in 1926. He found the farmers had no spring income; he offered an evening course on potato growing and helped organize the Sweet Potato Company. The year 1927 marked the beginning of the sweet potato industry in the entire county. Farmers in the Ellenboro community grew, cured, and sold more than 20,000 bushels of potatoes by 1936. Bushong developed a chick hatchery that produced 25,000 chicks per year; organized the Ellenboro Canning Association that had 15 local units and a yield of 18,000 cans per year and even more preserved units in glass jars; arranged a soil improvement project that resulted in several hundred acres of vetch, soybeans, and lespedeza for the community; instituted the Colfax Free Fair to improve the social life and pride in the area; educated the members of the community on poultry raising so the yield was 25,000 additional hens per year; helped to double the yield of cotton with a decrease of 1,000 acres needed for this production; and helped farmers sell 200 carloads of hay instead of importing the hay.

Local community reports credit Mr. Bushong with having brought about better living conditions during the depression; less money borrowed from the government; better community co-operation; school enrollment doubled; complete consolidation of township schools; farmers able to buy for cash; small community bank in excellent shape while seven in the county failed in one day; the elimination of town taxes; payment of 10 percent cash dividend on sweet potato company stock and all lint cotton selling at a premium [*Forest City Courier*, September 3, 1936, C 1, 4].

**The tourist industry.** Governor Clyde R. Hoey was able to announce that tourism in the state had grown from $36 million in 1936 to $102 million in 1940. He attributed this growth to advertisement. North Carolina actually had become a popular place to visit for several reasons: better roads, an improved economy, and the development of tourist sites [Powell, p. 497]. Improved transportation by rail and bus also made travel easier for tourists. Diesel engines made travel faster for those needing to economize on time.

**Summary.** The resources of water, soil, and their related industries were all important to the State of North Carolina and the nation — particularly during the Great Depression. Many problems surrounded the resources and their related industries. The solution to those problems, however, was not accomplished before the end of the decade of the 1930s.

## CHAPTER TWO

# *Population*

In the 1930s North Carolina and the South, in particular, were rich in many natural resources. Their most important asset, however, was their people. The South, especially North Carolina, possessed a rich endowment in its population. During his administrations, President Franklin Delano Roosevelt often expressed concern particularly about the South — its economy, its people, and its problems. He considered the South to be "the Nation's No. 1 economic problem — the Nation's problem, not merely the South's" (National Emergency Council, Roosevelt's letter to the Members of the Conference on Economic Conditions in the South, p. 1).

## I. *The Population of North Carolina*

To explore the problems and their solutions, President Roosevelt appointed a group that he called the National Emergency Council (NEC) and which included from North Carolina Frank Porter Graham, President of the University of North Carolina. In 1938 President Roosevelt wrote to the group and requested from them a detailed report on the economic problems of the South. He did not ask for the history or the causes of the problems; he merely asked for a report on the conditions and requested that they deliver the report directly to him (National Emergency Council, pp. 1, 3). The NEC titled its response *The Report on Economic Conditions of the South* and centered the report around several main topics, including the Southern people — a vital natural resource.

**Disapproval of the words of the NEC.** Some Carolinians were offended by the catch phrase "the Nation's No. 1 economic problem." These Southerners had seen the progress that the South and the state had made and saw the phrase as

> ...tailored to the headlines, but so easily misinterpreted as another purblind stereotype of the benighted South. It was almost as if the President had rung a bell that activated the conditioned reflex of the sensitive South. The region had accomplished much in the past seventy-five years, North Carolina's Senator Josiah W. Bailey declared indignantly, because of "our forefathers who rebuilt the South after the Civil War" [Tindall, p. 599].

Many Carolinians saw the South — and North Carolina, in particular — as the nation's greatest opportunity for improvement and development. These citizens objected to the words of the President and did not consider the South a problem.

> In the clamor of that political summer the import of the President's commitment to regional development was lost, and his effort to harness the power of sectional feeling to the New Deal cause failed completely [Tindall, 599].

Others, however, remained loyal to the President and his recovery plans.

the West" and as "the most fertile source for replenishing the population of the United States" (National Emergency Council, p. 5).

The National Emergency Council recognized there were population problems in the South. The Council considered the problems not to be local, Southern problems but problems affecting the entire nation. The NEC emphasized these population problems in its report to President Roosevelt (National Emergency Council, p. 20).

Of the four regions (South, West, Northeast, and North Central) of the nation, the South had the second largest population in 1930 (37,858,000). Only the North Central Region had a larger population (38,594,000). Even though many Southerners moved to other areas, by 1940 the population of the South (41,666,000) surpassed even the population of the North Central region (40,143,000). During the 1930s the growth rate of the South was more than 9 percent — largely because of new births. In fact, in the 1930s the Southern region had the highest birth rate in the nation (Dodd, *Historical Statistics of the States of the United States*, pp. 22, 32).

**Low birth rate in North Carolina during the 1930s.** It is significant that while the South had the highest birth rate of any region in the nation in the 1930s, North Carolina did not. In fact, North Carolina experienced a decrease in those younger than 5 years of age from the year 1930 (391,000) until the year 1940 (376,000) (Dodd, *Historical Statistics of the States of the United States*, p. 32).

One reason for the low birth rate in North Carolina was its stand on birth control. North Carolina and New Mexico were the only two states that had not imitated the Comstock Law, which Congress enacted in 1873 to arrest the distribution of birth control information, birth control devices, information on sexuality and sexually transmitted diseases, "obscene literature," and "immoral articles" (Lewis).

North Carolina inaugurated the first contraceptive plan into its public health programs at the expense of philanthropist Dr. Clarence J. Gamble, heir of the Procter and Gamble soap fortune. Dr. Gamble donated

*Frank Porter Graham, member of the National Emergency Council set up by President Roosevelt, was President of the University of North Carolina during the entire decade of the 1930s.*

In December of 1938 Governor Clyde Roark Hoey spoke in Washington, D.C., to the North Carolina Society of Washington, D.C. He made a subtle reference to Roosevelt's calling the South "the Nation's No. 1 economic problem."

> I must insist, however that a state that has required less for relief during the depression than most of the states of the Union and one that has contributed more to support the Federal Government per capita than any other state, save Delaware, is not properly in the class of a problem child [Corbitt, *Hoey*, "Address Delivered before the North Carolina Society of Washington, D.C., Washington, D. C., December 16, 1938," p. 233].

**The Population of the South.** The National Emergency Council's *Report to the President* referred to the South as both "a huge crescent embracing 552 million acres in 13 States from Virginia on the East to Texas on

the first check of $2,250 on March 15, 1937 (Wharton, pp. 463–465). Within three years the clinics were giving medical counsel to 4 out of every 100 indigent wives in 75 of the 100 North Carolina counties. By the year 1940, 75 percent of the public health units in North Carolina (61 of 81) had added birth control to the services offered (Wecter, pp. 179–180, 253–254).

**Age distribution.** Another reason for the slower population growth in North Carolina in the 1930s was the age distribution of its people. In 1930 those under 15 in the state numbered 1,200,000; those 65 and older numbered 116,000. These figures meant that a total of 1,316,000 of the 3,170,000 people (42 percent) in the state were either very young or very old at the beginning of the Great Depression. This distribution is significant because more than 40 percent were not of what is usually considered a child-bearing age.

These figures also imply that more than 40 percent were not of an age usual for seeking gainful employment; these people often relied on those in the employed portion of the population. This dependence of the very young and the very old on the working population increased the burdens of many Carolina workers during the Great Depression (Dodd, *Historical Statistics of the States of the United States*, p. 32).

By the year 1940 the number of older people in North Carolina had increased in both numbers and percentages. Those 65 and older in 1940 numbered 157,000 (5 percent of the total population of 3,072,000) as compared to 116,000 (4 percent of the total population of 3,170,000) in 1930. By the year 1940 the number of children 14 and under had actually declined in North Carolina from 1,200,000 to 1,161,000. Because the total population had also declined from 3,170,000 to 3,072,000, however, the percentage remained about the same: 38 percent (Dodd, *Historical Statistics of the States of the United States*, p. 32).

**Infant mortality.** Still another reason for the low birth rate and the slow population growth in North Carolina was high infant mortality. In North Carolina, 66 of every 1,000 infants died in their first year of life, and many of these died at birth; the national average was 54 (Reed, p. 252). The health conditions for infants in North Carolina and the nation left much to be desired.

**Migration of African Americans.** Further, the migration of African Americans to the North may have been another reason for the slower population growth percentage of North Carolina in comparison with other Southern states. This relocation forever changed the urban North, the South from which they migrated, and the lives of those who chose to migrate. Many African Americans hoped to find better living conditions and to leave the humility of segregation through this move.

To illustrate the decrease in the percentage of "Negroes," the U.S. census gives the following census statistics:

| Year | Total | White* | % | "Negro"* | % | "Other"* | % |
|------|-------|--------|---|----------|---|----------|---|
| 1930 | 3,170,000 | 2,235,000 | 70.5% | 919,000 | 29% | 23,000 | 1% |
| 1940 | 3,572,000 | 2,568,000 | 71.8% | 981,000 | 27.5% | 31,000 | 1% |

*The Census Bureau used these terms (Barabba, p. 32).

**African Americans in North Carolina in the 1930s.** North Carolina had a diverse population in the 1930s. The 1930 census showed little unemployment among African Americans. The proportion of African Americans working in the state was, according to the 1930 figures, much higher than that of other groups. This segment of the population constituted about one-fourth of the population and about one-third of the work force. The number seeking employment through the six federal-state employment offices, however, was probably much higher than that of whites (Bell, p. 71).

Opposite: *Children of a sharecropper. Part of a sequence of North Carolina images from September 1935. Photograph by Arthur Rothstein, Farm Security Administration.*

*Fannie Lou Hamrick (March 4, 1866–June 11, 1939) was a North Carolina resident all her life.*

North Carolina relief agencies were completely segregated in the 1930s. The state was, however, the first to establish a public welfare program for African Americans. Lt. Lawrence Augustus Oxley was the Director of Negro Welfare, State Board of Public Welfare, beginning in 1925. By 1930 he had helped to place twenty-three trained African American social workers in welfare departments throughout North Carolina. Oxley helped to organize forty-six counties for relief. He helped to establish and staff one statewide committee and twelve district committees to advise the governor. Because of the limited

2,159 as porters, laborers, and helpers in stores; and 2,774 as laundry operatives in 1930 (Henry, pp. 37).

When federal relief came in 1932, more adequate aid for African Americans in the state of North Carolina became available. Flour, material for clothing, highway construction jobs administered by the State of North Carolina, and local make-work jobs helped provide needed assistance. In Raleigh and Mount Olive, for example, a large proportion of the make-work jobs went to African Americans (Bell, pp. 71–72).

In 1932 Raleigh employed 258 whites and 640 blacks while Mount Olive employed no whites and forty blacks, mainly to dig drainage canals. In Scotland County about two hundred black women and children canned the produce from the "welfare garden" in return for their free government flour. When Durham distributed this flour from the city market building, the press of blacks at the "Negro entrance" was so great that they broke out a plate-glass window [Bell, p. 73].

Despite these figures, the Great Depression threatened the lives of many and the existence of certain businesses throughout the State.

*The child of a sharecropper in rural North Carolina in September 1935. Photograph by Arthur Rothstein, Farm Security Administration.*

funds, however, even these efforts were meager; North Carolina relief agencies were completely segregated at first (Bell, p. 72).

"Facts on Negro Life in the 1930s" reports that African American farmers numbered 80,966. Of these, 22,081 (26.03 percent) owned their own farms. The number of stores operated by African Americans was 1,907. About 54 percent of the 365,544 African Americans ten years or older in the state were gainfully employed: 178,256 in agriculture; 45,440 as servants; 6,600 as teachers; 163 as physicians; 1,547 as clergy; 9,502 as cigar and tobacco factory workers; 4,637 as chauffeurs and truck and tractor drivers; 8,510 in saw and planing mills; 4,440 in road and steel;

One of the most important [threatened] businesses was insurance. Early in 1930 the state insurance commissioner, Dan C. Boney, placed some thirty black fraternal orders on notice to raise their rates for burial insurance and put their finances in order or else he would stop their insurance business. This order was made necessary because young blacks no longer wanted expensive "all-day funerals with lodge officials in full regalia and armed with pikes and banners marching to their grave." As a result, young people bought life insurance from regular companies. The lodges were left with an older membership whose premiums were inadequate to pay for increasing numbers of burials. Boney placed the Pythian Order of Greensboro and Lodge No. 7 of the Grand United Order of Odd Fellows in receivership when they failed to increase their insurance premiums. He also barred the

National Benefit Company, a black insurance company, from doing business in North Carolina because it was near bankruptcy.

The North Carolina Mutual Life Insurance Company of Durham, the largest black business in the state, was also near bankruptcy by 1933. [Bell, p. 73].

The Great Depression heaped a disproportionate amount of pain on the African Americans. The decade was particularly sobering to many because they had just begun to make some progress. Tension — begun during slavery — increased among the races as a result of the "hard times." Many felt that a continued backward slide was all that they could expect (Henry, pp. 30–31).

The unemployment figures for the African Americans began to increase steadily during the 1930s. The estimate is that in urban areas black unemployment was 30 percent to 60 percent greater than white unemployment. Urban areas with significant African American populations tended to have a higher proportion of persons on relief. Contributing to black unemployment were (1) the dismissal of African Americans to make jobs for white employees, (2) the preferential treatment for white applicants, (3) the stagnant construction jobs that normally employed African Americans, (4) the reduction in domestic service jobs during the lean times, and (5) the competition of the unemployed, skilled whites with African Americans for unskilled positions.

Reduced-rent government housing constructed during the Depression was a boon to many African Americans. To ensure that there was little discrimination, a clause in the construction contracts specified that a certain percentage of the payroll must go to African Americans (Henry, pp. 30–31).

Within the African American society was a class system much like that of the "white" society. There was, however, a unifying feeling of identity among African Americans of all classes because they all felt

*Drinking fountain on county courthouse lawn, Halifax. Photograph by John Vachon, Farm Security Administration.*

the discrimination; all the "whites" did not have this cohesiveness (Federal Writer's Project, *North Carolina: A Guide,* p. 55).

Registration and voting were still difficult for African Americans in the 1930s. As a result of the Scottsboro case, attorneys began to draw African Americans for their jury panels, but few African Americans had actually served by 1939. Working in law enforcement and holding public office were almost nonexistent among the African Americans in the decade. Segregated drinking fountains, public conveyances, movie theatres, waiting rooms, restaurants, and restrooms were typical in much of the state. Some of the federal legislation did not serve African Americans very well; for example, about 90 percent of the African American workers were in occupations not covered by the codes of the National Recovery Administration, created by the federal government in June of 1933. Other legislative acts were more helpful, however. Although there was much room for progress in North Carolina, the reputation for favorable race relations persisted. The education, social, and economic advances had helped foster these relations (Federal Writer's Project, *North Carolina: A Guide,* p. 57).

**The Ku Klux Klan.** During the 1920s and early 1930s there was a revival of the second Ku Klux Klan (KKK). The first KKK had "ceased activities" after the Civil War, partly because of "the restoration of 'white supremacy'" and partly because of federal legislation (Lefler, 1963, p. 564).

The Republican Congress of the United States, concerned about the loss of Republican strength in the South and outraged by the actions of the KKK, took action after the close of the Civil War. First, they investigated the Klan. Next, the Congress passed the Force Act of 1870, the Federal Election Law of 1871, and the 1871 Ku Klux Klan Act. These laws declared that secret societies were illegal. The laws also suspended the writs of habeas corpus (which protected people from being detained without a hearing) "in disorderly areas," increased penalties for violation of the Fourteenth and Fifteenth Amendments, and gave military commanders more control over elections (Lefler, 1963, p. 470).

The "new" Ku Klux Klan in the 1920s and 1930s was weaker in North Carolina than in some other states, like Georgia and Indiana. Nevertheless, it was quite active in some portions of the state (Lefler, 1963, p. 564).

The KKK entered the fight in 1928 against the Democratic candidate Alfred E. Smith,

*A North Carolina Ku Klux Klan meeting.*

who ran against Herbert Hoover. Forest City, North Carolina, was the headquarters for the Klan in the state. Dr. A. C. Duncan directed the Klan in Carolina; he sent speakers into the most remote portions of the state to speak against Smith and campaign for Hoover. The Klan allied with community leaders across the state and conducted an anti–Smith campaign. The campaign was a bitter one. In some counties — like Rutherford — solid control by the Democrats broke for the first time in thirty years (Griffith, *The History of Old Tryon and Rutherford Counties,* p. 506).

Rutherford resident Nell Burns recalled the nature of the Klan in her area:

> The names of the members of the Ku Klux Klan in our area were unknown to the general public. The KKK remained quiet on most occasions, but at times the organization took actions against any person who was not behaving "respectably." The organization served as judge and jury.
>
> One of the white members of our local community was abusive to his wife when he was intoxicated. The Ku Klux Klan came to their home one night in full attire and burned a cross on his front lawn. They called him out and threatened to harm him physically the next time that this occurred, according to the rumors I heard. The ashes from the fire stayed on his lawn for some time; we rode by to see the remains— as did everyone else.
>
> I never knew of anyone else being threatened or harmed by the Klan in our area of North Carolina. Such acts of violence and threats of violence were unusual here.

Chapter Seven gives more information on civic, religious, social, and political organizations, including the National Association for the Advancement of Colored People, in the 1930s.

**The North Carolina Cherokee.** North Carolina during the Great Depression was the setting of ethnic diversity. The original inhabitants of North Carolina, of course, were the Native Americans, referred to as *Indians* in the 1930s. More than twenty tribes were in North Carolina, but the two most important numerically were the Cherokee — from the Iroquoian family — and the Tuscarora — also from the Iroquois and known as the Skaruren or "hemp gatherers." The Cherokee Indian Reservation (the Qualla Reserve) in Western North Carolina was the residence of many of these Carolinians, but other Native Americans resided throughout the state.

The Cherokee tribe was the subject of an 1889 state act, which established their legal rights and a reservation. The communal lands in Swain, Cherokee, Jackson, and Graham counties amounted to more than 56,000 acres. The increase in the North Carolina Cherokee Indian population by county during the 1930s increased the strain on resources of the Eastern Band and enhanced the suffering of the Native Americans (Perdue, p. 43). The increase is evident by the figures below:

| Year | Graham County | Cherokee | Jackson | Swain | Total |
|---|---|---|---|---|---|
| 1930 | 42 (2.4%) | 60 (3.5%) | 553 (32.2%) | 1,060 (61.8%) | 1,715 |
| 1940 | 172 (7.1%) | 29 (1.2%) | 841 (34.9%) | 1,368 (56.8%) | 2,410 |

*(Neely, p. 45)*

Perdue accounts for part of this increase in population as being the inclusion of some whites in the area.

> [M]any whites in western North Carolina became envious of the Indians' resources and benefits. As a result, the Eastern Band was inundated by whites who wanted to get on the tribal roll, or list of recognized Cherokee, in order to share in proceeds from the sale of timber on tribal land and in a rumored division of the band's communally owned territory. This dramatic increase in population severely strained the resources of the Eastern Band, and by the Great Depression of the 1930s the Cherokee were suffering acutely [Perdue, p. 43].

In the 1930s, however, the legal status of the Eastern Band was still not clear. These Native Americans were at the same time wards of the United States, citizens of the United States, and a corporate body under North Carolina state laws (Federal Writer's Project, *North Carolina: A Guide to the Old North State,* p. 30). As late as 1930, only one county in the state of North Carolina permitted members of the Cherokee tribe to cast their ballots (Neely, p. 30).

In the 1930s the government initiated a number of programs to help members of the Cherokee tribe. Federally paid teachers offered Cherokee children a better education in a new school (Perdue, pp. 58–59). This New Deal education plan was different from previous education plans; it did not attempt to change the Cherokee culture dramatically or to deprive the children of their native culture (Neely, p. 30).

Even in the 1930s it was not unusual to see residents of the Qualla Reserve plowing with oxen. Gradually, modern housing and scientific farming techniques helped to improve the lives of many Carolina residents. The government in the 1930s helped organize a cooperative. Through this organization the residents of the Cherokee Indian Reservations were able to market the crafts, including woodcarvings, pottery, and baskets. The opening of the Great Smoky Mountains National Park in 1934 brought thousands of tourists to Cherokee, the town at the eastern entrance. The tribe that had tried to preserve its traditional way of life outside the mainstream had become one of the most accessible, visited tribes in the United States (Perdue, p. 44).

The individuals in the Cherokee tribe did not have a clear title to the land on which they resided; rather they had only possessory rights. They could sell none of this land without the permission of the president of the United States and the Cherokee Council (Perdue, pp. 58–59).

**Other Native Americans in North Carolina.** Native Americans resided throughout the state. Many did not live on a reservation. These Carolina residents received no special privileges. Many encountered strict segregation laws. The segregation of drinking fountains, restaurants, buses, and trains was the

*Qualla Reservation resident who is plowing with ox.*

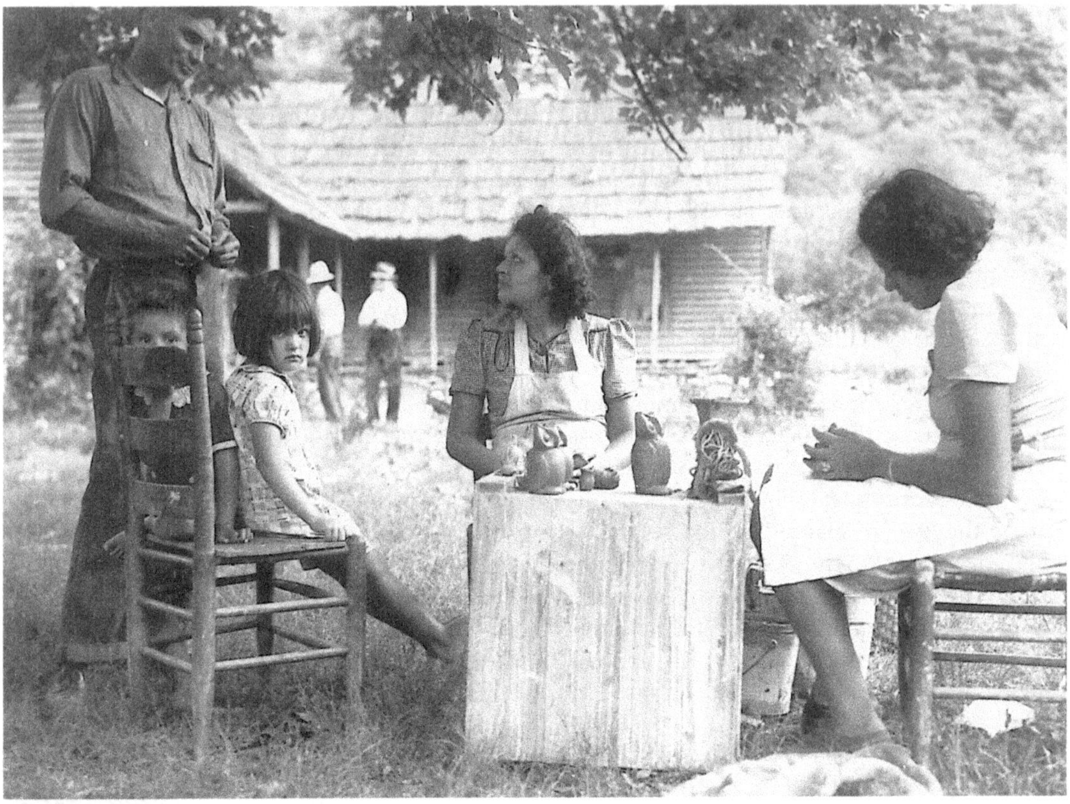

C AND D 2604-A. COURTESY NORTH CAROLINA DIVISION OF ARCHIES AND HISTORY

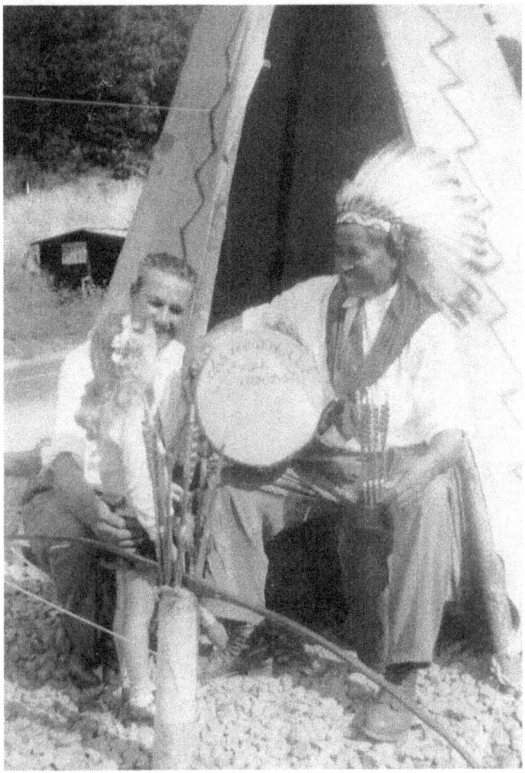

Top: *Pottery selling at the Cherokee Indian Reservation.* Left: *Tourists at the Cherokee Indian Reservation near the end of the 1930s. Chief Walking Stick is the resident in the photograph.*

rule. Some establishments even housed six bathrooms: one for each sex and "race" (Perdue, p. 51).

**On the road and the rails.** All the people of the 1930s, however, did not remain at home during this troubled time. People on the rails—legally and illegally—and on the road, with and without their own transportation, marked the era of the 1930s. Many individuals and families sought their fortunes away from their home.

More than 250,000 boxcar children marked the 1930s. The boys and girls of the rails were often as young as thirteen. The reasons for their travels were many: crumbling families, job searches, adventure, and desertion by parents. The Interstate Commerce Commission reported that 5,962 "railroad trespassers" suffered death or injury in the first ten months of 1932; 1,508 of these

*Family of African Americans, whites, and Native Americans located near Pembroke Farms. Photograph by Marion Post Wolcott, Farm Security Administration.*

approximate 6,000 deaths and injuries were under twenty-one years of age. Kingsley Davis states, "Half a million American boys [and girls] set out to look for the pot of gold at the end of the rainbow. They found it, but instead of gold it contained only traces of mulligan stew" (Uys, pp. 9, 11, 14, 21).

T. W. Martin and his parents lived near the railroad tracks. He remembers that his family often had visitors who asked for work and food. He actually saw some men walking the road and rails with their possessions tied up in a handkerchief and attached to a stick; some travelers carried a valise. Times were hard for many Carolinians; "city cousins" often went to visit "country cousins" who might have some vegetables and meat to share.

Unemployed men and women left home to ride the rails, to seek employment, and to find adventure. Bertha Thompson wrote of her life on the tracks in her autobiography,

*Composite photo of Lumbee Indians, including Dr. Fuller Lowry.*

*Sister of the Road* (1988), and the movie *Boxcar Bertha* records her story on film. All the travelers, however, did not travel alone.

Thompson hints at a reason that hoboes (unattached men and women looking for work), tramps (unattached penniless people looking for excitement), and bums (those addicted to drugs and drink and who have lost respectability) did not often select Southern cities as ideal destinations. She notes:

> In practically every large city that I have visited, except those in the South, I found hobo colleges, unemployed councils, and radical forums that were run especially for the hoboes and the unemployed. They were nothing new to me [Thompson, p. 73].

Thompson estimates there were in the 1930s "between five hundred thousand and two million hoboes in the United States, at least a tenth of whom were women" (Thompson, pp. vii, 48).

Family units also traveled by road and rail seeking work. Dorothea Lange in 1935 encountered a family—"just kids themselves"—on the road. The young mother, 17, the father, 24, and the child were hitchhiking on U.S. Highway 99 in California. The family came from Winston-Salem, North Carolina. Their baby was born early in 1935 in the Imperial Valley, where they were working as field laborers (Uys, p. 144–h; LC USF34-016099-E).

Of course many of the travelers of the thirties told of this life on the road and rails; *Tobacco Road*, a well-known book and movie depicting the era, told of the difficult lives of many of the common people. Migrant workers knew well the life of the rail and road.

**Migrant workers.** Migrant workers were important to the state. Their seasonal labor was essential to the planting, cultivating, and harvesting of the crops. The Coastal and Piedmont portions of North Carolina relied much more heavily on migrant workers or seasonal workers than did the Mountain region. The federal photographs of the 1930s

*Seaboard Airline Railway (SAL) 2401 (2-10-2) and another locomotive on a westbound freight at Ellenboro in 1936 or 1937. Photograph by Paul Price.*

reflect the workers engaged in diverse activities in various sections of the country — particularly in the coastal areas. Although the North Carolina census did not always reflect the presence of this part of the work force, tobacco farmers and producers of vegetables and fruits, in particular, could attest to their value.

**The rural-urban profile of North Carolina.** North Carolina farms had a population of 1,604,000 in 1930 and a population of 1,659,000 by 1940. The percent of rural population, however, decreased from 1930 to 1940 (Dodd, *Historical Statistics of the States of the United States*, p. 457). The percentage of the rural population dropped from 74.2 percent in 1930 to 72.7 percent in 1940; many farm workers moved to jobs in urban areas or joined the ranks of the unemployed (Lefler, 1963 edition, pp. 544, 604–605). During the Great Depression the state's population increased, but not as rapidly as before, and the birth rate dropped sharply (Lefler, 1954 edition, p. 605).

T. W. Martin reported that Carolinians on the farm probably had an easier life than many of the residents in the cities; those who resided in the country were able to raise fruits and vegetables to help provide nourishment for their families. Martin remembered that the country dwellers often had unexpected visits from their hungry "city cousins."

**Per capita income for the North Carolina population in the 1930s.** Much about the people of North Carolina is evident from the earlier information in this chapter. An additional facet of the population gem is per capita income during the era of the Great Depression — particularly as compared to the nation as a whole.

During 1929 the average per capita income of the United States was $705. The average income for the North Carolinian in the same year was $333; this was 47 percent of that of the nation as a whole (Barabba, pp. 243–244).

By 1940 the average per capita income

in the United States had decreased to $592. The average North Carolinian's per capita income was $320, 54 percent of that of the nation as a whole. The average per capita income of a North Carolina resident in 1929, however, was only 47 percent of the national average. North Carolinians had dropped their income only $13 from 1929 until 1940; the per capita income of the rest of the country had dropped over $100. North Carolina had long experienced the sting of the Great Depression. North Carolina's percentage of the national per capital income had increased, but the amount had dropped — a reflection of the poor economic condition of the nation as a whole (Barabba, pp. 243–244; Lefler, 1954 edition, pp. 552, 602–603, 605).

**Unemployment compensation.** North Carolina, after federal stimulus, established the Unemployment Compensation Commission in 1936 to administer the funds collected from taxes on payrolls and maintain an employment service for the State of North Carolina (Lefler, 1963 edition, p. 583). By 1939 Congress — with the endorsement of the states — increased federal appropriations (Wecter, p. 181). As a result, many of the unemployed had some funds to help provide for their children, other family members, and themselves.

**The National Industrial Recovery Act.** Perhaps the cornerstone of the New Deal for workers and businesses was the National Industrial Recovery Act (NIRA), which Congress passed in June of 1933, and the National Recovery Administration, which the NIRA created and which Hugh Johnson led. The NIRA encouraged cooperation among businesses, suspended antitrust laws to facilitate this cooperation, and allowed businesses to fix prices. The ultimate goal of the NRA and the NIRA was the self-regulation of business and the development of fair prices, wages, hours, and working conditions. Section 7-a of the NRA permitted collective bargaining for workers; laborers would test the federal support for their bargaining in the days to come.

To demonstrate support of the NRA, committed individuals wore metal buttons and badges which read, "Doing our part." Businesses also wanted to demonstrate their subscription to the NRA. Those businesses that were abiding by the NRA codes received a 5¼" × 7" decal with a screaming blue eagle for display in their window (Rittner). The federal government encouraged consumers to patronize only NRA businesses that professed, "We do our part."

**Public attitude toward President Roosevelt during the 1930s.** The substantial majority of those in America, particularly working class people, admired and supported President Roosevelt in the early days of the 1930s (McElvaine, *Down and Out*, p. 217). Even at the Convention in Chicago, his presence electrified the delegates. To the cheering audience he made his pledge,

> "I pledge you, I pledge myself, to a new deal for the American people." The band struck up the Roosevelt campaign song, "Happy Days are Here Again!", and for a moment in Chicago that summer, the pall of gloom lifted from American hearts....
> Everywhere the people came to see FDR in huge throngs. They gathered at lonely little railroad crossings in the West just to catch a glimpse of the campaign train; they lined the streets of towns and cities in dense masses; they filled to overflowing the public stadiums and arenas where he spoke. Their faces were grave at first, their eyes searching with quiet intensity the face of the man who might just possibly supply a few answers to agonizing questions. But soon they would begin to smile, to catch the jaunty enthusiasm behind the uptilted cigarette holder, the infectious grin, the voice (it seemed made for radio) which could so well express stern disapproval (of heartless corporations), poke satiric jibes (at humorless Republicans), and speak warmly and directly to people in the language of hope [Goldston, pp. 104–105].

Of course, the election results indicate his popularity. In November of 1932, for instance, Roosevelt received 497,566 votes; Hoover received only 208,344 (Powell, p. 490). In 1936 Roosevelt carried the state over Republican Alfred M. Landon with 615,000 votes to Landon's 223,000. In 1940 Roosevelt's 609,000 votes surpassed Wendell Wilkie's by 214,000 (Lefler, 1963 edition, pp. 584–585). William Randolph Hearst flattered Roosevelt by saying, "I guess at your next election we will make it unanimous" (Time-Life, *This Fabulous Century: 1930–1940*, p. 116).

Top: *This first-day cover and postage stamp commemorate the NRA, August 15, 1933.* Left: *These two pins indicate that the wearer is a sustaining member of the NRA and an NRA employee.*

Another indication that the working class people admired Roosevelt is the number of artifacts remaining from the era. A recent auction sold a chimney flue with a picture of Roosevelt for almost $100. Plaques with his likeness hung on walls of homes beside family and religious pictures. Children's toys included references to Franklin Delano Roosevelt. Even picture puzzles, children's books, movies, and paper dolls from the era had Roosevelt's picture on them. (Chapter Seven includes photographs and descriptions of some of these relics of the Great Depression.) Letters and the crowds that came to see him evidenced his popularity. A common saying about Southern Democrats was that "when they died, they believed that they went to Roosevelt."

Letters to President Roosevelt were many. McElvaine reports that in the week following his election, Roosevelt received 450,000 letters; the average remained 5,000 to 8,000 each day. After adjusting for population changes and literacy rates, he concludes that FDR received four times as many letters as the two previously most popular presidents: Wilson and Lincoln. President Roosevelt found it necessary to hire fifty people to answer the correspondence; in past years only one person was necessary. McElvaine found more than 15 million letters in the Franklin Delano Roosevelt Library. Undeniably the dominant personality of the 1930s was Franklin Delano Roosevelt. He was the focal point of the feelings of Americans. Americans either liked him or disliked him; everyone noticed him (McElvaine, *Down and Out*, pp. 6–7, 205).

**The photographs of the population of North Carolina during the Great Depression.** The photographs of North Carolinians during the decade of the 1930s reflect the population: the rural and the urban residents; the young, the middle-aged, and the elderly; the

*The NRA decal depicts a screaming, blue eagle on a yellow background. The business manager could place this decal on a window or on another flat surface; both sides had adhesive.*

## II. The Men

As a Southern state, North Carolina was in some respects like its Southern neighbors; in other ways, however, it was unique.

**Statistics.** North Carolina, for instance, did experience a population increase during the 1930s. In fact, growth in population characterized the state for each decade from the original 1790 census through 1940. The population of the Tar Heel State grew from 3,170,000 in 1930 to 3,572,000 in 1940 (Dodd, *Historical Statistics of the States of the United States*, p. 32).

North Carolina differed in several respects from many of its Southern neighbors, however. At a time when many residents were moving from the South, others were moving to the Tar Heel State. A large part of the increase in population for the state, in fact, came from those 15 years of age and above — not newborns. Whereas the unemployed were exiting other states, many were coming to and remaining in North Carolina for jobs. This increase in those above the age of 15 was apparent in both rural and urban areas across the State of North Carolina (Dodd, *Historical Statistics of the States of the United States*, pp. 22, 32).

Gainful workers in North Carolina in 1930 numbered 1,141,000 — about 62 percent of those who were of employable age. By 1940 the gainful workers had increased to 1,279,400 — 84.6 percent of those who were of employable age. The total population of North Carolina in 1940 was 6,908,000 (Dodd, *Historical Statistics of the States of the United States*, p. 130).

In North Carolina the number of males and females was almost equally divided. In 1930 the number of males in the state was 1,575,000 (49.7 percent), and the number of females was 1,595,000 (50.3 percent). By 1940 the number of males had increased to 1,773,000, but the percent had dropped slightly to 49.6 percent; both the number (1,799,000)

employed and the unemployed; the forester, the industrial worker, the migrant worker, and the farmer; residents of the Mountain, the Piedmont, and the Coastal regions; North Carolina natives and those who migrated to the state in search of a chance, a better life, and hope; and Native Americans, whites, and African Americans. These Carolina portraits of Tugwell's "important human beings" and their environment are an irreplaceable part of the records of the 1930s.

Each of the important population segments — men, women and children — is deserving of further investigation. Separate sections feature these important natural resources.

---

Opposite: *Campaign buttons for Franklin Delano Roosevelt; John N. Garner for Vice President; Henry Wallace for Vice President; Harry Truman for Vice President; Herbert Hoover for President; Alfred Landon for President; Wendell Wilkie for President; and Thomas E. Dewey for President.*

1933-1936 Election Term
Franklin Delano Roosevelt, President
John N. Garner, Vice President
Herbert Hoover, Republican Candidate

1937-1940 Election Term
Franklin Delano Roosevelt, President
John N. Garner, Vice President
Alfred Landon, Republican Candidate

1941-1944 Election Term
Franklin Delano Roosevelt, President
Henry Wallace, Vice President
Wendell Wilkie, Republican Candidate

1945-1948 Election Term
Franklin Delano Roosevelt, President
Harry Truman, Vice President
Thomas E. Dewey, Republican Candidate

and the percent (50.4 percent) of females in North Carolina had increased slightly by 1940 (Dodd, *Historical Statistics of the States of the United States*, p. 32).

**Marriages.** The rate of marriages throughout the United States dropped during the Great Depression from 10.14 marriages per thousand in 1929 to 7.87 marriages per thousand in 1932. The Great Depression was altering the family unit of the nation and the lives of men (McCutcheon, p. 73).

**Crime.** Wanda Robbins remembers many rural North Carolinians telling of not having to lock doors or windows during the 1930s. Crime rates in rural areas have always been below crime rates in urban areas (Donnermeyer, p. 1). Not everyone felt safe, however.

Prohibition and the Depression resulted in an increase in crime, particularly in the large urban areas of the United States. In New York City, for example, there were 222 homicides in 1929; in 1930 there were 316. During the first seven months of 1931 alone there were 200 murders. Robberies, looting, drive-by shootings, and other crimes filled the headlines (McCutcheon, pp. 121–140).

To explain this difference in crime between the rural and urban areas, McElvaine describes despair as the dominant mood among the unemployed "little man." He describes those without jobs as being docile; he notes that sullenness, not bitterness, and despair, not violence, were typical among the forgotten, common people. He sees these victims as blaming the era and becoming dispirited; he notes little violence among them (McElvaine, *Down and Out*, p, 3).

**Employment of men.** An often-altered image during the 1930s was that of the man as the chief breadwinner for the family. Some men had to share this role or relinquish it entirely to others in the family. Many textile mills and other industries of the decade chose to hire women instead of men. These employers had found that women were often more submissive than men and usually drew lower wages than their male counterparts; this employment practice was one that caused

*Chain gang at work on a road in Western North Carolina in the 1930s.*

many males to lose their employment (Byerly, pp. 11–12).

Another employment practice that resulted in the loss of employment for men was the hiring of children. Child labor undermined the security of some adult males—and some females. In fact, in the South of the 1930s, 148 children out of every thousand (14.8 percent) worked on the farm or in the textile mills (National Emergency Council, pp. 41–42).

This practice of hiring children and women in the mills enabled—or required—some men to seek farm labor or other employment while the other family members worked in the factories. The loss of a part of their traditional role was debilitating for some of the men; others took it in stride and helped keep the family unit strong in any way that they could.

Many men, of course, were unemployed; others continued to labor on the farm, in the sawmills, in the textile mills, and wherever they could find employment.

**Education of males during the Great Depression.** In many families during the Great Depression, the boys found it necessary to stop their schooling to help support the family. These young men dropped out of school. The overall dropout rate in the United States in 1940—at the end of the Great Depression—was 76 percent. Of course the dropout rate at the beginning of the Great Depression before compulsory attendance laws was much greater than 76 percent (Trelease).

In other families the parents might deem it more necessary for a young man to get an education than the girls. The boy with the best "head for schooling" might, therefore,

*Lumber-pulp industry at Plymouth Box and Panel Company and McCann Erickson Company, 1937.*

remain in school while the rest of the family would work in the fields, the factories, the forests, or wherever income was available. The 1930s, then, was a time to focus on work; there was some time for entertainment as Chapter Seven attests, but the lean times were primarily a time to make ends meet.

**New careers for men.** Many men tried alternative ways of making a living during the Great Depression. Plato Rollins Price, for instance, mined feldspar in Spruce Pine, North Carolina, for 10 cents an hour during the early years of the decade. Because he had no lease on the land in Spruce Pine, however, he lost his mining job when the owner tightened his purse strings; his son, Edward Rollins Price, tells of his father and family during the Great Depression.

*Store of Mr. P. R. Price, Mooresboro, 1939.*

My father moved with our family from Spruce Pine to Plum Tree, North Carolina. There he worked as a barber. When times became leaner for the mountain residents, however, they could no longer pay 15 cents for a hair cut. My father had to seek another way to make a living. He moved us again to Rutherford County, North Carolina, where I found a job at Spindale Mills and my sister Jessie went to work at Caroleen.

My father found a service station for rent in Cleveland County, but he did not have the money initially to lease the business and stock the store. I sold my own car and, with that money and a loan from his son-in-law Ervin Grindstaff, my father was able to begin a new business: running a store.

Price's Store, located at the Cleveland County–Rutherford County Line, was primarily a service station. In addition, however, my father stocked socks, gloves, work clothing, and groceries. With the patronage of the community, the help of his family, and the ideal location, Price's Store became a success.

By the time of his retirement in the early 1960s, a one-stop shopping center — an idea ahead of its time — replaced the original wooden building. I had built and now ran an antique store at the location. My father's granddaughter Carolyn owned a restaurant on the same lot. My brother Roy managed a shoe store. The general store itself, however, remained the work of my dad until he sold the store and went to live with my brother Falls; in the mountain community my dad "helped" with my brother's store in Drexel.

Finding work was difficult during the era. Dewey Carpenter, a Wake Forest graduate, had difficulty finding employment for his wife and son. He was able, however, to find work selling Watkins Products. His family and he were very proud of his new job.

Other men, especially those near tourist areas like the Outer Banks and the Great Smoky Mountains National Park, often were

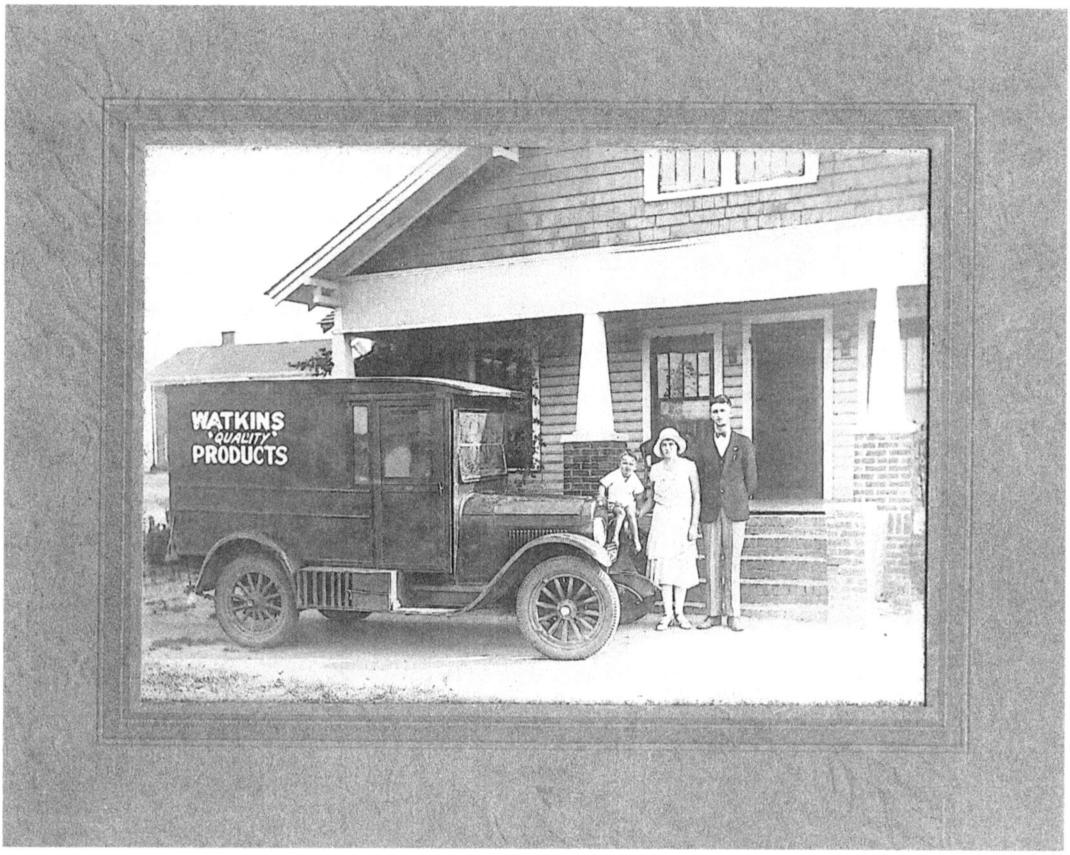


COURTESY WALDA CARPENTER

ROBERT WATKINS STUDIO

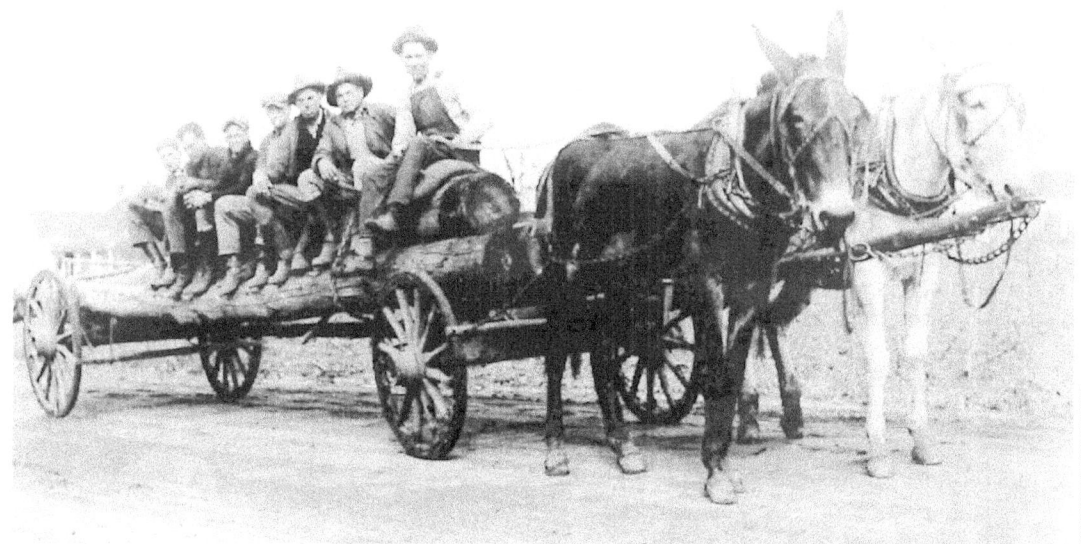

Top: *Walda Carpenter and Dewey Carpenter, Sr. with their young son Dewey Carpenter, Jr. and the Watkins truck, a Chevrolet, during the 1930s. Dewey sold Watkins during the Great Depression when jobs were scarce.* Bottom: *North Carolina loggers. Photograph was in the collection of Beulah Pruett.*

able to increase their income by running roadside vegetable stands, making woodcarvings, creating pottery, training hunting dogs, and even breeding livestock, rabbits, and poultry. Occupations were as varied as the imagination and the Carolina land permitted; most of the North Carolina men were able to maintain their self-respect as they tried to provide for their families during the Great Depression.

**Images of men.** The federal photographers preserved on film the images of Carolina men at work and at play. The viewer sees the men laboring in the fields; at the textile mills; in the smoke house; in the sawmills; in the mines and quarries across the state; on the picket lines; on farm machinery and in vehicles; in the milling companies; on ships and boats; at the local stores; at neighborhood hog killings; in the office; on house calls to the sick and injured; building; making pottery, wooden implements, and woodcarvings; grading and tying tobacco; at the auctions; in the cities and towns; playing checkers and the violin, and in the construction of woodcarvings, barns, buildings, and homes.

## III. The Women

The images of the Carolina woman during the Great Depression are many and everchanging. Many women of the time were primarily wives and mothers, but the image of the single woman and the working woman are important, too. When times became hard, the Southern woman revealed her true mettle.

**Home responsibilities.** In addition to any outside employment they might hold, Southern wives and mothers were largely responsible for the housework and the rearing of the children. Women's jobs were not usually complete after a 10-hour shift in a restaurant, factory, or hospital; after the work in the field or office; or after a day of work at a typewriter or cash register (Byerly, p. 76).

**Mutual aid networks.** Selma Best remembers growing up on a Carolina dairy farm during the Great Depression. Even as a child, she learned to help others and to assist her family make a living during the "tough times."

> We always had a garden, and my mother pickled beets and cucumbers, dried peas, canned fruits and vegetables, and hung onions tied in bunches in the space under the house.
> Aunt Nannie and Uncle Bynum would often harvest their green beans, break the beans at night, and then sell them in the mill villages the next day. Women who worked all day in the mills often did not have time for gardens and preparing vegetables after returning home at night. Our work helped them — but it also made our produce more attractive to the prospective buyers and helped to supplement our income.
> I remember how we helped other people. Frequently we would gather at a friend's home and help them with breaking beans or shelling peas. They would reciprocate our help. Some families had corn shuckings.

Best's remembrance of helping others was not an isolated incident.

> In these crisis years, women's responsibilities did not end with their own families, however. Women were primarily responsible for the complex, reciprocal support that had formed the basis of rural "social services" for generations. In order to cope with the downturn, farm women relied on the same kin, friends, and neighbors as always. They intensified organized efforts to provide community relief. In short, as was the case with urban and suburban women, when economic crisis struck, it was up to farm women to stretch scarce resources so that farm families could survive. Yet even as most of the burden for family and community survival fell on women, men's commercial activities continued to be seen as the highest priority because farm families believed that commercial agriculture was the key to a more secure future on the land [Walker, *All We Knew Was to Farm,* pp. 34–35].
> Rural Southern women maintained the social ties which formed the bedrock of mutual aid networks. Women organized the informal visiting that built ties between neighboring families as well as more formal school and church activities such as Christmas pageants or "dinner-on-the-ground" after Sunday services.... Although maintaining mutual aid networks would later be dismissed as simply socializing, these social ties were crucial to farm families [Walker, *Southern Women,* p. 6].

**African American women.** Segregation and entrenched discrimination circumscribed the lives of rural women. The South's peculiar racial caste system shaped the social lives and responsibilities of Carolinians (Walker, *Southern Women*, p. 2). It was not unusual, however, to see Carolina women — regardless of whether they were African American, white, migrant, immigrant, or Native American — working together in the field, at the "hog killings," and in the tobacco barns. In times of death, illness, and family disasters, rural women usually "helped each other out." This womanhood, sisterhood, and motherhood formed a necessary bond in many communities. Getty Davis told of an African American midwife assisting until the doctor arrived to deliver her child. The midwife placed scissors under the bed "to cut the pain."

Although African American women had limited access to other than domestic jobs, the strength that many showed in providing for their families was a model for everyone during the "hard times." Some took washing

*Tobacco "putting in" near Wilson, July 1938.*

*Women shucking corn in Durham County, 1934.*

and ironing into their own homes, rather than going to another home to perform the labor; working at home was especially convenient if there were young children to care for at home (Byerly, p. 75).

**Cottage or fireside industries.** Pottery, basket making, and weaving were skills often passed down from generation to generation. When the government in the 1930s helped the Cherokees to organize a cooperative to market their crafts, the women — like the men — began to produce items for sale. With the tourist industry, the market for these items increased (Perdue, p. 58).

Similar cottage industries or fireside industries helped add income to other families throughout the state. Women in some parts of the state took work into their own homes for the farms and factories; tying loops together for rug mills (looping) often supplied income. These working women sometimes enlisted other family members — the children, the older parents, and grandparents who lived with them — to help with this additional source of income. The making of quilts and the weaving of rugs in the home were other examples of the creative energies of the Carolina woman. Between the household chores and the care of the young or elderly in their home, many women tied together loops for the rug mills or stripped, graded, and tied tobacco in their homes (Nell Burns; Wecter, p. 27; FSA photographs).

A North Carolina Extension Service brochure called *Chair Caning* (1935) describes the steps in this process. Many women — and men — perfected the skill and were able to add to the income of their family by practicing this cottage industry and repairing the chairs for people in the area (Wilson and Workman, pp. 1–8).

**Domestic workers.** Although most fam-

*The Titus Oakley family stripping, tying, and grading tobacco in their bedroom in Granville County, November 1939. Photograph by Marion Post Wolcott, Farm Security Administration.*

ilies were doing all their own work, some rural and urban families were able to employ outside, inexpensive, domestic help — most often African American women — to assist with the household work and the care of the children. These African American domestic workers could use their hands to stir the dough of the family for which they worked; they could lie down with the children at naptime to add security; they could discipline the young people in the family; but they could not use the front door of the house where they worked each day. A social hierarchy with its own peculiar rules and regulations existed in much of the South — and North, as well (Stoney and Helfand, *Uprising of '34*). In other parts of the state and in "troubled times," women bound together to help each other regardless of caste, class, religion, ethnicity, or social class; working side by side at the canneries and in the fields was not unusual for these women trying to "make ends meet" (Grim).

**The rural woman.** For the rural woman, "the seasonal rhythms of the land and the needs of her family" and others dominated her life.

> The precarious and unpredictable Southern agricultural economy forced women to become experts in doing without, making do, and stretching scarce resources [Walker, *Southern Women*, p. 2].

When the family earned its livelihood on the farm, the work of the wife was essential. Often she farmed the land alongside her husband, reared the children, prepared meals, sewed and laundered the clothing, cleaned, and maintained the home; her labors helped produce and harvest the crops the family needed to survive. Most farm wives also generated some income selling eggs, milk, butter, and garden produce. Only rarely could the rural, agrarian family hire domestic help. Other money-making endeavors included opening stands and novelty stores; raising bees; sewing for others, making and selling quilts, bonnets, and aprons; and accommodating boarders (Byerly, p. 75).

There was a drop of 63 percent in the business of commercial restaurants as families gave up the luxury of "eating out." Despite this drop, many women could still supplement the family income by preparing and serving food to others outside their family. In the rural community of Ellenboro, for instance, Beulah Pruett helped support her family through a restaurant.

**Conserving and preserving foods.** The pinch of the Great Depression meant that many already busy wives, mothers, and female workers had to conserve food safely by pickling, preserving, canning, smoking, drying, and curing. Most women baked the bread — often cornbread or biscuits — for the family, and some made their own soap. It was not unusual for a woman to make and sell molasses, jellies, jams, and baked goods. Community canneries assisted women who brought their own tins and food and who helped with the canning work (Wecter, p. 27).

Pickling was another important way of ensuring food for the winter. Rural women pickled watermelon rinds, cucumbers, beets, onions, okra, and beans. Getty Davis's own recipe for pickled cucumbers required preparation steps for nine days: 5 days the pickles soaked in salt brine and had to be stirred periodically, 2 days in alum with cooking each

*Boarding house run during the 1930s primarily by Sarah Harrill Martin and her family to supplement the family income.*

*Beulah Pruett's Sandwich Shop in Ellenboro.*

day, and 2 days in vinegar, sugar and spices with additional heating each day. With many women beginning to work away from the home, however, recipes changed. By the 1940s recipe books began to have titles like Ruth Berolzheimer's *The Quick Dinners for the Woman in a Hurry Cook Book.*

**Storing food.** Donnis Curtis remembers how her family stored their sweet potatoes for an entire year.

> We would take some small poles and make a triangular structure in the yard near our house. We would cover this foundation of poles with burlap bags. The resulting structure looked like the pictures of wigwams one sometimes sees in books.
> We put the potatoes inside the space; sometimes we added some dirt around the potatoes to help protect them from temperature changes. Next we covered the burlap covering with a layer of mud. This helped to insulate the potatoes against freezing. We added another layer of burlap to finish the protection of our potatoes.
> Somewhere at the bottom of the "tepee potato house," we left a flap. We could fold the flap back, reach inside, and remove some potatoes for our meal. Sometimes we children would reach inside, remove a sweet potato, wash it off, peel it, hold it like an ice cream cone, and eat it for a snack.
> Have you heard people saying that raw potatoes will make a child have a stomach ache? Well, that is not true. My sisters and brothers and I have eaten many raw potatoes as a child. Of course, our tummies were younger at the time!

Not all Carolinians stored their sweet potato yield at their own home.

The year 1927 marked the beginning of the sweet potato industry in Rutherford County. Under sponsorship and insistence of the Farmers Federation and the various vocational agricultural teachers [particularly A. B. Bushong] in the county's schools, the development of a new cash crop was urged. The county was found to be particularly adapted to the growing of sweet potatoes. In March the Colfax township com-

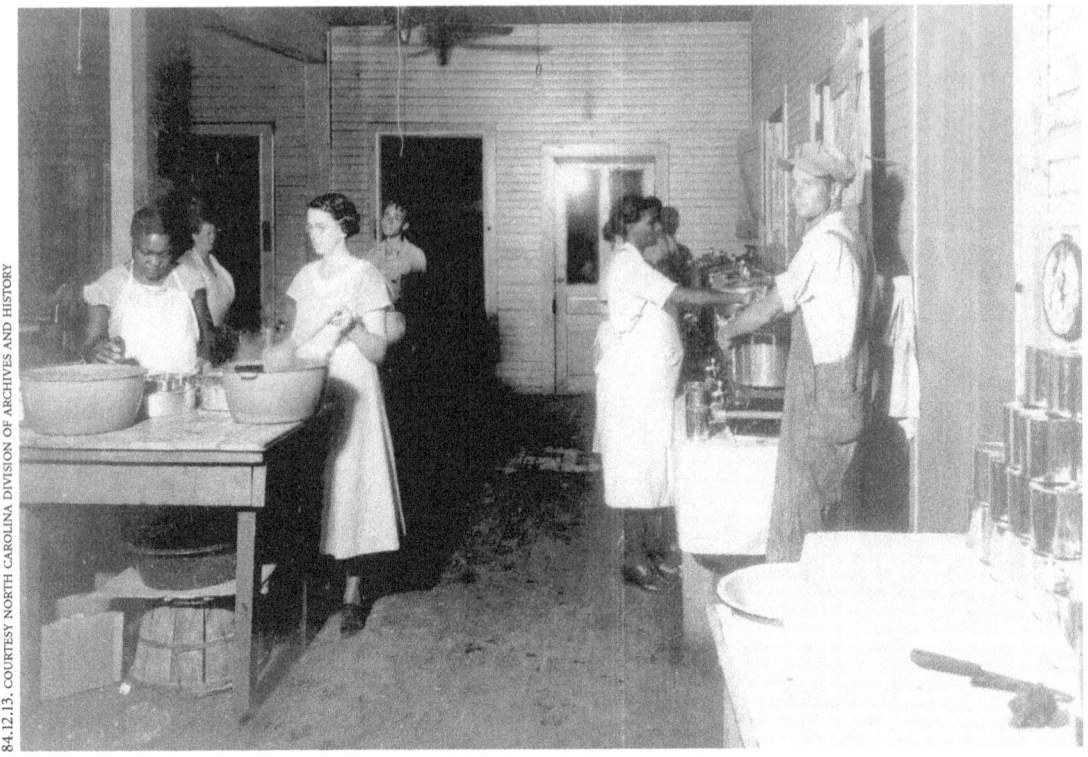

*McGowan Community Cannery, Rocky Mount, 1930s.*

munity decided to build a 3,000 bushel sweet potato curing house, the first of a series in that section. Toward the end of the year the Farmers Federation erected a 12,000 bushel capacity curing house in Forest City, after having profitably sold a large quantity of imported potatoes the previous year. Sweet potato growing is now one of the most profitable crops in the county [Griffith, *A History of Old Tryon and Rutherford Counties,* p. 504.].

Jessie Gibbs remembers how her family preserved apples for the winter.

> Our family found a way to preserve for many months the apples we gathered. My father would take wooden boxes he had built and put in a layer of cottonseed. Next we would add some apples and pack the cottonseeds tightly around them. We would continue to alternate the seeds with the apples until we had filled the box. We would store this box under the house. We frequently had an apple in our Christmas stocking from this supply of apples packed in cottonseed.

**Hog killings.** After the first heavy frost — usually in December or January — the rural family, often with helpful neighbors, would gather for the slaughtering of the hog; the cold weather was necessary to help the meat "keep." The men would go to the pen, which had usually been located far from the house to decrease the smells and flies, and would kill the hog by shooting it or by using a heavy mallet or axe to crush its skull. They would hang the huge animal — usually weighing several hundred pounds — from a gallows and "bleed" it.

Some families kept the blood for blood pudding. Other families in the "Bible Belt" insisted that using the blood "went against the scriptures"; these fundamentalist families might quote verses when someone asked why they did not save or use the blood that they took from the hog.

> And whatsoever man there be of the house of Israel, or of the strangers that sojourn among you, that eateth any manner of blood; I will even set my face against that soul that eateth blood, and will cut him off from among his people.
>
> For the life of the flesh is in the blood; and I have given it to you upon the altar to make an atonement for your souls; for it is the blood that maketh an atonement for the soul.

## Two: Population

Top: *A. B. Bushong, agriculture teacher at Ellenboro High School, was instrumental in starting sweet potato houses such as these in Ellenboro. The Farmers Federation helped finance the buildings.* Right: *C. D. Grant hangs his hog in the smokehouse that he will use for his winter meat supply at Penderlea Homesteads, a Farm Security Administration Project near Willard, December 1936. Photograph by Arthur Rothstein, Farm Security Administration.*

Therefore I said unto the children of Israel, No soul of you shall eat blood, neither shall any stranger that sojourneth among you eat blood.

And whatsoever man there be of the children of Israel, or of the strangers that sojourn among you, which hunteth and catcheth any beast or fowl that may be eaten; he shall even pour out the blood thereof, and cover it with dust.

For it is the life of all flesh; the blood of it is for the life thereof; therefore I said unto the children of Israel, Ye shall eat the blood of no manner of flesh: for the life of all flesh is the blood thereof: whosoever eateth it shall be cut off [Leviticus 17: 10–14].

The same persons who objected to the use of blood often overlooked prior verses which forbade eating the pig, a cloven-hoofed animal which did not chew the cud.

> [T]hese shall ye not eat of them that chew the cud, or of them that divide the hoof ... the swine, though he divide the hoof, and be cloven-footed, yet he cheweth not the cud; he is unclean to you.
> Of their flesh shall ye not eat, and their carcase shall ye not touch; they are unclean to you [Leviticus 11: 4, 7–8].

After most of the blood had been drained, the carcass was scalded in a huge vat of boiling water to loosen the hair. The hide was scraped to remove the rest of the hairs. Next the workers cut the body into smaller pieces for ease in handling. Almost nothing was wasted.

The cooks boiled the liver, combined it with corn meal and spices for preservatives and taste, and formed the mixture into blocks of livermush. When the workers combined the liver with the snout and other parts before forming the blocks, the resulting loaf was scrapple. The workforce might wash, clean, and fry the intestines for chitlins; these chitlins could be eaten alone or added to cornbread for cracklin' bread. When stuffed with ground meat and spices, the thin skin of

*Women stirring kettles over a fire during hog killing.*

the intestines could form the casing for link sausage. The brains from the skull were a delicacy when mixed with eggs and fried for breakfast. Much of the fat was rendered, or cooked down, for lard; the lard would later be heated for frying, as a main ingredient in biscuits, and as a seasoning for vegetables.

The family often packed the hams, shoulder, and side meat in salt and seasonings; later these portions would be covered with cloth and hung in the smoke house. This carefully preserved meat would keep for several months until warm weather arrived (Donnis Curtis; Parramore, *Express Lanes,* p. 8; Buren Davis; Dan Martin).

The "fatback" cooked with vegetables would provide seasoning or, when fried, would serve as "Arkansas ham." Annette Martin shared her mother-in-law's unique recipe for cooking the fatback:

> Before going to the field in the morning, we would slice some of the fatback and leave it in buttermilk to marinate. When we came in at dinner or supper, we would batter the meat in cornmeal and flour and fry it until it was crisp.

Annette said she had tried the batter-fried meat and found it quite good.

Ham, fried until tender, often had as its accompaniment "red eye gravy." The usual method of preparing the side item was to remove the cooked meat from the pan and add some coffee from the pot brewing on the back of the stove to the drippings. Poured on the grits commonly ground at the local gristmill, red eye gravy was standard fare for a special Carolina breakfast.

**Native American women.** Native American women labored alongside the men in the fields. Like other rural women, they often made the clothing for the family, did the cooking, preserved food for the "off season," dressed the chickens and other animals, ground the corn and acorns for meal, cleaned, laundered, cared for the children and sick, made items for family use and for sale, and still found time for working with the tourist industry.

**Home Demonstration Clubs.** In North Carolina in 1920 the State Organization of Home Demonstration Clubs began; the pur-

*Cherokees on Qualla Reservation, July 1939.*

pose of this group was to expand the work of the canning clubs of the Farmers' Cooperative. Before that time, certain individual counties had already begun local "Women's Auxiliaries" or "Women's Clubs." In Rutherford County, the first of these clubs was the Tomato Club in the Mt. Pleasant Community in 1918 (Public Records from Rutherford County Cooperative Extension Office; Mrs. Mae Blanton, Tracy Davis).

O. Max Gardner, North Carolina Governor from 1929 until 1933, encouraged the work of the Home Demonstration Clubs—particularly to help with his "Live at Home" program, which encouraged families to grow or make what they needed and to rely on themselves. The Live at Home Program was a decided change because many of the farmers in the state usually grew crops to sell for cash. Now Gardner urged farmers to produce grains and hay for the livestock and food for their families. He encouraged families to dry and preserve what was not immediately needed. Home demonstration agents offered advice and encouragement (Powell, p. 488).

> In those early years of the home demonstration agent [in Cleveland County, in particular], there were some objections to the college-trained women, for it was felt that the experienced housewives knew more and were better qualified to instruct their daughters and neighbors [Weathers, Henry, 258].

Other clubs had developed and formed across the county and state; for instance, the Ellenboro Home Demonstration Club had as its first president Miss Cleo Burns (August 21, 1882–November 29, 1966). Beginning with her successful leadership, the club was still active in 2002. The Ellenboro Club gave many demonstrations on canning, quilting, etiquette, cooking, health care, crafts, feeding and bathing invalids, and arts (Public Records from Rutherford County Cooperative Extension Office; Mrs. Mae Blanton; Tracy Davis). In 1936 the North Carolina Federation of Home Demonstration Clubs became a charter member of the National Home Demonstration Council (*North Carolina Yearbook*, p. 1).

During the lean times the Carolina

*Miss Cleo Burns (August 21, 1882–November 29, 1966) was the first President of the Ellenboro Woman's Club.*

women especially needed the services of these clubs. The programs offered suggestions on nutrition, economical dishes, meal preparation, home problems, care of the sick, and food preservation. County fairs often featured displays of the Home Demonstration Clubs.

During this time, thrifty women even used the rinds of watermelons for pickles, as this adaptation of a family recipe indicates:

### Watermelon Rind Pickles

Cut the watermelon rind into 2" cubes. Be sure to trim away the dark green and the pink parts. Weigh the cubes. Soak the cubes overnight in line water. (Use about 1 ounce of lime to each 2 quarts of water.) Drain the cubes, rinse them well, and allow them to stand 2 hours in cold water. Cook the cubes until tender.

Combine 1 cup of water, 2 cups of sugar, and 1 cup white vinegar for each pound of rind. Tie in a bag 1 tablespoon cinnamon and 1½ teaspoon whole cloves. Drop into the container with the sugar and vinegar mixture. Simmer 10 minutes. Remove the spice bag.

Add watermelon cubes and ½ lemon thinly cut to hot mixture. Place in jars and seal well [Adapted from a family recipe of Helen Collins].

*Home demonstration booth at Caswell County Fair in Yanceyville in October 1940. Photograph by Marion Post Wolcott.*

During 1930 the programs for the Rutherford County Women's Clubs included preparing foods for the sick, making candy and inexpensive gifts, preparing cucumber pickles, making jellies and jams, proper table setting, and preparing bread from fermented potatoes (Public Records from Rutherford County Cooperative Extension Office; Mrs. Mae Blanton; Tracy Davis).

**Potato bread.** One of the recipes for making bread from fermented potatoes involved the preparation of a starter. This type recipe was economical because yeast had to be purchased only once. Below is one such example:

### Aunt Blanch's Potato Starter

1 large potato, peeled and sliced
3 cups water
2 tablespoons sugar
½ teaspoon salt
1 cake of yeast

Mix the sugar, salt, yeast, and water. Pour over the potato in a 1 quart jar. The next day again add the mixture of water, sugar, and salt again. The starter is ready to use [Courtesy of Lucille Carpenter].

**Sewing.** Many women, during the Depression years, began or continued to make their own clothing—and even hats—if they could afford the material. They attempted to "copy" expensive clothes by using cheaper materials. Longer skirts and more feminine styles began to replace the shorter, more boyish dresses of the 1920s. By the mid–1930s, however, skirt lengths began to rise again. Slacks, shorts, and beach pajamas began to find acceptance in many communities (Wecter, p. 28). Some unemployed, rural, and urban women who were truly experiencing "lean times" sought merely to stay warm and ceased to appear in public because of their worn, tattered clothing (Wecter, p. 30).

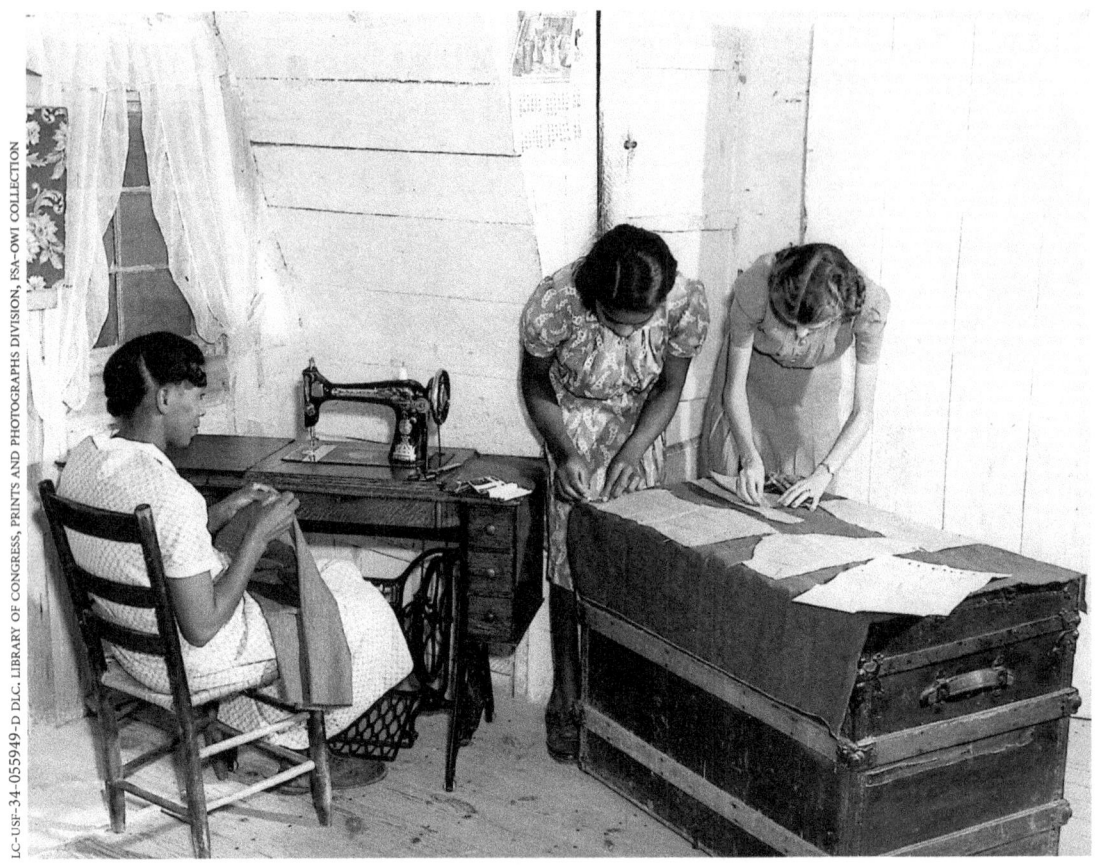

*FSA (Farm Security Administration) home supervisor Miss Harton helping one of the borrowers' families cut patterns and make their own clothes in Caswell County in October 1940. Photograph by Marion Post Wolcott.*

**Etiquette.** It may seem surprising that during a time of severe economic hardship the Women's Club should give programs on etiquette. Mrs. Ed (Mae) Blanton, who was born in 1919, grew up in North Carolina during the Great Depression and had served as president of the Ellenboro Home Demonstration Club for four years, explains:

> Even though many members of the Ellenboro Club were dirt poor, the people had pride and dignity. The Home Demonstration Club tried to maintain this self-respect in its people. Good manners, how to entertain properly, and how to preserve style through a difficult time were important to us. Even in homes where the diet was limited, the Club encouraged the women to assemble their families together around the table, to maintain a family unit, and to serve from left to right.

Community service activities were a top priority of the Ellenboro Club — especially during the Great Depression. Its 1934 activities included donating to the needy 63 cans of fruits and vegetables, 1 can of sausage, a half bushel of peas, 1 gallon of molasses, and 1 bushel of sweet potatoes. In 1939 the Ellenboro Club donated to the Cancer Campaign; to the bookmobile; to the Ellenboro School Library and to the Ellenboro School grounds; and to the old church all the following: a piano, a cook stove, window curtains, and an outdoor fireplace. In addition, each year the Club planted something new on the grounds of the Ellenboro Depot (Public Records from Rutherford County Cooperative Extension Office).

Many clubs provided suggestions and patterns for sewing and for making wardrobe items; not all women, however, had the time and acceptable attire to attend the meetings. Some club leaders shared information with individuals in their homes (Mae Blanton).

*The Seaboard Airline Railway (SAL) Depot in Ellenboro was constructed about 1905 and was an important depot and train stop during the 1930s.*

Governor Clyde Roark Hoey addressed the Home Demonstration Clubs of Currituck County on April 6, 1938. His praise of the clubs follow:

> Much of the real progress and development of rural life in North Carolina can be directly attributable to the organization of Home Demonstration Clubs and the work of the agents throughout the State. When you form a club you directly affect the lives of all the people in the community, because these clubs are made up of either present or prospective home-keepers, and hence vitally concerned [about] the welfare of the whole community....
>
> The Home Demonstration Clubs have been making the rural home keep pace with the progress on the farm, and in many instances leading the way for a fuller and richer rural life. The farm will not surpass the home. Both need to be developed and improved together and the farm women of North Carolina are proving equal to the task of keeping fully abreast with the educational progress of the State and the development of a well-balanced farm program which includes the canning and preserving of farm products, as well as the raising of all foods necessary for home consumption.
>
> Definite achievements in beautifying the homes and garments in the rural sections have resulted from your Club activities. Roadside improvement will naturally follow. It should be your constant purpose to unite in making our countryside even more beautiful. Beauty adds to the joy of life, and there is incomparable beauty in the simple things, even the wild flowers and the dogwood blooming in such rich profusion along the roadside and through the woods. Let's make North Carolina a beautiful state [Corbitt, *Hoey*, "Address Delivered at a Meeting of the Home Demonstration Clubs of Currituck County, Currituck Courthouse, April 6, 1938," pp. 195–196].

**Women in the work force.** The Carolina woman was an important part of the labor force. By 1930 one out of every five women — nearly eleven million — worked outside the home (Wecter, pp. 25). Some women near factories went to work for the first time outside their home when times got harder — provided jobs were available.

The roles of women (rural or urban, industrial or agrarian) in the work force were important to society. Some industries preferred

*Skein winding, or running the yarn from a skein to a spool, at the Southern Combed Yarn Industry in Gastonia in 1938.*

to hire the female; her salary was lower, and she was often more submissive. In those homes where the wife was the sole provider, she often assumed greater family command. Sometimes the result of the working wife and the jobless husband was a greater closeness; other couples, however, became embittered by want, insecurity, and reproaches (Wecter, pp. 31–32). Women worked frequently also as nurses, secretaries, and teachers, in particular.

Some social reformers encouraged employed women to give up their jobs and stay at home so men could work. These reformers ignored the important fact that many women were the head of their household and had a family to support (Fisher, p. 138). The National Federation of Business and Professional Women's Clubs reported that 48 percent of 12,000 female employees surveyed had dependents; more than 17 percent had the sole responsibility for households ranging from two to eight persons. The number of dependents per woman increased between 1930 and 1936 while the average earnings decreased. By the end of the decade, 95 percent of American women ran their homes without the benefit of outside aid or domestic help. This, of course, meant that many African American women lost positions as domestics (Wecter, pp. 25–26).

At first the Great Depression did not affect the employment of women workers because employees favored hiring females. As the Depression years continued, however, many women, too, lost their jobs; these jobless, now older women found new employment difficult to attain.

**The women with white collar jobs.** Although women occupied many unskilled positions, they also worked in occupations like secretarial, clerical, teaching, and other "white collar" jobs. Walda Carpenter, for instance, applied for a position with the Welfare Department in Rutherford County for the summer of 1937. Walda was a teacher in the county schools and hoped to secure a summer job temporarily until school began and her paid position re-opened again in the late summer. An important part of the job of the "welfare worker" who assumed this position would be to identify blind, homeless, crippled, and dependent children who would receive assistance through the Social Security Act of 1935; the Supreme Court had upheld this act on May 24, 1937, and Rutherford County wanted to have its paperwork in place when assured funds were available. Walda Carpenter recalled:

> My interview for the position was to be with Dr. Ellen Winston and Dr. Roy Brown in Raleigh, North Carolina. Mrs. O. C. Turner, Superintendent of Welfare for Rutherford County, advised me that dress for this interview and for the job itself was to be "very conservative."
> 
> Not sure just what "very conservative" meant, I consulted a friend in Winston-Salem who was working with the Welfare Department there. I asked her to help me in selecting the appropriate attire.
> 
> She told me that I should wear no jewelry and no earrings; she advised me that a wedding band should be my only ornaments. My dress and my shoes should be very plain.
> 
> I purchased a plain blue dress for the job interview and bought a new pair of shoes: lace up oxfords. My only "frill" was a plain handkerchief in my dress pocket. I passed the interview and the test with "flying colors."

Walda, however, found that before the Board of County Commissioners of Rutherford County would hire her, they would first ask the permission of her husband:

> Joseph Beam, who was a County Commissioner, came to talk with my husband about my employment before they would hire me. My husband replied, "She will do what she wants to do. She makes up her own mind."
> 
> The Board hired me, and I went to work for Mrs. O. C. Turner, Superintendent of Welfare for Rutherford County, on June 13, 1937. The temporary position turned into a full-time job. I did not return to teaching in the fall.

Walda had many duties in her new Welfare Department position — a position which she kept even after the new school year began. Instead of teaching, she was now — among other things — certifying men for work with the CCC camps and individuals for "old age pensions."

> I had to identify which individuals would be eligible for the old age assistance funds, when they became available from the state and federal

*Walda Carpenter went to work for the Welfare Department in 1937 and used this photo for her application.*

the time. The movie, based on the book, starred Ginger Rogers, who won the Academy Award in 1940 for her performance as Kitty.

Even female teachers began to feel the impact of the Great Depression. In 1931 the National Education Association reported that three-fourths of all cities were excluding married women from employment (Wecter, pp. 25). In North Carolina many of the unemployed teachers—like Cleo Burns—taught adult education classes; adult education raised the literacy level of the state and contributed to the income of teachers.

**Gender identities.** Many of the programs of the government reinforced gender identities. In 1932 the federal government ruled that public service could employ only one spouse per household; the woman was invariably the one who stepped down because of the higher wages paid to men and because of the tradition of the male breadwinner. New Deal legislation enforced wage differentials between men and women and regulated both wages and maximum hours (Fisher, p. 7).

**Images of women.** Fisher noted the images of women captured in the photographs of the FSA. Whereas the male had been the traditional economic provider, during the Great Depression the staggering levels of unemployment were somewhat lower for women than for men. The Great Depression altered the traditional roles of the male and of the female.

When many females became the source of income for their families, their traditionally dependent roles grew clouded. At times the women in the photographic and written records appear particularly strong, as in the North Carolina picket lines (Stoney and Helfand, *Uprising of '34*). At other times the women appear tender and feminine, as when they hold their children—perhaps a "widely felt nostalgia for a mythic American past...." The photographs of the FSA capture these dual images of women during the decade of the 1930s (Fisher, p. 138).

Stryker never specifically asked his photographers to emphasize in their photography women and their roles; yet many photographs

government, and determine the total for our county. For eligibility for this aid, the person had to have lived in the county at least five years, had to be at least 65 years old, and had to furnish two documented proofs of age. The two written documents usually furnished were a birth certificate and a record of birth from the Bible. In lieu of one written proof of age, a person could recall three public events. In our community many people recalled seeing the "high water" at Cliffside in 1916 as an important public event.

Our office sometimes used notarized statements to verify eligibility when written evidence or remembrances of public events were not appropriate. Miss Cleo Burns—teacher, adult education instructor, long-time county resident, and the first president of the Ellenboro Home Demonstration Club—was an excellent resource. Born in 1882, she had been teaching since 1900. Her honesty and integrity were unquestionable, and her willingness to help others made her an important asset to the community.

A popular book in the 1930s was *Kitty Foyle* by Christopher Morley; Kitty was a female white-collar worker, still a novelty at of women appear. Some show them in poses traditionally assumed by men and in jobs and places heretofore frequented primarily by men. Other photographs show women as teachers and rural mothers, the "universal touchstone" (Fisher, p. 138).

The Carolina women, then, varied greatly from region to region and from time to time during the decade. The important photographs of women in their settings—Coastal, Piedmont, and Mountain regions—capture the diversity of this important group and depict the oppression, the depression, the dignity, the hope, and the strength that was theirs.

## IV. The Children

The Great Depression signaled the end of childhood for many young people. Millions of children in the 1930s felt hunger, want, and harshness. Many of them dropped out of school and went to work at an early age. Others left home to ease the burden for their families. It was a time when some families had to separate, often never to reunite. Some children became ill and even died. All children of the 1930s were affected in some way by the times (Raper, p. 24).

**Children of the Great Depression.** Some adults who were children of the Great Depression, however, view themselves, their families, and their communities as better for their experiences. Dr. H. G. Jones states emphatically that the period taught him the difference between needs and wants (Interview with Dr. Jones, product of the Great Depression and Professor Emeritus at the University of North Carolina). Often the children were proud that they were able to contribute to the family unit; these children gained spiritually what they lacked materially. The Great Depression brought many families closer; families working together sometimes softened the harsh effects of hard

*The daughter of a sharecropper in rural North Carolina in September 1935. Photograph by Arthur Rothstein, Farm Security Administration.*

times. The community feeling in some areas helped the young and the old to survive their deprivation. This cohesion resulted in a sharing that lessened the oppression and built a trust that permitted many families in certain areas to sleep with open windows and unlocked doors in the summer (Wormser, pp. 13, 118).

Many of the children of the Great Depression suffered the worst that the decade could give and yet they still survived. Often they faced their futures with bravery and hope. Some considered these hardships a way to learn perseverance and faith (Wormser, pp. 118–119).

Although many saw the Great Depression Era as a time to learn the value of family, community, and cooperation, others learned a different lesson from the decade:

> For some, the lesson was that society should abandon altogether collective efforts to remake itself in any image and leave it to individuals once more to strive as best they could for themselves. For others, the state seemed infinitely richer in spirit and talent as a consequence of the barriers broken and programs created through social struggle. Perhaps all North Carolinians might begin to look to their own peculiar heritage for guidance and inspiration. For there were values in that heritage that had nothing to do with oppression of the weak or exploitation of the underprivileged [Parramore, *Express Lanes*, p. 5].

**"The Greatest Generation."** Tom Brokaw regards the "men and women [who] came of age in the Great Depression, when economic despair hovered over the land like a plague" as "The Greatest Generation" (Brokaw, p. xix). He notes how the youth of the 1930s

> ...had watched their parents lose their businesses, their farms, their jobs, their hopes. They had learned to accept a future that played out one day at a time. Then just as there was a glimmer of economic recovery, war exploded across Europe and Asia ... this generation was summoned to the parade ground and told to train for war.... They answered the call to help save the

*Children in Sunday School at the Penderlea Resettlement at Willard, North Carolina, in 1937. Photograph by Ben Shahn, Farm Security Administration.*

world.... They faced great odds and a late start, but they did not protest. At a time in their lives when their days and nights should have been filled with innocent adventure, love and the lessons of the workaday world, they were fighting.... Without their efforts and sacrifices our world would be a far different place today [Brokaw, p. 6].

**Child labor in Carolina.** Children were instrumental in making North Carolina the largest producer of textiles and tobacco products in the nation. The children often began a life of picking cotton, harvesting tobacco, or working in a factory at an early age. Since many of them did not have the clothes that they needed, they put cardboard in their shoes to cover the holes in the soles. Clothing made from flour sacks or handed-down was typical (Wormser, p. 11). Yet these children typically maintained their dignity and their belief in themselves. Only a few years later the children of the Great Depression answered with pride the call of their nation to rally and to fight a world war (Wolfe, p. 145).

Many Southern entrepreneurs were interested in hiring children, not adults who commanded higher wages. Child labor, then, affected the child and at the same time undermined the security of the adult male, the adult female, and families. In the South 148 children out of every thousand (14.8 percent) worked on the farm or in the textile mills; for the nation as a whole, however, only 47 of every one thousand children (4.7 percent) engaged in manual labor (National Emergency Council, pp. 41–42). This practice of selectively hiring children and women in the mills enabled — or required — some men to continue with their farm labor or seek other employment while the other family members worked in the factories (Byerly, pp. 11–12).

**Child labor in the factories.** The North

*This Rhodes Manufacturing Company spinner said she was 11 years old and had been working for over a year. Photograph by Lewis Hine.*

Carolina Labor Law of 1903 both prohibited the employment of children less than twelve years of age and limited the work week for those less than eighteen years of age to sixty-six hours. However, the State of North Carolina did not provide for the adequate enforcement of its labor laws (Lefler, 1963 edition, 564; Byerly, p. 169).

This inadequate enforcement of labor laws for children was typical of most of the states at that time (Wormser, p. 48). In 1930, 23 percent of the girls between the ages of fourteen and nineteen in the nation were working; 40 percent of the boys within this age group held jobs (Wecter, p. 181). Both the state and the federal government began work to improve the plight of children.

At the beginning of the decade of the 1930s, jobs for children increased dramatically while jobs for adults decreased. Factories, farms, and small businesses began to look for laborers who would work for low wages and for long hours without complaint. Children — and some women — met these qualifications (Wormser, p. 47).

In 1933 the textile manufacturers offered an amendment abolishing labor in the mills for those under sixteen years of age; many cheers and much applause in the committee chamber and throughout the nation greeted this amendment. Some manufacturers, however, mourned losing cheap labor, and some families regretted not having the additional wages, small though they were.

From federal funds and from state and local coffers, North Carolina began a system of monthly payments to the needy — including children. The Supreme Court upheld the law when businesses complained that the taxes they paid were detrimental and that the plan was unconstitutional. From August 8, 1933, to December 5, 1935, 11.8 percent of North Carolinians were on relief; this percentage was an increase over the 10.7 percent for the first six months of 1935 (Lefler, 1963 edition, p. 581).

Wormser estimated that by 1935 there were still over two million children (about 20 percent) laboring in the work force across the United States (p. 48). By 1940 the 1930 percentages (23 percent for girls and 40 percent for boys) had dropped to 19 percent for girls and 35 percent for boys. The legal restraints against child labor and the compulsory school attendance laws had lessened the employment of children (Wecter, p. 181).

**Child labor on the cotton farms.** Dirt farmers sought cheap wage labor also. Because most laws neglected child labor in agriculture, many landowners leaped at the chance to hire the youth in the area. Estimates are that half a million children between the ages of ten and fifteen worked in the fields. Some children began their toil even earlier (Wecter, p. 182). Donnis Curtis explained:

> As soon as the children in my family turned six years of age, we were expected to do two things: go to school and work in the fields. We had to do the same amount of work in the fields that our father did. In other words, when he reached the end of a row hoeing or picking cotton, we should be reaching the end of our row at the same time. I can tell you that the burrs on a cotton stalk used as a switch were very sticky if we did not work hard!

Nell Burns had a different perspective on the work in the field:

> I always thought it was my duty to tell stories to my brothers and sisters in the field and to keep them entertained while they worked. I saw my job in a different way than my father did. I preferred to sit on the lower limb of a shade tree and give a summary of the latest books that I had read. I sometimes sat up late at night reading in order to have new stories to share. When my father came to the field, however, he often gave me a new job description.

Two of the field jobs that were most demeaning and brutal for the young were hoeing and picking cotton. Tenant farmers — particularly in the South — needed the work of their children to help them produce the crops and pay their debts. If the landlord noted that one of the tenant farmer's children was not working well, the whole family might have to leave the land — and their shelter. Yet the landlords seldom paid the child laborers; most dropped out of school or attended school around the schedule of the crops. The working day for these young field laborers was from "can see to can't see" (Wormser, p. 48–50).

*Two of the children of J. A. Johnson in the cotton field in Statesville, October 1939. Photograph by Marion Post Wolcott, Farm Security Administration.*

**Child labor on the tobacco farm.** Tobacco farming engaged many child laborers. A broken tobacco leaf could mean the job of a child — and the loss of work and a home for the rest of the family (Wormser, p. 51). The work became even more tedious as the stinging tobacco worms called "packsaddles" inflicted their venom on tender, young skins and as the temperature climbed to over 100 degrees in some Carolina fields (Interview with Buren Davis).

**The barn.** Despite the work associated with the farm, many farm children of the Great Depression look with nostalgia on the earlier time and place. The barn held particular fondness for some rural children. With its tin roof, the sound of the rain was accentuated for those in its warmth and safety inside. On the days of rainy weather when farm work was at a standstill, "[You could] listen to the rain on the roof while you communicated with your soul" (Parramore, *Express Lanes*, p. 9). Wanda Robbins, who grew up during the Great Depression, remembers her mother's reference to their barn.

When we children became too loud and boisterous, our mother would threaten, "If you children don't get quiet and do as I asked, I am going to take my old hat and go to the barn."

We always immediately settled down when she made this half-humorous threat.

The barn was also a place where farm children played. Nell Burns recalled that her brothers built an "airplane" from a large wooden potato crate in the early 1930s.

They added wings and nailed a piece of wood to the front for a propeller. When the construction was through, my two brothers began to argue about who would get to take the first solo flight. Finally, they decided that the younger would push the older one out of the loft. The older brother promised the younger that he would "fly around and pick you up."

All of us younger children sat down to watch the flight. We hoped that the plane would make several circles, and we, too, might get to ride. Of course, the plane fell immediately to the hay below.

My older brother was afraid to tell my parents what had happened. He had a very bad cut on his arm from the fall, but he was particularly afraid that the younger brother would get in trouble for pushing him out of the loft.

*Billy, the son of Mr. Compton, a sharecropper, is taking off tobacco for grading and stripping in the strip house in Carrboro, September 1939. Photograph by Marion Post Wolcott, Farm Security Administration.*

To prevent further problems from occurring, the two brothers decided to sew up the cut themselves. They first held a needle in the flame of a match before making two stitches with the thread that they had washed. Somehow the cut did not get infected, the two boys successfully removed the stitches when the wound healed, and my mother never knew of the home doctoring.

When I felt daring, I would yell to my younger sisters that I was going to jump out of the barn loft. Feeling a little frightened when I looked down, I would add some conditions. "I am going to spit; if my spit splashes, I will jump." They would come running to see me jump, but I would not see my saliva splash. I would change the conditions: "If my spit doesn't splash, I will jump." Again the *spit* was never right for my magnificent leap.

I often look back on this "vision" with laughter because I was extremely myopic and could not see the ground. I realize now that I was making sure that the time was never right to jump.

Parramore describes the livestock barn on many Carolina farms as a place that

> ...usually included a central passageway that separated cow stalls on one side from mule or horse stalls on the other. But the gambrel roof also covered storage space for feed, tools, and machinery. Here cows were milked, horses shoed, equipment repaired, sick animals treated.... It was where children played hide-and-seek ... where dignity was recovered after a personal setback, and, like as not, where love was made [Parramore, *Express Lanes,* pp. 8–9].

*Charlotte's Web*, the children's classic, describes a barn in detail. E. B. White, the author and winner of the Newbery Award, repeated the *s* sound to convey the hushed, peaceful feeling there.

> The barn was very large. It was very old. It smelled of hay and it smelled of manure. It smelled of the perspiration of tired horses and the wonderful sweet breath of patient cows. It

*The barn of Robert Ewart Burns and Nell Burns with a corn crib over 125 years old and a barn over 100 years old.*

often had a sort of peaceful smell — as though nothing bad could happen ever again in the world. It smelled of grain and of harness dressing and of axle grease and of rubber boots and of new rope. And whenever the cat was given a fish-head to eat, the barn would smell of fish. But mostly it smelled of hay, for there was always hay in the great loft up overhead. And there was always hay being pitched down to the cows and the horses and the sheep [White, p. 13].

**School dropouts.** Both rural and urban children faced problems in securing an education during the Great Depression. Not all youth were able to remain in school. Many had already begun their employment and their formal schooling had ended. Many felt some regret that they had to end their formal education. The New Deal attempted to help these children.

**The National Youth Administration.** The New Deal directed many special programs directly to the youth of the nation. The Federal Government, in June of 1935, created the National Youth Administration (NYA). Until 1943, this program supplied funds to pay for part-time workers in high school and college (Watkins, p. 258). By June of 1936, there were some 475 NYA projects in the state of North Carolina alone (Lefler, 1963 edition, p. 581). About two million students in the nation received an average of $6.00 per month (Wecter, p. 188).

**Letters from and about children to President Roosevelt.** In his broadcast Fireside Chats, President Roosevelt encouraged the public to write to him. The needy, the poor, and the oppressed — regardless of age — often wrote directly to President Roosevelt, and he personally signed most of the replies either because of his concern or to quiet the discontent (McElvaine, *Down and Out*, pp. 6, 26).

More than 15 million letters to President Roosevelt and his First Lady remain. McElvaine considers these letters to President Franklin Roosevelt and Eleanor Roosevelt to be one of the few and best means available to obtain immediate testimony on the Great Depression. Remembrances can fade. Interviewers of people of the period too often used their memory and their interpretation — not verbatim accounts— when they recorded the conversations. Census figures and statistics are very important, but letters give the testimony one needs for accuracy (McElvaine, *Down and Out*, pp. 4–6).

Some of the letters were from children, and many were from adults on behalf of children. One such letter came from High Point, North Carolina:

> Mr Roosevelte   I am In nead Bad Please help me I have 7 children and is Sick all thje time one of my children is Sick and has Ben for a lone time and I have No under clothes for none of the famiely we cant harly hide I self with top cloths I ned Milk and my Boy need milk Please give my childrens and my Self Some under cloths or we will freze to Deth this cold wethr we can work But my husBan he make $6.75 per week no way I can get any under cloths for the famely please help me I have not a teeth in My head wen I Eat I nely Dieys no way to get any please help me please [McElvaine, *Down and Out*, p. 138].

**Children and the President's visit.** When President Roosevelt toured in North Carolina, young and old alike came out to wave to him, to speak to him, or to shake his hand. Many North Carolina public schools closed so that the children could see the President of the United States. One such visit was the one that came in the middle 1930s.

**The Federal Emergency Relief Administration.** The Federal Emergency Relief Administration (FERA), begun in May of 1933, was a program of both work and direct relief.

*Mill village in Gastonia in 1938.*

Certain aspects of FERA directly affected children. For instance, the program hired unemployed nurses to tend small children (work relief) and began a free lunch program (direct relief) (Wecter, p. 181).

**The Social Security Act of 1935.** The Social Security Act of 1935 made funds ($24,750,000) available for dependent children in need of aid, for maternal and child health ($3,800,000), for homeless and neglected children ($1,500,000), and for crippled children (2,850,000) (Wecter, p. 181). On May 24, 1937, the Supreme Court upheld the act. North Carolinians availed themselves of their entitlements although many viewed the aid contemptuously as "handouts."

**Child labor laws in North Carolina (1937).** By 1937 North Carolina had raised the prohibitory age for child labor generally to sixteen years; the state had also set the minimum age for employment in hazardous occupations to eighteen (Lefler, 1963 edition, p. 564.) Clyde Roark Hoey, North Carolina Governor from 1937 until 1941, considered the North Carolina Labor Law "one of the best child labor laws in the Nation" and one "which has received universal commendation throughout the country" (Corbitt, *Clyde R. Hoey*, "Review of Four Years, December 29, 1940," p. 604). The state began to enforce these laws more diligently than it had in the past (Lefler, 1963 edition, p. 564).

**The Federal Wages and Hours Act of 1938.** The Federal Wages and Hours Act of 1938 governed businesses that produced goods for interstate commerce; this Wages and Hours Act, together with the North Carolina Labor Law of 1937, helped many workers—particularly children—in the Tar Heel State. By 1939 Mildred Gwin Barnwell was able to write that in North Carolina "a child under 16 can't even take a sight-seeing tour through a cotton mill" (Barnwell, p. 15).

**Child labor and the mill villages.** The consolidation and sale of many of the North Carolina textile villages, the demise of family labor in the mills, the strictly regulated salaries and hours, and particularly the abolition of child labor convinced many North Carolina mill owners that they should use their profits for the wages of their employees rather than for subsidizing mill village housing. Federal and state child labor laws, then, helped ring the death knell for subsidized mill housing for textile workers; North Carolina was one of the first states to begin the trend of abolishing such villages (Glass, pp. 84–85).

The faces of North Carolina's population—its men, women and children, as they worked and as they played—are an important part of the portrait of the Great Depression in the Tar Heel State. Their images tell their own story.

## Chapter Three

# *Education*

North Carolinians in the late 1930s could take pride in much — particularly the educational system of the state. Although there was still a need for improvement, public schools had progressed to the point that Governor Clyde R. Hoey was able to say that the "history of education in North Carolina reads like a romance" (Corbitt, *Hoey*, "Address Delivered before the North Carolina Teachers Association, March 19, 1938," p. 190).

**History of education in North Carolina.** The state had begun its public school system in 1837. Its state university, the University of North Carolina, ranked among the oldest and most respected of all the state universities. North Carolina had long recognized the need for higher education for women in the state and was attempting to provide educational opportunities for all people (Corbitt, *Hoey*, "Address Delivered before the North Carolina Adult Education Advisory Council, Raleigh, March 16, 1938," p. 190).

## I. Under O. Max Gardner, North Carolina Governor from 1929 until 1933

The nation and the state had much room for improvement at the beginning of the decade of the 1930s. O. Max Gardner, from Shelby, was eager to improve education. In 1931, shortly after his term as Governor began, the state put into use complete state support of public schools for a six months' term (Van Noppen, p. 140).

**Equalization.** In 1901 the General Assembly doubled the $100,000 that the legislature of 1899 had appropriated; loud cheering accompanied the announcement. At the same session the legislature adopted a program of equalization; with this program, the legislature would distribute money to the counties in inverse proportion to the value of the county's taxable income. The reasoning was that poorer counties could raise — or equalize — the quality of their schools to at least begin to approach the quality of the wealthier counties. Disgruntled wealthier counties complained that the burdens of the poorer counties were not theirs to carry. The public school system was an obvious solution: the state — not the counties — would maintain the school system (Powell, pp. 446–447).

**Two school systems reduced to one.** The newly adopted, state-supported public school system meant that North Carolina would have two systems: the state school system of six months and the system of local control in those counties where there was an extended term supported by local levies and the Tax Reduction Fund. The extended terms ranged from one to three months (Van Noppen, pp. 140–141).

In 1933 the legislature declared non-

*Old Well and South Building, University of North Carolina, 1939.*

existent all special tax districts and special charters; the state would completely support the schools (Van Noppen, pp. 140–143). This was possible because of the adoption of a 3 percent sales tax on virtually everything people bought except for meat, bread, and flour (Powell, p. 485).

Further actions increased state school funds and teaching loads and decreased salaries, education costs, and the number of principals. The state assumed entire responsibility for the management and control of the buses and rearranged the bus routes. The two school systems had become one.

Many of the rural schools of Western North Carolina benefited from the school law of 1933. Some cities, however, viewed the law as catastrophic to the education of their children. Asheville, for example, had an excellent school program; the 1933 law reduced its budget for the city school system from the $763,628 of 1929–30 to $183,761 for 1934–35 — a severe blow to the residents of the area. The law eliminated manual training, music, and physical education, courses that the Asheville schools had taught since 1905 (Van Noppen, pp. 140–143).

**Dropouts and illiteracy in North Carolina in 1930.** The United States Census Bureau applied the term *illiterate* to those over age ten who could not read and write. The 1930 Census determined that 4.3 percent of the national population was illiterate. North Carolina, however, had a much higher illiteracy rate by this older definition. Ten percent of those in the state who were over the age of ten could not read (Corbitt, *Hoey*, "Address Delivered before the North Carolina Adult Education Advisory Council, Raleigh, March 16, 1938," p. 190).

The state with the highest rate of illiteracy in 1930 was South Carolina, which had a 26.9 percent rate (Raper, p. 237). It is difficult, however, to determine if the rate of illiteracy was higher at the end of the Great Depression than at the beginning because the 1940 Census did not define illiteracy in the same way as had the 1930 Census; the 1940 Census and the reports thereafter attempted to determine the number of years in school (grades completed), rather than using the term *illiteracy* or *nonreaders.* In 1940 in North Carolina 95,414 persons had completed no school years and 337,639 had completed only 1 to 4 years of school; the total (433,053) comprises 26 percent of the total population of those 25 and over (1,649,820) in the State of North Carolina (Ullman, *Statistical Abstract,* pp. 104, 113). Jim Trelease notes that the dropout rate for the nation in 1940 was about 75 percent; during the worst years of the Great Depression, however, the percentage was probably even higher. These 1940 statistics are, at best, very difficult to compare with the 1930 Census.

**Mill village schools.** Many of the textile workers lived in isolated mill villages. The companies owned the houses, sometimes ran the stores, usually built the churches, and even helped to provide whatever schools they deemed necessary. In addition, the mill owners might help to subsidize the ministers, administer the sheriff's department, and contribute to the pay of the teacher — or teachers— for the school.

Not all village schools, however, were of inferior quality. Some mill owners sought to educate the offspring of their employees. These concerned mill owners helped subsidize only the best teachers and attempted to construct school buildings which kept the children warm; some of these proprietors tried, whenever possible, to equip the school with adequate lighting to make reading and writing easier for those enrolled. The managers even attempted at times to provide activities at the village community center for the local children.

In North Carolina, however, the support of the plant owners for education was some-

*Cliffside School was built in 1920–1921 for a quarter of a million dollars. Charles H. Haynes (Haynes Mills) built the school to carry out his father's interest in education. Photograph is made by James M. Walker.*

*Mrs. Stroup, director of Community House, reading to children in Gastonia, 1938.*

what lower. Harriet L. Herring in 1926 attempted to survey 322 North Carolina plants. She found that most of the owners of the plants had contributed to the building and the support of the churches; only 28, however, had supplemented the support of the schools. Of the 322 plant owners, only 49 employed community workers.

In the early part of the 1930s, however, children of North Carolina textile workers often did not attend school; they, too, went to work at the local mill in order to contribute to their family's income. Later, the State of North Carolina would legislate and strictly enforce attendance laws for all its youth. It would also be much later before the initiation of a statewide program for testing the achievement of Carolina youth (Herring, *Welfare Work in Mill Villages*, pp. 27–31, 135). By 1931 North Carolina, like all Southern states, had laws against the employment of children under fourteen and against night work by those under the age of sixteen (Tindall, p. 323).

**Gardner's desire for an eight months' school term.** When the decade of the 1930s began, North Carolina Governor O. Max Gardner expressed his desire for an eight months' school term for all children in the state. He considered such an extension — provided that it was possible at an expense less than the current effort — to be one of the highest public services that the General Assembly of North Carolina could render to its constituency (Lanier, pp. 183–184). It was 1933, however, before the state passed a law to extend the school term.

George Brown Tindall praises the actions of North Carolina. He states that

> North Carolina went further than any other state, with the assumption of state responsibility for a six-month term in 1931 and eight months in 1933, and became the only state with "truly a state system of public education" [Tindall, pp. 495–496].

William S. Powell notes that among Gardner's achievements that attracted national attention [were] uniting the three state-supported institutions of higher education as the Consolidated University of North Carolina; and taking responsibility for operating the public schools for the required six-month term, further easing the burden on local government. Continuation of the latter was possible largely through the adoption very early in the next administration of a 3 percent sales tax on virtually everything people bought except bread, flour, and meat [Powell, p. 489].

**Money-saving measures, including salary cuts for teachers, in education.** During the 1930s the state endured many problems with education. Some people in government began to talk of closing all the state's public schools for a year or two; this action would allow the state to save the money to make sure the schools had the same standard as before the Great Depression began. Instead many of the schools shut down cafeterias, closed laboratories, discontinued foreign languages, music art, typing, home economics, and other "nonessential" courses; many schools, however, had never had these "frills" in the first place (Powell, p. 485). At a time when classroom size increased because of consolidation of schools and classrooms, North Carolina still found it necessary to cut teacher salaries 10 percent in 1931. Some regarded these money-saving measures as economic policies, not educational policies (Lanier, p. 193).

Education faced many hardships as did the entire state. The salaries of state employees were cut 20 percent under Governor Gardner and by an additional 25 percent under Governor Ehringhaus (Powell, pp. 485–586).

**One-room schoolhouses.** In 1931 there were 1,600 one-room schoolhouses in the state; the total schools for North Carolina in that year was 6,720. There were 935 one-room schools for African Americans and 665 one-room schools for whites (Lanier, p. 190).

Walda Carpenter was a teacher in a one-teacher school in Rutherford County and recalls:

> I taught seven grades in the one-teacher school in the Brittian Community. I was expected to provide all supplies for my students. I went about gathering the supplies in earnest. I went to the local hardware store and asked for horseshoes for the students to play with at recess. I asked the Coca-Cola Plant for pencils. I was ready when school began each year.
>
> Our schedule for a school year was different than a regular year today. We started to school in the hot summer and stopped school when the cotton bloomed for cotton-picking break. School resumed when the cotton harvest was complete. Times have changed!

Donnis Curtis, who attended a small school in North Carolina during the Great Depression, remembered the split schedule to allow students to help with the field work. She recalls also her school being temporarily transformed into a hospital; Chapter Four, "Health," tells more about this transformation from educational institution to health care facility. Donnis recalls her education in a small, rural school during the 1930s:

> I did not attend a one-room schoolhouse; the school I attended was more sophisticated: a two-room schoolhouse with all eight grades in the one building. The school, Palmer's School, was located almost at the South Carolina line, and I attended there for several years.

**Unique problems of rural youth.** Children of the rural areas faced unique problems in securing an education. Many had to rise early enough to milk cows, feed farm animals, draw water, build fires in the wood cook stoves, bring in firewood, and perform other chores before boarding the bus for the long ride to school — if the adults decided school was in order that day. Classmates poked fun at the smell of those who had worked in the barns before arriving at school. Tattered clothing, attendance based on the maturation of the crops, derisive comments from those who did not live in the country, and inadequate school supplies and lunches were only a few of the hardships, embarrassments, and hurdles many farm children and migratory workers faced in their pursuit of a free, public education (Nell Burns).

**Education of Native Americans.** The education of Native Americans in the state varied. For instance, Cherokees in the western part of the state often attended schools established by missionaries. The schools were

*A public school house at Wilson Mills in Johnston County.*

in several communities; the missionaries also established a boarding school in the town of Cherokee. Many of these schools

> attempted to eradicate traditional practices and beliefs. Among other things, they forced children to speak English, and many Indians began to abandon their native tongue.
>
> During the 1930s the United States government initiated a number of programs to help the Cherokee. A new school staffed by federally paid teachers offered children a better education [Perdue, pp. 42, 44].

This New Deal assistance provided a different education from that of earlier days; the new curriculum did not seek to change the Cherokee culture dramatically or to force the Cherokee students to abide by a different norm (Neely, p. 30).

Many Native Americans did not oppose the strict segregation that they encountered.

> The Lumbee did not oppose segregation in the [early 1900s].... Instead, they welcomed an opportunity to develop an Indian consciousness and to manage their own affairs. Indian churches established a Baptist Association and a Methodist Conference separate from white organizations. An Indian school committeeman directed the Lumbee educational system, and a local leader bargained with the white political establishment in the county to acquire public services for the Indian community.
>
> Although racial segregation did help engender an Indian identity that had earlier been assailed, exclusion from white institutions and full participation in the political process denied Indians opportunities and real control of their lives. Segregation made them second-class citizens.... Furthermore many ... establishments had three water fountains—one for each race—and six bathrooms—one for each race and sex [Perdue, pp. 50–51].

**Consolidation.** Parents, lawmakers, and educators argued about consolidation of the scattered schools. Consolidation could increase the average number of students for each teacher and reduce costs, but the location of the one-room schools made this a difficult goal to achieve in the state. Many of these one-room schools were in isolated areas; consequently consolidation would require the building of new schools in isolated areas. The law, however, made it clear that for financial reasons North Carolina needed some consolidation because an elementary school could not operate if the average daily attendance during the preceding year was below twenty-two (Lanier, p. 190).

## II. Under John C. B. Ehringhaus, North Carolina Governor from 1933 until 1937

The people of North Carolina elected John C. B. Ehringhaus of Pasquotank County as governor in 1932. Former Governor O. Max Gardner and his brother-in-law Clyde R. Hoey worked hard to ensure the election of this candidate. "The Shelby Dynasty," including Hoey and Gardner, was helping to determine the political climate of the state.

**Governor Ehringhaus and education.** On January 5, 1933, the new North Carolina Governor, John C. B. Ehringhaus, addressed throngs of citizens in the new Memorial Auditorium in Raleigh. He described deficits, distress, and decreasing funds in the Tar Heel State. He expressed the hope that the state would adjust all other economies before cutting back on public education and defaulting the children of the state. By May of the same year the House and Senate finally set aside a $16,000,000 appropriation for an eight-months' school term (Lanier, pp. 199, 200).

**Education for African Americans.** Equalization was not apparent in the education of North Carolina African Americans. By 1933–34 only ten high schools for African Americans existed in the twenty-four counties of Western North Carolina; most of the ten, however, were inadequate. Although the African American high schools of Buncombe County had thirteen teachers, most of the other counties had only one or two teachers for the entire high school (Van Noppen, p. 143). By 1935–36, however, the value of Negro public school property, not including colleges, was slightly more than $11,000,000 (Henry, p. 37).

**Unique problems of youth in securing an education.** Although many Depression era youth dropped out of school, some were able to remain. Even those still enrolled, however, often attended school only sporadically. Reasons for irregular attendance included a lack of sufficient clothing, inadequate school supplies, embarrassment at having no lunch to take to school and being teased for poverty, laxly enforced attendance laws, a need to work, and a lack of encouragement from others. Some children lied about their ages so they could secure employment or help at home instead of attending school. Some of the dropouts and some of the other children enrolled still hungered for an education.

**Adult education in North Carolina.** The date of the Federal Emergency Relief Act was May 12, 1933 — about 60 days after the inauguration of President Roosevelt. In 1933 Harry L. Hopkins, Administrator of the Federal Emergency Relief Administration, began the Federal Emergency Adult Education Program. North Carolina, as well as the other states, began increasingly to emphasize adult education. This nationwide program, using teachers without jobs to instruct other unemployed groups, had 1,190,131 enrollees by April of 1935 and had employed 43,722 jobless teachers. The Works Progress Administration (WPA) continued these programs when the FERA ended (Wecter, p. 190). Adult North Carolinians profited from these federal programs and from the available colleges about the state; the unemployed teacher also benefited from the salary.

**Salaries for teachers.** North Carolina provided a graduated teacher scale that recognized experience with an increased salary. The maximum teacher salary in North Carolina was $90 per month; the minimum was $45 per month. African American teachers had a different scale: $35 to $70 per month (Lanier, p. 203). Salaries for teachers did not

*Hollis Elementary classes of 1932. These students are not identified.*

increase in 1934; the increase was 10 percent for 1935 and 5 percent for 1936 (Corbitt, Hoey, "Address Delivered before the North Carolina Teachers Association, Raleigh, March 19, 1938," p. 192). This granted increase was largely because a group of 1,000 people gathered and demanded a fair wage for its teachers. The percentages given for teacher salaries by the General Assembly were 20 percent for 1935 and 25 percent for 1936 (Lanier, p. 209).

**National Youth Administration.** The National Youth Administration Act of 1935 assisted high school and college youths seeking to secure an education. Nell Burns remembered vividly the help that the NYA gave to help her secure a high school education; she described her work in an interview:

> I worked in the office at Hollis High School in North Carolina for seven months. I graded papers for the teachers, filled in reports for the school, mended library books, catalogued books for the library, and helped in any way I could. I was very grateful for the NYA.
> My Papa would allow me to accept the money because I had worked for it. He would not allow his family to accept free lunch or anything we had not worked directly to earn.
> I used the NYA money to buy clothes to wear to school and even saved enough to buy my own class ring when I graduated. I was very proud that I did not have to ask anyone for money. I did not waste a single penny of anything I earned.

**Works Progress Administration.** Congress established the Works Progress Administration (WPA) in April of 1935. This agency took over the relief aspects of PWA and superseded FERA. The program paid for work rendered rather than merely distributing a "dole." The building of baseball fields for schools and communities, the constructing of municipal buildings, and even the painting of murals were some of the activities that the government compensated.

The program financed writers who traveled about the state to collect historical information and local folklore; *These Are Our Lives* and *North Carolina: A Guide to the Old North State* were two volumes from North Carolina that resulted from the relief project. Other projects of the WPA included conducting nursery schools; serving school lunches; and giving plays and concerts (Lefler, 1963 edition, pp. 581–582).

Nell Burns vividly recalled seeing the play *Snow White* at her elementary school; her teacher explained that the program was free to all students and that "the government had paid for the performance." Always a reader and lover of fairy tales, Nell was convinced that the characters were real. After much begging and coaxing, her teacher allowed Nell to go backstage and meet the character of "Snow White." Nell begged to go with "Snow White." When "Snow White" said that Nell would miss her family, Nell hugged her and said that she would never miss home if she could go with the lovely young lady. Without the "government," such dramatic programs would never have come to schoolchildren in the rural area of Rutherford County, North Carolina.

## III. Under Clyde R. Hoey, North Carolina Governor from 1937 until 1941

Clyde R. Hoey, native of Shelby, received the mandate of the people of North Carolina to serve as their governor for a four-year term. Instrumental in his election were members of the "Shelby Dynasty" and the former governors Ehringhaus and O. Max Gardner, his brother-in-law. Hoey, a former textile manager, understood the "common" folk and had several goals for the state.

**Governor Hoey and education.** In 1937 North Carolina Governor Clyde Roark Hoey expressed his interest in education. He advocated a twelfth grade, the furnishing of free texts for elementary schools, and restoring the salaries of teachers to the pre–1929 level. Although the North Carolina Legislature was not able to increase the salaries as much as Hoey wanted, it increased the salaries 10 percent (Corbitt, *Hoey*, "Address Delivered before the North Carolina Teachers Association, Raleigh, March 19, 1938," p. 192).

**The education of tenant children.** Hoey recognized the problems of shifting farm tenancy as late in the decade as 1937:

> [A] matter of prime concern to the State and the landowners is that under our present plan of farm tenancy there is a disposition to change tenants with great frequency.... Statistics as compiled by the Department of Agriculture show that more than one-half of all the tenants in the State have lived on their present farms only one year. One-fourth of these tenants move every year and one-third of the croppers move each year [Corbitt, *Hoey*, "Address Delivered at the Cotton and Peanut Festival, Enfield, November 4, 1937," p. 152].

The children of tenant farmers faced unique problems in securing their education. Their lightweight, scant, well-worn clothing kept many away from school on all but the mildest days. Many farm family budgets could not provide even the paper and pencils the students needed for completing assignments. The school attendance of many of these rural children was dependent on the cotton fields, the tobacco fields, and the demands of their families. Furthermore, the moves of tenant families from one area to another sometimes disrupted school attendance (Raper, p. 24). Coupled with jeers from their city counterparts, a family focus on work above education, and little time to study, these rural students had many disadvantages.

**School transportation.** In 1937 North Carolina transported more children to school by bus than any other state in the nation. About 287,676 North Carolina children per day arrived at their schools on 4,139 buses; the average child in North Carolina traveled 20 miles per day at a cost of $5.34 per child, the lowest cost in the nation; the next lowest cost of transportation per child for a state was $10.29 in the State of Arkansas. The District of Columbia had a cost per child of $96.07; fourteen states had a cost of more than $30.00 per child for transporting children to school. Of tremendous importance to Hoey and to North Carolina was the fact that not a single child lost a life in bus transportation to and from school during the whole school term (Corbitt, *Hoey*, "Address Delivered at the State Meeting of the Adult Educational Group, Roanoke Island, July 8, 1938," p. 200).

*Governors Ehringhaus, Gardner, Hoey, and Morrison.*

**Free texts and four-year programs.** By 1938 the state had funds to begin issuing free basal texts for the elementary grades; in addition, the state authorized textbook rental for the high schools. The appropriations for education in North Carolina were "around" $25,000,000 (Corbitt, *Hoey*, "Address Delivered before the North Carolina Teachers Association, Raleigh, March 19, 1938," p. 192). Hoey recognized that by 1938 there were over 800 high schools in North Carolina with four-year programs as compared to only 14 in 1907 (Corbitt, *Hoey*, "Address Delivered at the Dedication of the New High School Building, Shelby, February 11, 1938," p. 177).

**The teacherage.** To help teachers make ends meet and to provide an income to certain families, teacherages sprang up throughout North Carolina. The teacherage was in use throughout the decade. T. W. Martin stayed at one.

> My first year teaching in 1939 was at Green Creek High School, in the breadbasket of Polk County. The principal and his wife ran the teacherage, and I boarded there. I paid the family a set amount, and the teacherage supplied a room to me, provided all of my meals, and furnished laundry service for the towels and bed linens.

**Salaries for African American teachers in 1939.** In 1939 the most pressing matter for the North Carolina State Salary Committee was a petition from African American teachers to adjust the differences in salary between African American and white teachers. The committee made a slight adjustment in both 1939 and 1940. Still, the salary differential was a cause for concern (Lanier, p. 215).

**Continued gains with adult education.** In that same year Governor Hoey praised highly the Adult Educational Group and could cite outstanding examples of progress in the state. For instance, Swain County had reduced its number of illiterates from 1,848 to only 400. Dare County had the lowest percentage of illiteracy of any county in the state. Hoey noted how the Adult Educational Group touched the life of Carolinians; he encouraged local communities to cooperate with the state and federal governments to advance the work of the group and to enhance the life of those in the state (Corbitt, *Hoey*, "Address Delivered at the State Meeting of the Adult Educational Group, Roanoke Island, July 8, 1938," p. 201).

**North Carolina education during the Great Depression.** During the Great Depres-

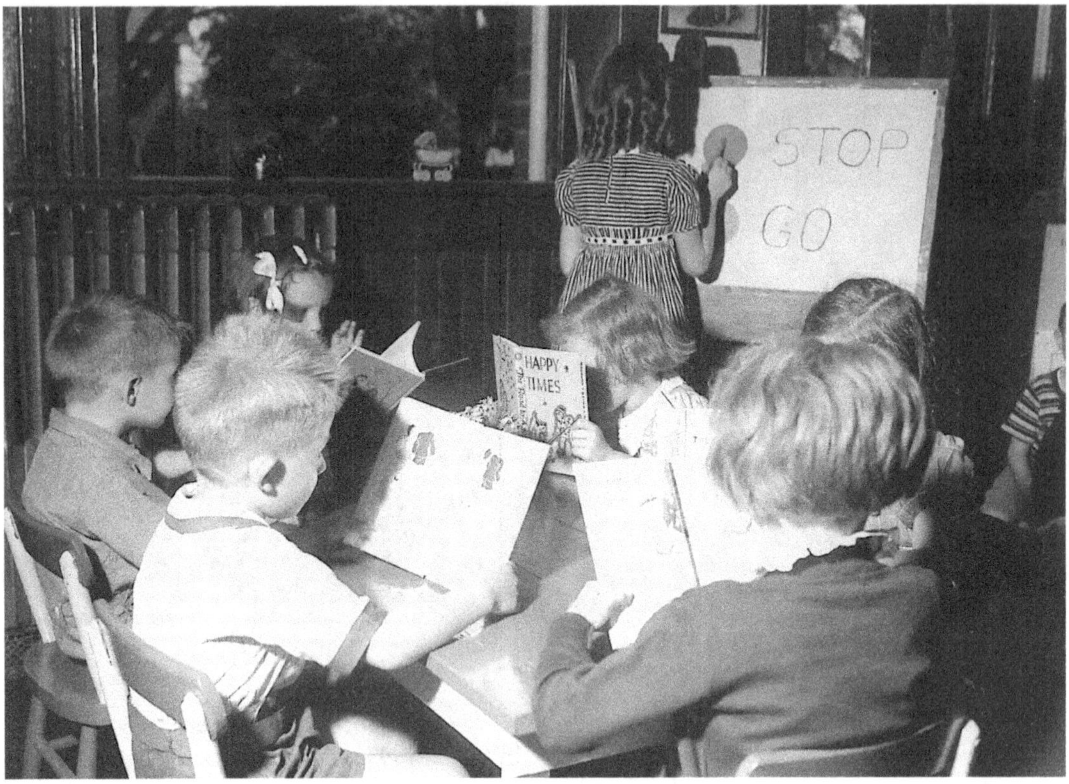


C AND D 2665-B. COURTESY NORTH CAROLINA DIVISION OF ARCHIVES AND HISTORY

LC-USF-33-30518-M4. LIBRARY OF CONGRESS, PRINTS AND PHOTOGRAPHS DIVISION, FSA-OWI COLLECTION

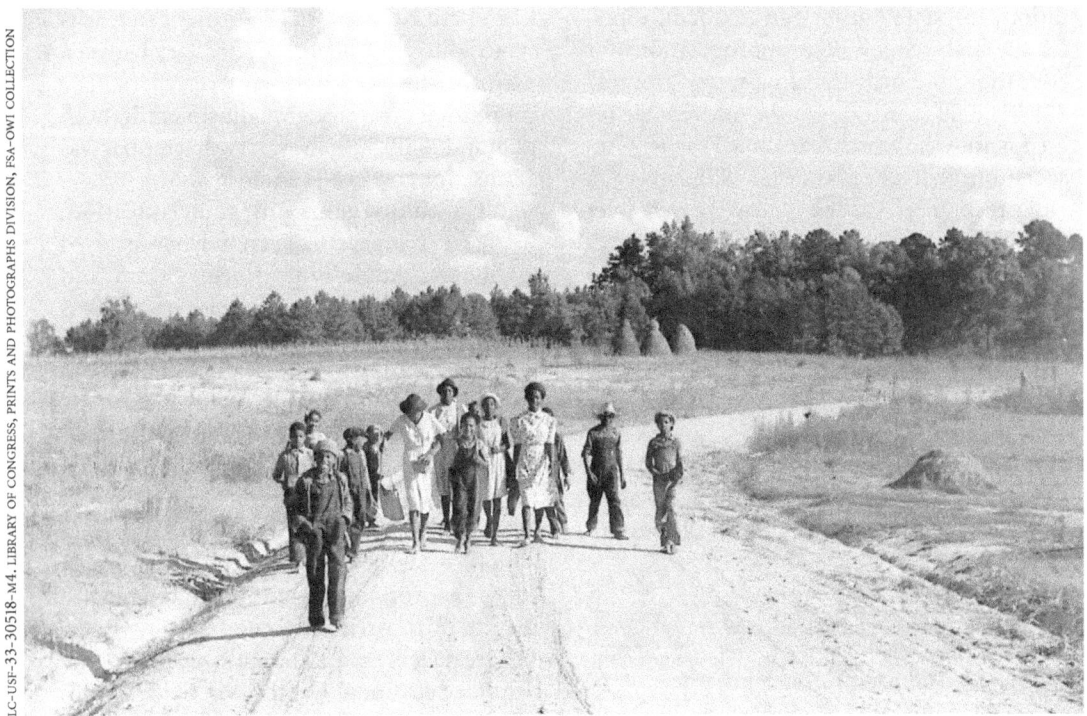

Top: *Classroom in Oxford, October 1940.* Bottom: *Children walking home from school in Frogboro, North Carolina, in September 1939. Photography by Marion Post Wolcott, Farm Security Administration.*

sion schools across the country closed because of a lack of funding. However, not a single public school in North Carolina failed to operate on full schedule (Corbitt, *Hoey*, "Address Delivered in Opening North Carolina's Participation in the New York World's Fair, New York, June 19, 1939," p. 279).

**School events.** Even though times were hard, funds limited, and many schools deprived of resources, the opportunities that they provided meant much to the children enrolled and to the community, which often attended the events faithfully. Nell Burns remembered working in the office, playing basketball, participating in the Glee Club and going to state finals, debating and going to state competition, receiving honors for her grades, attending the yearly fair on the grounds of a neighboring school, and going to see President Roosevelt. She participated in programs and attended the senior banquet, which was called a "prom" in some areas but not in an area where the term implied dancing. She recalls:

> The thing that I remember most fondly about my participation in school events was the recitation that I gave in the elocution program at Hollis School. My teacher read "How the La Rue Stakes Were Lost" by Charles Newton Hood — a 10-page recitation. When she finished, I raised my hand and asked to recite the first paragraphs of it verbatim. She was very surprised at how fast I had learned it, and she asked me to practice it for the talent program at our school.
>
> The recitation is still very touching to me. I can still recite every word of it after more than 60 years — and I still cry every time I say it. A beautiful medal that is still one of my dearest possessions and the recognition of my family, friends, and neighbors were my rewards for doing what I wanted to do.

*Safety Patrol in Oxford, October 1940.*

*Hollis High School Girls' Basketball Team, 1939. Left to right, Nell Waters, Gertrude Black, Frances McFarland, Nell Daves (Burns), Buna Daves, Sadie Bradley, Maude Whitener, Tewie Bradley, Inez Hunt. The photograph came from the album of Nell Burns.*

## IV. Higher Education in the 1930s

Higher education, like public education for grades one through twelve, changed drastically in the state of North Carolina during the decade of the 1930s.

**Consolidation of the three major state higher education institutions.** Governor Gardner in the early summer of 1930 turned to the Brookings Institution in Washington, D.C., for counsel; this independent organization had successfully helped the state of Virginia. By December the Brookings Institution had submitted its suggestions, and Governor Gardner shared the report with the legislature, state officers, the press, and other interested individuals (Powell, p. 483).

Gardner recommended favorable action on a number of the proposals at the General Assembly on January 9, 1931. The adopted proposals included using a short ballot that called for the election of fewer state officers and the appointment of more officers by the governor. Another suggestion was establishing within the governor's office a Division of Purchase and Contract with broad powers

*Hollis High School, Class of 1940. Left to right, row 1: Mrs. Ruth Jones (teacher), Nell Waters, Eloise McFarland, Frances McFarland, Nell Daves (Burns), Jessie Davis, Tewie Bradley, Mrs. Mozelle Warlick (teacher). Row 2: Mr. Glenard Warlick (principal), Frank Ervin, J. O. Gettys, Martin Martin, Earl Moore, Hyatt Melton, Edith Robbins, Doris Campbell, Mr. S. T. Teague (teacher).*

over state purchases and with the tasks of disposing profitably of any obsolete or unused state properties, using competitive bidding, and identifying sources of materials. Other agencies established by the General Assembly were the Department of Personnel; a Department of Banking to supervise banking functions and the insurance industry; a Department of Labor with a Division of Statistics, a Division of Standards and Inspections to replace the Child Welfare Commission and the Department of Labor and Printing; and a changed State Board of Health (Powell, pp. 483–485).

One of the most important changes, however, was the consolidation of the three major North Carolina higher education institutions—the University of North Carolina at Chapel Hill, North Carolina State College in Raleigh, and the North Carolina College for Women in Greensboro. This achievement attracted national attention (Powell, pp. 483–485; Tindall, p. 368).

**Governing the consolidated institution.** To control and manage the three branches as one university, a single board of one hundred trustees had final authority. The desired result was the end of the duplication of programs, reduced costs, and decreased educational rivalry. A Commission on Consolidation planned the transition. On November 14, 1932, Frank P. Graham became president of the Consolidated University of North Carolina (Powell, p. 483).

**Frank Porter Graham.** Frank Porter Graham served as president of the University of North Carolina from 1930 until 1932 and the Consolidated University of North Carolina from 1932 until 1949 (Tindall, p. 368). He became perhaps the best-known president of a state university during the decade of the 1930s. President Roosevelt asked Graham to be a part of the National Emergency Council, and Graham helped prepare *The Report on Economic Conditions of the South* toward the end of the decade.

Graham was a controversial but powerful figure in the state and nation.

> At five-feet-six and one hundred thirty pounds, Frank Graham was known as a man of courage and sincerity. Most of his friends deeply resented such labels as "pink-tinted" or radical for their candidate. In many ways ... [he] seemed quite moderate in his politics. He neither drank nor smoked. He was even known to frown on coffee.... He advocated continued price supports for farmers and federal assistance in conservation and education....
>
> The radical thinking of which Graham was accused was mainly an outgrowth of his support for well-meaning causes. At one time or another, he had supported some two hundred different organizations which were aimed at some kind of social improvement.... While president of the university from 1930 to 1949, he had allowed Communists among the student body. He dared to invite radical philosopher Bertrand Russell and black poet Langston Hughes to the campus as speakers. "The Fighting Half Pint," as he was called, had once defended a University of North Carolina professor for eating lunch with a black Communist [Parramore, *Carolina Quest*, pp. 409–410].

The enrollment of the Communists in the University of North Carolina was an issue in the labor movement in the state of North Carolina. Chapter Six, which is titled "Labor and Labor Organizations," treats the Communist enrollment. In the history of the decade, however, the matriculation was a somewhat unimportant occurrence. Nevertheless, Frank Porter Graham was one of the persons that the later McCarthy investigations reviewed (Parramore, *Carolina Quest*, pp. 409–420).

**Higher education for African Americans in North Carolina.** The education of African Americans was important to the state and the nation.

> Three four-year public colleges and two three-year public normal schools for Negroes report an enrollment of 2,333 (1936–1937). Five private four-year colleges and three two-year private colleges list an enrollment of 1,701 in 1936–1937 [Henry, p. 37].

By the end of the 1930s advanced degrees were also possible through the state-supported colleges for African Americans. Both graduate and professional programs in certain areas were now available for enabling African Americans to fulfill their potential with programs within the state.

**Aid to youth for higher education in the 1930s.** The NYA (National Youth Administration) and the FERA (Federal Emergency Relief Administration) were two federal programs that helped make higher education possible for many in the state and nation during the Great Depression. In fact, by 1940 one out of every six or seven college-age students attended some college. This was a record for the nation and world (Wecter, p. 191).

T. W. Martin, retired principal and classroom teacher, took advantage of the financial help offered through the NYA to secure his college education:

> I entered junior college in 1935. My job was to fire the boiler at 4:00 a.m. for the kitchen. I also swept floors and performed many other odd jobs to earn my wages. I was able to secure my education.
>
> I attended Wake Forest and earned my diploma from that institution. I still had the help of NYA as I worked to earn my college education.

**Enrollments in institutions of higher education.** From 1930 until about 1934 the enrollment in most institutions of higher education in the nation dropped, but beginning with the 1934–35 school year, the tide turned (Wecter, p. 191). North Carolina had twelve state-supported colleges that survived the Depression; Western Carolina Teachers College at Cullowhee actually increased its enrollment (Bell, p. 6).

Many teachers of the time did not attend a formal four-year college program to meet the requirements for teaching. Walda Carpenter explains the procedure in one county:

> Although some teachers in the area in the 1930s did possess a college diploma, one might

secure a teaching position in my county by passing a test administered by the superintendent.

In Rutherford County, Roundhill Academy offered some of the courses that would enable one to become a proficient teacher. I personally attended college in Asheville and took some courses at Roundhill. I passed the test that the local superintendent administered to me and taught for five years before going to work for the Welfare Department.

My education was unusual for a North Carolina woman of the time. I had social work training above my teacher's certification. My final paper became a part of the book *Concepts of Social Work* by Alan Keith Lucas.

**Carolina teachers as models.** Miss Cleo Burns (1882–1966), who served as first president of the Ellenboro Home Demonstration Club, began her career in education in 1898–1899. She began teaching while she was attending Piedmont High School at Lawndale; at Walls School, she was the only teacher for first through fifth grades. Like many beginning teachers, she had little higher education and large classes; one year she taught a class of 65 children in grades one through seven.

In many ways, however, she was very much not typical of other teachers. Cleo was partially paralyzed from polio. Her education over the next 54 years consisted of many courses from various colleges: Roundhill Academy, Limestone College in South Carolina, Women's College, and other institutions. By the time of her retirement, she had taught every grade in school and during the Great Depression she taught adult education classes. Because Miss Cleo, as her students called her, never married, she did not have to face the decision of whether the school board would re-employ a married teacher. Miss Cleo retired from the school system in 1953; she had taught in the public schools for 37 years—a long career by any standard. She had served also as a Sunday School teacher almost all of her adult life, as an adult educator and an art teacher, and as a respected leader in local clubs and the community (Biggerstaff, May 28, 1953).

*Cleo Burns was a teacher in Carolina's public schools for 37 years and served as an adult educator and art teacher during the Great Depression.*

A. B. Bushong was another outstanding educator. Educated at Virginia Polytechnic Institute, this agriculture teacher in Ellenboro received the title Master Vocational Agricultural Teacher of the South and of the State from the Federal Board of Vocational Agriculture. He competed against 2,000 other teachers from 12 states for the award; chapter one lists some of his accomplishments to benefit the community, the farmers, the state, and the nation.

**Summary.** Education in both remote and crowded areas, for young and old, for rich or poor was a goal in the State of North Carolina. The photographs of the decade show the progress of the state toward this goal.

CHAPTER FOUR

# *Health*

The *Report on the Economic Conditions of the South* described the South as a "belt of sickness, misery, and unnecessary death." The *Report* noted that ill health affected "even the height and weight of school children" (National Emergency Council, p. 29). Certainly hunger was widespread. Photographers to the state of North Carolina documented cases of rickets, malaria, pellagra, tuberculosis, and other diseases. Public health doctors found that of the 140,000 school children examined in 41 Carolina counties, 23,000 were malnourished (Powell, p. 486).

Author Jack Temple Kirby gives one unassailable generalization:

> Because of their climate and their poverty, southerners were less healthy than other Americans, and they looked it. Malaria, one of the three enervating "lazy" diseases peculiar to the Southeast, was well understood in the nineteenth century but before World War II only limited progress was made toward ditching and draining mosquito-breeding pools from which the disease spread.... Hookworm, another of the diseases that made southerners seem good-for-nothing, is an intestinal parasite common to barefoot people who step in feces containing worm larvae. Pellagra [is] the third of the lazy diseases... [Kirby, pp. 186–187].

## *I. Pellagra, One of the Lazy Diseases*

Kirby notes the shortened and uncomfortable lives of many Southerners. He describes them as "a corn-and-pork-consuming folk":

> Had the corn been leavened with other vegetables, and had the pork been lean instead of fat, they might have been healthy. But tradition, ignorance, and especially economic circumstances permitted in the main a diet only of "white" food—that is, fat pork; corn in the form of bread, or "pone," fried in pork grease; and molasses made from corn or sorghum. This diet was central to what Rupert Vance termed the "cotton culture complex," but it ... [existed] to varying degrees outside the cotton-growing areas, too. During the late 1920s, Vance found, the "maize kernel" constituted 32.5 percent of all the food intake of southern blacks. The figure for whites (which Vance did not report) must have been near this....
>
> [S]outherners of both races relished corn and pork and never apologized to outsiders. "We eat our hogs, fat-back and all," declared a North Carolina sharecropper in 1938; "I like fat-back." He went on to relate a tale of a campaigning politician who promised the electorate beefsteak if he were sent to Congress. "That kind er talk hurt him and lost him the precinct" [Kirby, p. 188].

Of course, despite Kirby's implications, necessity, the lack of money, and the limited availability of other foods made the "white diet" compulsory for many. It was this unbalanced diet that was to cause, particularly in the South, a great sickness: pellagra. Pellagra, however, was not fully understood by the general population of North Carolina and the South until much later.

*A child with symptoms of rickets in December 1938. Photograph by Marion Post Wolcott, Farm Security Administration.*

**Conrad Elevjhem, Dr. Joseph Goldberger, and pellagra.** In the 1920s the surgeon in the United States Public Health Service was very concerned about a disease called pellagra. This disease of the four D's—dermatitis, diarrhea, dementia, and death—was particularly prominent in the South; in 1912 South Carolina alone reported 30,000 cases and a mortality rate of 40 percent. Goldberger headed the investigation to determine the cause of this disease whose skin condition resembled leprosy; his theory was that germs did not cause the disease, but critics disagreed. Goldberger and his assistant George Wheeler conducted "filth parties" to convince the skeptics. On April 26, 1916, they shot 5–6 cubic centimeters of blood from infected pellagra victims into their own bodies to show that they would not contract the disease. They swabbed secretions from the nose and throat of pellagra victims and rubbed the secretions into their own throats and noses. They put scabs from the rashes of the victims into capsules and swallowed them. Even Goldberger's wife Mary submitted to the inoculations. None of the three became infected with pellagra (Kraut, pp. 1–6).

Goldberger's experiment was to feed

*Mrs. Lloyd, on the left, who is 91 years old, has lived in the same place, Carboro, for 69 years. Her daughter, in the doorway, suffers from pellagra (a severe niacin deficiency caused by improper diets, especially those consisting largely of corn). Photograph by Marion Post Wolcott, Farm Security Administration.*

children in two Mississippi orphanages and in the Georgia State Asylum fresh meat, milk and vegetables instead of a corn-based diet; the dramatic result was pellagra victims who recovered on the balanced diet. Skeptics called the experiment a fraud; believers talked of a Nobel Prize Nomination.

With the hard times in the South in the 1920s, the pellagra cases spiked. Goldberger predicted 100,000 cases and 10,000 deaths from pellagra for 1921; his predictions of famine and plague for the South were correct. Still the public did not believe (Kraut, pp. 1–6). A Spartanburg, South Carolina, newspaper reports on a recent book about research of the era:

> Public health officials headquartered their pellagra research efforts in Spartanburg [near the North Carolina line] because of the large number of textile mills in the county and the high number of cases of the disease.... "Spartanburg was the epicenter for the disease." ...Goldberger and his helpers worked night and day, canvassing 24 mill villages and an unknown number of farm families. They wanted to know what people ate, and the places where they bought their food....
>
> "It was one of the greatest epidemiological studies ever completed in this country, and it was done right here in Spartanburg," said Charles Gershon, an Asheville urologist who's writing a book about Goldberger and the work he did at Public Health Service Hospital at the corner of College and Forest streets.
>
> What made Goldberger controversial was his claim that poor diets on the dining tables of poverty-stricken textile workers and sharecroppers were causing a scourge of pellagra to sweep across Spartanburg County and communities throughout the South [Henderson, pp. A-1, A-6].

The South, however, was not grateful for Goldberger's work, his predictions, or his pleas for relief, supplies, and hospitalization for the poor. Some enraged Southerners protested that the negative characterization of their area would discourage tourism and investments. "They believed that Southern pride and Southern prosperity were on the line" (Henderson, p. A-1). The newspaper article states:

> "The politicians had a vested reason to keep people in a certain position," Gershon said.
> Gershon said Goldberger was appalled by the living conditions he saw on ... sharecropping farms and in the area's mill villages. "Dr. Goldberger realized immediately there was a direct relation to how much money a person earned and pellagra," Gershon said. "This was a disease of the poor."
> Goldberger's belief that pellagra was the direct result of bad diet defied the long-standing notion the disease was caused by bacteria, and it challenged the economic and social structures that were the cultural backbone of ... the South [Henderson, p. A-1].

Goldberger continued his research to identify the "pellagra preventive factor." He learned that brewer's yeast prevented the disease as effectively as and more economically than meat, milk, and vegetables. He was not to complete his study, however; he died on January 17, 1929. It was Conrad Elevjhem who found that a deficiency in niacin — a B vitamin — caused a similar disease in canines; Tom Spies found that nicotinic acid could cure the dreaded disease of pellagra, one of the South's three lazy diseases. Tulane University scientists found that an amino acid called tryptophan was a precursor of niacin; their experiments showed that when it was added to bread, it could prevent pellagra. These findings helped relieve the suffering of many — especially Southerners — from a disease of poverty: pellagra (Kraut, pp. 1–6).

The pellagra epidemic lasted from 1906 to 1940. The South was hit hardest as were African American residents of the area (Henderson, p. A-6).

**Planning diets wisely.** Even those with some money might not know how to plan their diet wisely. With the beginning of their old age assistance on July 1, 1937, many older Carolinians were receiving their first income in some time. With this income available to them, however, the recipients might not know how to spend the money and plan their diet wisely, and there were strict guidelines on how they could spend the $5.00.

Walda Carpenter, welfare worker from Rutherford County, remembers one man who called her at the Department of Welfare. He was at Grady Withrow's General Store in Hollis, North Carolina, and had a question.

> He asked, "I know once I begin drawing my pension, I have to give a strict accounting of all purchases. I just wanted to ask if I could buy my wife and me 'one square meal' before I draw my first check."
> I replied that he could; then I asked, "Just what do you call a 'square meal'?"
> "A square meal is a tin of sardines, a pack of crackers, and a can of pork 'n beans."
> I reassured him that the 'square meal' would be fine.

The Home Demonstration Clubs throughout the state helped to guide homemakers in the components of a healthy diet and how to plan nutritious menus for a family even on a limited income. The Home Demonstration Clubs and community canneries helped Carolinians preserve foods safely.

When some of the federal programs began to limit the production of the staple cash crops of the South, agricultural families began to plan a variety of crops for their families. A. B. Bushong, the outstanding agriculture teacher in the South, was instrumental in helping encourage raising additional crops and livestock to increase variety in the menus of the family and to improve the health of Southerners, particularly Carolinians.

## II. Hookworm, the Second Lazy Disease

As late as 1956 C. E. Turner reported that hookworm disease (ancylostomiasis) caused by the *Nector americanus* was still a common occurrence — particularly in the southeastern

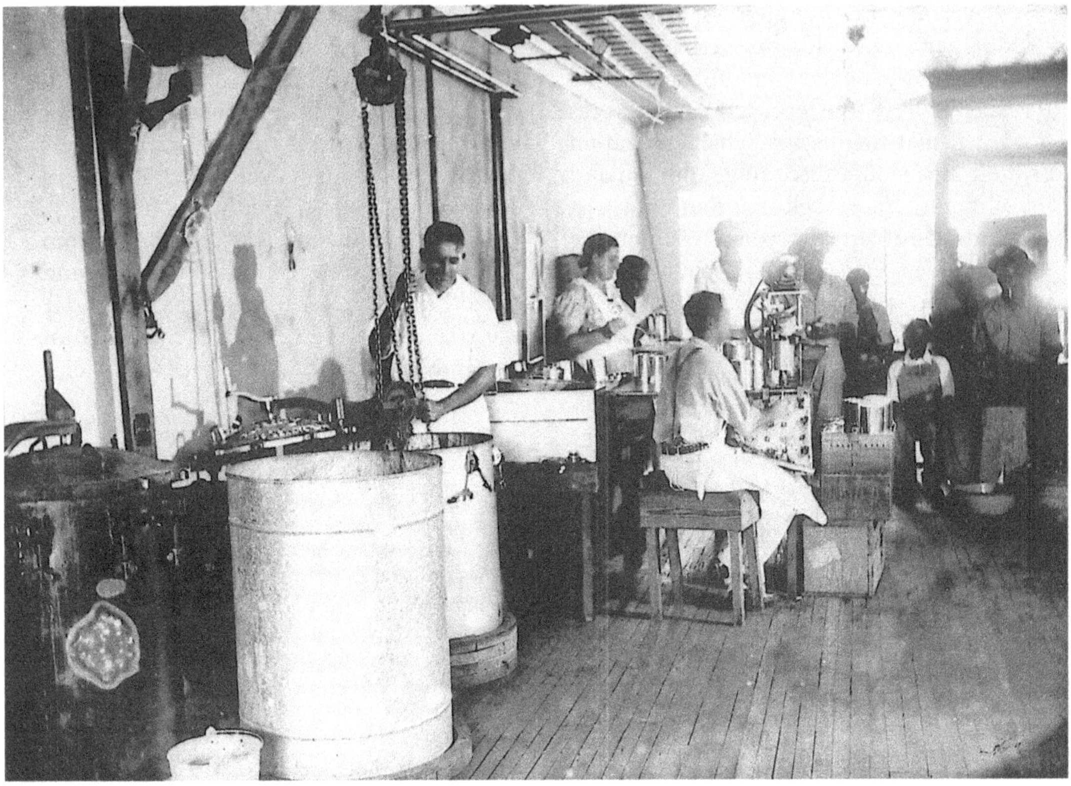

COURTESY W. H. MCARTHUR

COURTESY ANNETTE MARTIN

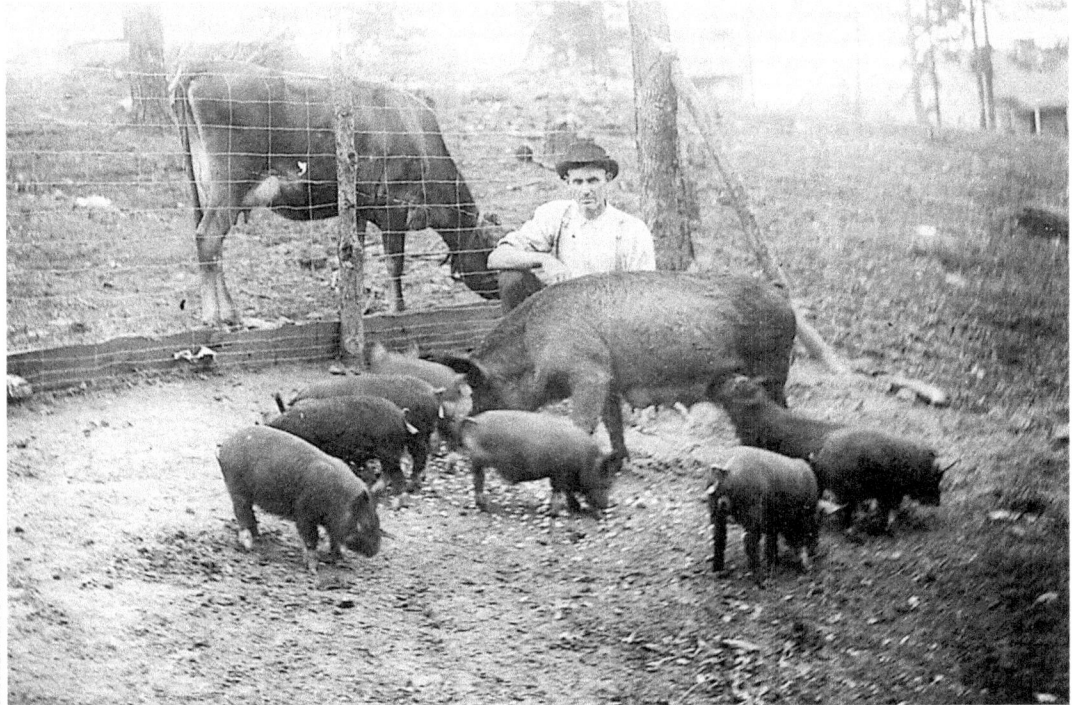

Top: *McArthur's Metal Shop in Rutherford County made the vats used in this 1930 community cannery.* Bottom: *A farmer and his "prize" litter of pigs.*

parts of the United States (Turner, p. 549). Its occurrence in the South in the 1930s was a major health hazard, particularly to the children.

**Pathology.** Hookworm is an intestinal parasite of humans. Heavy infection can create serious health problems for newborns, for children, for pregnant women, and for people who are already malnourished — as the statistics on pellagra indicate that many Southerners were in the 1930s.

Victims become infested with the worm by direct contact with contaminated soil or with the larvae themselves. The most common ways of contamination are walking barefoot through the affected dirt — a common practice in the warm South — or ingesting the larvae through not washing well the vegetables grown in the soil, not washing one's hands after working or playing in the dirt, or not drinking from a clean water supply. Proper sanitation provisions were crucial to good health of the citizenry.

Hookworm eggs grow well in warm, moist, shady soil; there they hatch into larvae (Center for Disease Control and Prevention, "Fact Sheet: Hookworm Infection," p. 1). These barely visible larvae can penetrate the skin — often through the feet. The site of entry usually produces an itchy rash — sometimes

*Sanitation in Randolph County, circa 1930.*

called "ground itch." The infected person may even develop open sores around the places of entry—usually the ankles or legs. These open wounds seem to appear with no apparent cause and are difficult to cure on the outside of the body; what is going on inside the body is not at once evident to the host of these hook-worms. People in the South often referred to these slow-healing areas as "fall sores" or "dew sores." These common references indicate that the sites often contacted the morning dew and were more severe in the fall after a summer of exposure to the hookworm. The terms "fall sores" and "dew sores" suggest explanations that the victims were using to explain the presence of conditions they did not understand; the small parasites, the actual cause of these sores, were unknown to most residents.

After entry into the body through the skin, the larvae pass through the lymphatic system to the blood stream and move through the blood to the lungs. The larvae pierce the walls of the air sacs, pass through the breathing tubes to the mouth, are swallowed, and eventually reside in the small intestine. This long journey takes about a week. If the larvae are swallowed through contaminated water or food or are placed directly in the mouth, their journey is shorter and the larvae go directly to the intestine after being swallowed (Turner, p. 420).

The larvae develop into worms that are about one-half inch long and that attach themselves to the walls of the intestine and suck the blood of the victim. Anemia, abdominal pain, weight loss, diarrhea, appetite loss, difficulty breathing, enlargement of the heart, irregular heartbeat, and lethargy—hence the name "lazy disease"—can result.

An adult worm can produce thousands of eggs that are excreted. If the excretion contaminates the soil and if the conditions are right, the eggs can develop into larvae (Center for Disease Control and Prevention, "Fact Sheet: Hookworm Infection," p. 1).

**Dr. Benjamin Washburn.** One Carolina native and traveling doctor in the mountains of North Carolina gained international recognition in his fight against hookworm.

*Dr. Benjamin E. Washburn (about 1950).*

Dr. Benjamin Washburn—whose first book, *A Country Doctor in the South Mountains*, tells of his practice in North Carolina before his joining the Rockefeller Sanitary Commission in its campaigns against hookworm disease—served the state, the nation, and the world.

After his work in the Appalachian Mountains, Washburn stated that he wished he had hypothesized more about those whom he treated. The "dew sores" or "fall sores" that were slow healing among residents of the Rutherford County community were actually among the first stages of hookworm, a disease that Washburn sought to eradicate locally, nationally, and internationally (Washburn, *A Country Doctor in the South Mountains*, pp. 15–18).

Dr. Washburn attempted to share his knowledge and expertise with the state and world. He organized the Bureau of County Health Work of the North Carolina State Board of Health and became health officer of Nash County, one of the first counties of the United States to provide full-time health service (Washburn, *A Country Doctor in the*

*South Mountains*, back cover). Washburn was an officer of the International Health Division of the Rockefeller Foundation from 1915 until 1939; he served in North Carolina, Trinidad, Jamaica, the West Indies, and Central America (Le Gloahec).

Upon retiring, Dr. Washburn was health editor of the *Progressive Farmer* from 1940 until 1953 and served as a district health officer during World War II. He also was a member of the Governor's Committee on Hospitals and Medical Care and a Director of the North Carolina Good Health Association (Washburn, *A Country Doctor in the South Mountains*, back cover).

**Prevention and treatment of hookworm.** The County Health Departments in North Carolina, the Home Demonstration Clubs, doctors and nurses, and publications from the North Carolina State Board of Health helped to educate the public as to the cause, symptoms, treatment, and prevention of hookworm disease. Health Departments, publications, doctors, and nurses advocated provisions for adequate sanitation as an important part of decreasing the incidence of this "lazy disease." This education was important for a populace that had no knowledge of the significance of "ground itch," "dew sores," or "fall sores." Through education, sanitation, and treatment, the incidence of hookworm disease began to decline.

## III. Malaria, Another of the Lazy Diseases

Malaria, one of the three lazy diseases that Kirby notes, was a particular concern in North Carolina. During the 1930s and at the turn of the century period—before the days of insect sprays and bug killers—mosquitoes were very common in North Carolina with its mild, normally moist climate. Many people developed chills and malaria from the bite of the infected *Anopheles* mosquito. The only way at the time to treat the high fevers, quell the chills of the disease, and slow the growth of the parasite contracted from the mosquito bite was to use a bitter medicine called *quinine*.

**Edwin W. Grove and the fight against malaria.** Before the turn of the century, Edwin W. Grove, a native of Bolivar, Tennessee, worked at Paris Medicine Company in Tennessee. He began developing a more pleasant treatment for malaria.

By mixing iron, lemon, and sugar with the quinine, Grove developed a tasteless medicine called Grove's Tasteless Chill Tonic. Grove's tonic sold for 50 cents a bottle and carried Edwin's own guarantee: No cure, no pay. When bottles of his Tasteless Chill Tonic outsold bottles of Coca-Cola, Grove became a millionaire.

Edwin Grove's contributions to the health of Carolinians, Americans, and the world would continue. He moved to another phase of his life and work (Johnson, pp. 50–52). With his fortunes he built Grove Park Inn in Asheville, where he emphasized cleanliness and quiet.

## IV. Poliomyelitis

"The ride to the hospital with a feverish polio child was frequently one of the most difficult trips ever taken by a family," the Polio History Timeline reports. Unfortunately, it was a trip that many families made during the 1930s, a time before the medical profession had developed a prevention for the disease ("Polio History Timeline").

President Franklin Delano Roosevelt knew well the high fevers and the crippling effects of the disease. In 1921 he had contracted polio, and the disease had left him unable to walk unaided in the years to come. Established in 1927, the Warm Springs Foundation in Warm Springs, Georgia, was critical in helping many polio patients live comfortably. Often a visitor at Warm Springs, President Roosevelt sponsored the First Birthday Ball to benefit the facility; the ball raised one million dollars in 1934 ("Polio History Timeline").

The iron lung was the "difficult, tedious, and frequently frightening" aid for polio vic-

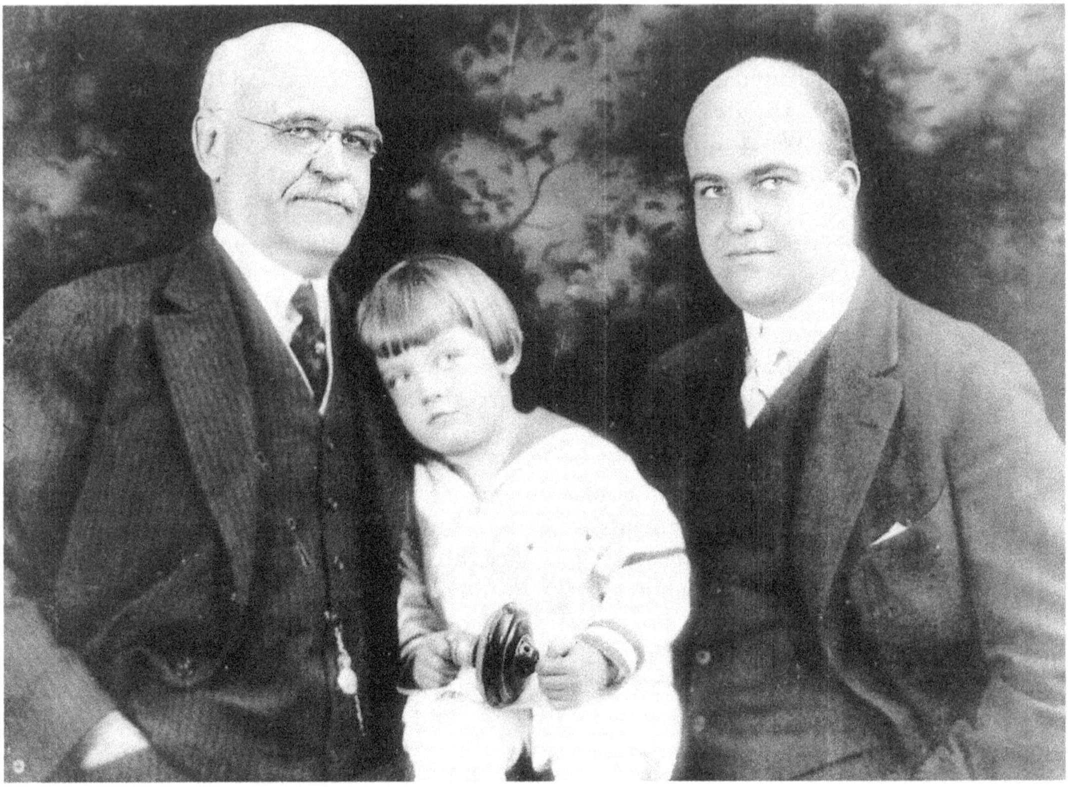

COURTESY GROVE PARK INN, 290 MACON AVENUE, ASHEVILLE, NORTH CAROLINA

COURTESY GROVE PARK INN, ASHEVILLE, NORTH CAROLINA

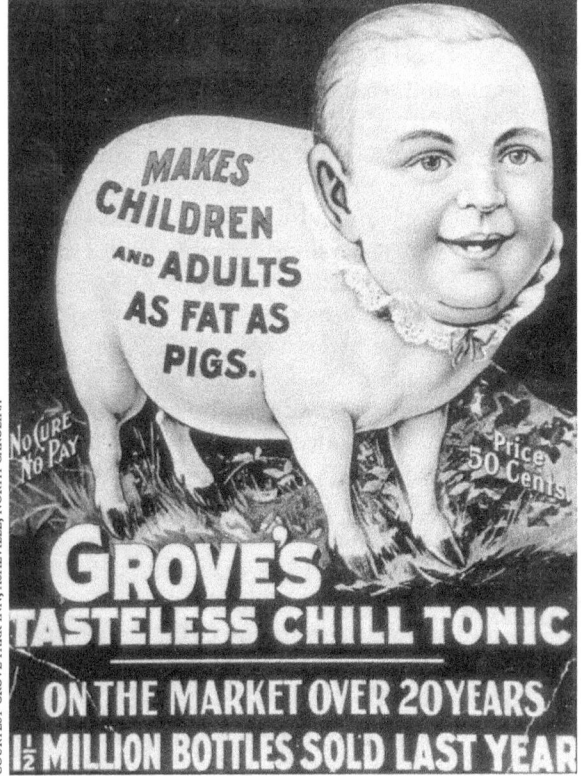

Top: *Three generations of Groves: Edwin W. Grove (1850–1927), Edwin W. Grove, Jr. (1890–1934), and Edwin W. Grove, III (1912–1967).* Left: *The famous Grove trademark was the face of a baby. In this advertisement the face appears on the body of a plump pig. The slogan "No Cure, No Pay," was, in effect, a money-back guarantee.*

tims. Unfortunately no cure was available or prevention possible during the decade of the 1930s. In 1935 vaccine trials of 17,000 children brought death to six and polio itself to twelve. A vaccine nasal spray developed by Edwin Schultz brought a permanent loss of the sense of smell to many of the 5,000 children tested. Concern for treatment and prevention continued. The National Foundation for Infantile Paralysis, created in 1938, had as its first president Basil O'Conner and as a radio spokesperson Eddie Canter. Canter coined the term "March of Dimes" and urged listeners to send their dimes to the foundation in the name of President Roosevelt ("Polio History Timeline").

Cleo Burns—a North Carolina

*The Grove Park Inn, built by Edwin Grove.*

teacher, first president of the Ellenboro Home Demonstration Club, and victim of polio — was typical of most North Carolinians who contracted the disease; one either survived — often with crippling — or succumbed to the illness. Cleo survived and was a contributing member of society and a public school teacher for thirty-four years (Biggerstaff, May 28, 1953). The end of the decade of the 1930s had brought no prevention for the dreaded affliction.

## V. Furthering the Health Care of Carolinians

Fortunately, North Carolina and the nation resolved to improve the health of all its citizens.

**The health of the child laborers of North Carolina.** As the Chapter Two sections on population, children, and the New Deal explain, the state and the nation passed various labor laws and programs that improved the working conditions, the provisions for caring for citizens, and, therefore, the health of children and adults.

**History of the State Board of Health.** The General Assembly created the North Carolina State Board of Health in 1877. Because of the friction among its members in 1930, Governor Gardner dismissed its members and named a new board. The board, now with the approval of the governor, would continue to name the secretary-treasurer — the head administrative officer. The duties of the board included making and enforcing the guidelines for quarantine and immunization and establishing the public health policy of the state. The State Board of Health was one of the largest and most important state departments (Powell, p. 484).

**North Carolina health departments after 1930.** North Carolina was forward-looking in the health departments it established.

By 1937 there were eighty-one health units in the state (Kirby, p. 168). Physical examinations, inoculations, and advice to families were an established part of the health department services.

As Chapter Two mentioned, North Carolina inaugurated the first contraceptive plan into its state health programs. Dr. Clarence J. Gamble of Procter and Gamble financed the program; he donated the first check on March 15, 1937 (Wharton, pp. 463–465). By the year 1940, 75 percent (61 of 81) of the public health units in North Carolina had added birth control to the services offered (Wecter, pp. 253–254).

Donnis Curtis recalls another service provided by public health departments at the time.

> Nurses from the health department visited our school periodically and examined us to make sure that we were in good health. When I was examined, my family was told that I had diseased tonsils. I had had frequent sore throats and had been very sick during the winter.
>
> One night in the summer before I went to bed, my parents told me that the next morning my daddy would be taking me to school to have my tonsils removed. What a sight that was! Children were going into the school with their parents holding their hands. Some were crying and pulling back. Parents were having to force some children inside. We were all scared to death. I simply held my father's hand and walked inside.
>
> The school had been converted into a hospital with beds where the desks had been. We were led to the operating area when our turn came. We each had ether and had our tonsils removed; we were returned to our bed. My daddy sat beside my bed in a straight chair all night. The next morning I was released, and we went back home. I have often thought about how unusual it was to have surgery in the school building!

Nell Burns remembered the vaccinations that the health department administered at Hollis School:

> I remember when they brought the typhoid vaccination to our school. I lined up with everyone else, but my feet started running and I just could not take the shot. My father was upset that I did not take the vaccination when I got home. Typhoid was a common problem at this time because of the pollution of many of the wells; livestock and privies often contaminated the drinking water at homes and at schools.
>
> The next time that the health department came with vaccinations, I submitted to the ordeal. This time the vaccination was a smallpox vaccination. When I came home, I told them, "You'll be proud of me today. I took a shot without running and crying." This time my family was upset because I took the vaccination. My older sister had had a very hard time with the smallpox vaccination some years before, and they feared the worst for me. They always believed that the serum had not been applied in a sterile manner. It seems strange to me now that the health department could administer these inoculations without the knowledge and consent of the parents.

**Health and safety.** Health and safety of North Carolinians became themes of even the Carolina power companies. In 1935 Duke Power issued statistics on how improved street lighting helped reduce traffic accidents in a metropolitan area.

> Cities spending over $1.50 per capita for street lighting have 130 night accidents per each 100 day accidents. At $1 and $1.50 per capita, 165 night accidents to 100 day. From 50 cents to $1 per capita, 205 night to 100 day. Less than 50 cents per capita, 235 night for 100 day... [Maynor, p. 72].

Many advertisements stressed the uses of electricity to improve health, safety, and sanitation. Feature stories in various publications extolled the virtues of good lighting for studying and reading. Sweepers, irons, and washing machines helped with sanitation — and the health of the user. "Reddy Kilowatt," the mascot of Duke Power Company, helped with conveying the message of the benefits of electrical power:

> To Reddy, we'll turn o'er the sweeping,
> He will dirt, dust, and germs take away.
> Thus the backaches, the pains,
> Oh! so tired, dear.
> You will think in a day turned to play [Maynor, pp. 72–73].

Duke Power and other power companies began to advise power consumers of the uses and advantages of electrical power to the health and well-being of the family.

> The company [Southern Power Company] hired home service advisors and agricultural specialists to help consumers with everything from money saving tips to extensive counseling and elaborate demonstrations [Maynor, p.68].

Top: *The Reddy Kilowatt pin was the logo that the Duke Power Company adopted. This pin was in the possession of Robert Ewart Burns, who retired from Duke Power Company.* Right: *Many homes in North Carolina did not have the electricity necessary to run a pump to bring water into the homes. Here Ola Mae Adams draws water from a well. This photograph was made in the late 1930s.*

Many Carolina families of the 1930s, however, had no access to electrical power for their homes — and would not have been able to afford the cost even if they had the access. Without electricity to pump the water, most residents used a windlass at their well to draw water.

**Traveling doctors.** Although doctors established offices in some Carolina towns, cities, and villages and although health departments existed in the 1930s, the traveling country doctor was very much a part of most communities. The professional personnel in the health departments made some house calls. Doctors like Dr. Benjamin Washburn and Dr. S. A. Malloy often traveled to outlying areas to help the sick and wounded.

Most residents called the doctor as a last resort. They usually tried first the home remedies of their ancestors, the advice of older residents, the services of the midwives of the area, and patent medicines before calling — and incurring the cost of — the doctor.

**Remedies.** Some of these home remedies did indeed work. Washburn describes a case of facial paralysis in one of his patients. In order to obtain the prescription for *Tr. Cimicifuga racemosa* to treat this condition, a member of the family would have to go by horseback to the nearest drug store in Forest City, which was more than twenty miles away — a forty-mile round trip. Because the

*Dr. S. A. Malloy examining Louis Graves and his family. The Graveses were Farm Security Administration borrowers. Photograph by Marion Post Wolcott, Farm Security Administration.*

patient had been recovering well with the tea made from the roots of "black crowhop," Washburn suggested that the patient continue with the home remedy. Later Washburn consulted his *materia medica* and found that the common name of *Cimicifuga* is "Black Crowhop" or "Black Cohosh." The folk remedy was the same as the prescription drug (Washburn, p. 18).

Had he been more observant, Washburn believed that he could have reported on the use of tannic acid for the treatment of burns long before the medical profession acknowledged this treatment. The members of the South Mountain community had traditionally used oak balls and oak leaves for wounds and burns, which were common since women's clothes often caught fire near the flames around the wash pots. The oak leaves and balls were rich in the tannic acid (Washburn, p. 18).

Jessie Gibbs remembers some of the home remedies that her mother used; Jessie's mother learned the remedies from the grandmother who reared her.

Mother emphasized cleanliness in our home at all times. I remember the reservoir in our wood stove was always filled with hot water for cleaning and washing the dishes.

My mother's grandmother was a midwife in the mountains of the North Carolina; she was very knowledgeable and greatly respected. She assisted in "laying out" bodies of those who died. She knew how to make poultices from cooked onions and mustard and how to place the remedy directly on the chests of those who had congestion from bronchitis, pneumonia, and deep colds.

Another remedy that she prescribed to children in the community who suffered from scabies ("itch") was rubbing the body in sulfur and lard. She was always careful to remind the parents to wash the bedding and clothing of the child in very hot water. She cautioned that treating the child alone was not sufficient; the child could easily become re-infected without proper

*Farmers listening to the sales talk of a patent medicine vendor in a warehouse during tobacco auctions in Durham. Photograph by Marion Post Wolcott, Farm Security Administration.*

hygiene. My mother would tell us not to hold hands with other children. An outbreak of scabies could spread quickly from child to child in a classroom.

Many people in our community would gather the foxglove plant and other plants and herbs and sell them for medicinal purposes to medical companies. Often the pharmacy would purchase the plants and sell them to the medical salesmen who came to the area. The foxglove was used to make digitalis for the heart.

Although many people in the community believed in a "spring tonic" of pokeberry shoots or watercress (cressie salad), my mother never prepared this for us.

Nell Burns remembers the remedy that her mother prescribed for children of the neighborhood who had contracted ringworm, a fungal infection.

Mother would suggest that their parents take the hulls of black walnuts and rub them over the affected area. This hull would stain the skin and kill the fungi causing the discomfort.

My father also knew how to cure thrush in babies. This disease is an infection of the mouth. The throat and tongue of the child becomes covered with a white coating. His remedy was a secret that passed from the father to one child in the family. He was the thirteenth child and because I was his thirteenth child, he was going to teach me to cure this problem. My father, however, suffered a sudden stroke and died before he could share this information with me.

Nell particularly remembered a life-saving remedy her mother helped her use.

My mother had pronounced veins on her legs. Many of these veins protruded from her leg as much as the width of one's finger. They must have given her much pain and discomfort, but she did not complain.

One day Mama was preparing biscuits for the family meal, and I was helping her. She opened the door of the wood cook stove and turned to get the two pans of biscuits from the counter. When she turned back to the oven, she bumped her leg *hard* against the corner of the oven door.

Blood began to spurt — not run, but spurt — from her leg.

She grabbed a clean dishtowel. I helped her press it tightly against her leg while my sister ran to the field for my father. Meanwhile the leg continued to bleed profusely, and the cloth was soaked through almost immediately.

My mother instructed me to take the clean, white flour and pack it on her leg. Immediately the first handful became a red, gooey mass. I continued to pack the leg with flour, wrapped the leg with clean cloths, and applied pressure.

Later, the doctor credited me with saving my mother's life, but it was her clear instructions and calm manner that helped us both get through the ordeal.

**Tobacco as a "remedy."** Tobacco was an important part of folk medicine; its many uses survived the passing of most other rituals. A "little snuff on a broom straw" placed in the mouth was the treatment of choice for nausea. To muster the strength for the final push in childbirth, midwives like Granny Lewis of Burlington, North Carolina, quilled the mother-to-be. With quilling, the midwife placed the snuff on one end of a straw and blew it into the nostril of the woman at the right time; the great sneeze that resulted from the woman was accompanied by the birth of the child. Granny Lewis and others used quilling well into the 1930s (Kirby, p. 192). Washburn and many other doctors, however, condemned this practice that often resulted in the tearing of the mother during childbirth (Washburn, p. 16).

During the decade of the 1930s rural people — especially those in the South — were able to buy cloth bags of loose, cut tobacco for cigarettes and to "roll their own." The cost of these bags of tobacco was usually five cents. Plugs of tobacco and powdered tobacco accounted for the "lumped lip or swollen jaw" that travelers often noted in the rural South. Chewing tobacco and snuff "defined rural southerners"; urban Americans were beginning to exchange pipes, cigars, snuff, and chewing tobacco for cigarettes. Although those who were more affluent tended to condemn the use of tobacco by the poor, there were reasons for its use. Tobacco was more than a "pernicious habit"; it was many Southerners' "drug of choice." "[T]obacco dulled the pain of hunger and aching teeth and gums, while providing a pleasant, gratifying sensation in the mouth" (Kirby, pp. 191–192).

There were guidelines on how the 1937 recipients of an "old age pension" could spend their pension; beneficiaries had to keep a close accounting of expenditures. Walda Carpenter, who worked with the Welfare Department in Rutherford County, had one client to refuse the old age assistance she could draw. When Walda told her client that there was to be strict accounting for the "pension," the woman told her flatly, "'After I eat, I have to have my dip. If I can't have my dip after I eat, I don't want the money for my food.'"

**Alcohol as a remedy.** Whether to use alcohol as a remedy — especially during Prohibition — was a frequently debated issue. Dr. C. W. Stiles, who had been sent to Raleigh by the United States Public Health Services, advocated the issuance of whiskey held in bonded warehouses and by the Internal Revenue Department as a medicine. Dr. R. L. Carlton, health officer of Winston-Salem, agreed with his view; a group of citizens who had opposed prohibition during the First World War endorsed their stand (Washburn, *As I Recall*, p. 171).

A resolution from the North Carolina Medical Society and the American Medical Association during the term of President Woodrow Wilson renounced whiskey for medicinal purposes. The statement declared that "alcohol as a drug can be eliminated from the pharmacoepia without in any degree crippling the efficiency of the doctors armamentarium." These resolutions caused the State Board of Health to take issue with Dr. Stiles; the temperance movement backed the opposition to whiskey for medicinal purposes. Some medical men who — like Dr. Carlton — professed to have noted "beneficial effects of whiskey in cases of lung involvement ... were bitterly denounced." The Methodist Church issued and distributed an editorial disapproving of the use of whiskey (Washburn, *As I Recall*, p. 172–173).

Dr. Stiles ended the debate by issuing a statement saying the use of whiskey was a

*A woman dipping snuff while watching the sorghum syrup at a cane unit on the Wes Chris property in Carrboro, September 1939. Photograph by Marion Post Wolcott, Farm Security Administration.*

remedy that he alone advocated; he disagreed with the belief that it had no medicinal value, noted that neither the State Board of Health nor any particular doctor had any part in advocating whiskey as a medicine, and returned to the Public Health Service in Washington.

The use of alcohol as a household remedy remained common in the 1930s for colds, women's complaints, "lung involvement," and high blood pressure — despite the actions of the State Board of Health and Prohibition (Washburn, *As I Recall*, pp. 172–173). Washburn tells of the discovery of a large, illegal copper distillery near High Point. Attached to the still was a note:

> If you happen to run across this still, please do not bother as every drop of liquor is to be used by the sick people of High Point. No one profits one cent on this liquor and it is given to the sick people absolutely free. The man running the still has nothing to do with the liquor. Mr. Crutchfield or any other Revenuer, please act accordingly. Will explain who I am when I see you in Asheboro at the District Attorney's office [Washburn, *As I Recall*, p. 171].

**The health of African Americans in North Carolina.** Through the cooperation of the Julius Rosenwald Fund, an African American Physician became a member of the North Carolina Division of County Health Work on January 1, 1936. This new field agent worked with local health officers to improve the public health education among African Americans. Health education was an important concern. The death rate for African Americans was 15.2 per thousand in 1925 and 12.2 in 1935; whites, on the other hand, had a death rate of 9.9 in 1925 and 8.7 in 1935. The lack of hospitals, doctors, and nursing care accounted for the higher rates for African Americans.

In 1930 a 50-bed unit for African Americans opened at the Benjamin N. Duke Memorial Ward. In 1938 there were 30 hospitals in North Carolina for "whites," 11 for African Americans only, and 114 for all people; the 24 hospitals in the state which were supported by city, county, or state funds were open to all people (Federal Writer's Project, *North Carolina: A Guide*, pp. 53–54).

Three diseases that were particularly high among Carolina African Americans were tuberculosis, malaria, and venereal disease (Federal Writer's Project, *North Carolina: A Guide*, pp. 53–54). The state made great gains in the treatment and prevention of these diseases among African Americans and all Carolinians during the 1930s.

**Health among the Native Americans.** A Cherokee medicine man, or *shaman*, was an important religious leader. Although the shaman had a natural ability, he had to serve an apprenticeship. The trainer guarded the information, kept it secret, and revealed it only to certain apprentices. Apprentices learned by observing, listening, and assisting. The accumulated knowledge of eight hundred or more plants might be available to several medicine men in a village. Cherokee medicine involved home remedies, the advice and treatment by the shaman, and communication with a greater power—Nun-wa-ti medicine. Chiltoskey noted that a clever medicine man "inspired confidence and applied the salve of attention to the wounded ego" (Hamel and Chiltoskey, pp. 5–6).

The *Swimmer Manuscript: Cherokee Sacred Formulas and Medicinal Prescriptions* by J. Mooney and F. M. Olbrechts (U. S. Bureau of Ethnology, Bulletin 99, 1932) includes the root of a fern as an ingredient in rheumatism cure (da-yi-u-wa-yi), the Indian cup-plant for fevers, and the yellow-rooted grass for toothache (Hamel and Chiltoskey, p. 63).

When Mooney gathered his information in the 1930s, he was skeptical of the medicinal properties of the plants. He compared a list of Cherokee medicinal plants with the plants listed in the *United States Dispensatory*, the pharmaceutical directory of the day, and found that 25 percent were included. Another 60 percent were either not listed or were used incorrectly according to the *United States Dispensatory*. He could not judge whether the remaining ones were used correctly or incorrectly according to the *Dispensatory* (Hamel and Chiltoskey, p. 6).

## VI. The Varied Diets of North Carolinians

Indeed diet was a major factor in the health problems of many Carolinians. Most North Carolina farms did not support all the basic needs of the family. Only in the Appalachian Mountains (at the border of Tennessee and North Carolina) and in a small area of the Piedmont did true subsistence farming exist (Kirby, p. 142).

**Subsistence farming.** The Davis family was an example of subsistence farmers who served also as tenants. Mrs. Getty Davis recalls:

> When John and I were tenant farmers, we planted corn for Mr. Joe; from this crop we were able to get corn meal for cornbread, corn meal mush, and hushpuppies. When Mr. Joe allowed us to plant our own area in wheat instead of just the cash crop, I could make biscuits and rolls that varied the diet of my family even more.
>
> Later, when we secured our own land in North Carolina, I preserved everything that I could from our garden and the fields. I canned a variety of vegetables that we raised ourselves, and we kept potatoes and turnips in our "potato hill" for many months. I made jellies and jams from fruits we gathered and pickled cucumbers by the gallon for my family.
>
> Malnutrition was never a problem since John planted a variety of foods in our garden, and I worked hard to give my family many different menus. Sauerkraut from cabbage was a good source of vitamin C for my family in the winter. I read the materials that the Health Department and Home Demonstration Clubs produced about canning, preserving, and good diets. Later I even worked in the local elementary lunchroom and used my knowledge of foods there.

We felt very fortunate to have gardens on our land to feed our family well.

Everyone in the area knew about John's cured hams and his homemade molasses. They sold well.

Indeed, molasses were a rich source of iron and added variety to the diet. The harvesting and crushing of the cane and the boiling of the sap required much work. The thick golden syrup was worth the effort to many; cane was a popular crop and improved the health of Carolinians.

*North Carolina: A Guide to the Old North State*, published in the 1930s by federal funds and written by writers employed by the federal government, notes that "cookery is as varied as the State topography. Every section ... offers a distinctive food to lure the gourmet. Yet all parts of the State shared many of the food customs of the old South" (Federal Writer's Project, *North Carolina: A Guide*, p. 106).

Charles Kuralt (1934–1997), who grew up in North Carolina and was a noted television journalist, believed that cookery was important. He said that if you wanted to find where you are, all you had to do was go into a kitchen and lift the lid. "If you are looking for the spirit of a place, head for the stove" (Kuralt, *American Moments*).

**Variations in meats.** Meats varied across the state. Pork, as described in Chapter Two, was important across the state. Barbecues, the *Guide* reports, were common throughout the state in the 1930s. Sometimes whole pigs, lambs, chickens, or cuts of beef were cooked over live coals. Baked hens—fat chickens of either sex—served with dressing made from crumbled cold biscuits and cornbread, onions, sage, and chicken broth were also found on many dinner tables on Sunday (Federal Writers Project, *North Carolina: A Guide*, p. 105).

Nell Burns recalls another Carolina way of preparing chicken and the weekly meal that her father cooked: chicken and dumplings. She remembers how each Sunday he "rolled the biscuit dough very, very thin and dropped it in the boiling broth." We children were always interested to see our father doing "woman's work" in the 1930s, but we eagerly looked forward to the delicious results for

*Making molasses. Photograph was in the collection of Mrs. Beulah Pruett.*

*Skimming the boiling cane juice that is being made into sorghum syrup in Carrboro. Photograph by Marion Post Wolcott, Farm Security Administration.*

Sunday dinner. "One chicken could go a long way when the recipe was chicken and dumplings!"

**East coast favorites.** On the east coast fish muddle—made from several kinds of fish, onion, and potatoes and cooked to a thick stew—was a frequent food for a large group; east coast gatherings might also center around oyster roasts or Brunswick stew made from chicken, beans, onion, corn, and tomatoes. In eastern North Carolina, the typical Sunday breakfast in the 1930s was broiled salt roe herring; in the spring, choice roe shad was common; in the summer, the easterners savored crabs and shrimps (Federal Writer's Project, *North Carolina: A Guide*, pp. 105–106).

**Specialties of the Native Americans.** On the Cherokee Reservation (Qualla Reserve) in North Carolina, a centuries-old recipe for bread made from acorns was typical. The preparation of the acorns for the meal, soup, or frying is a long process. Although the Cherokee women could use acorns from either the red or the white oak, acorns from the white oak were less bitter because they contain less tannic acid. Properly prepared, both have a pleasant nutty taste.

The Cherokee women knew how to exercise special care in selecting the acorns. Fall was the best time to gather the acorns; if they waited until later to pick the acorns from the ground, the shell was often filled with worms or bugs. If the acorn was lying on the ground without its cap, it was probably filled with a worm; the weight of the worm had probably caused the acorn to fall from the tree. The gatherers knew not to bother with the ones with little holes through which something had crawled out of or into the shell (Redhawk, William).

The gatherers soaked the crushed acorn meat in a clean, quickly running stream for several days to leach the tannic acid from the meat. An alternate way to remove the tannic acid was to boil the chunks from 15 to 30 minutes until the water turned brown; draining and boiling again and again might be necessary to remove the bitterness. The cooks deep fried the resulting meats or mixed them in a soup or in greens. After drying the damp particles in the sun or over a fire, the preparers sometimes ground the roasted meats finely into flour or more coarsely into grounds for acorn coffee (Rhema, p. 1).

By mixing the acorn meal with water, the Cherokee women made a stiff dough. They added salt, formed the dough into round loaves, and slowly cooked the mixture in the ashes. They also placed thick dough on sticks and cooked it over the hot coals. When baking powder and an oven were available, they combined the acorn flour with baking powder, eggs, and even regular wheat flour for a variation (Rhema, pp. 1–2).

Along the roads in the fall, they frequently set jugs of fresh apple cider out for sale. Smokehouses held curing pork, deer, and bear for the winter ahead. Mountain apples and cabbage, Sandhills peaches, and sourwood honey were delicacies favored by all who could secure them. Carolina food was varied — if the pocketbook allowed.

**Typical Carolina dishes.** The *Guide* reports that "southern cooks have a reputation for frying everything: meats, vegetables, breads, and even pies." Equally famous for the South, and for North Carolina in particular, were fried chicken, gravy, and hot biscuits — made with lard, soda, and buttermilk; kneaded to a fine texture; and baked until brown in the oven of a woodstove or less frequently a gas range or an electric cook stove. Served hot with fresh butter and with "sweet" milk or buttermilk to drink, biscuits and milk were very much a part of the meals of those who raised their own wheat, owned cows, or could afford to buy or barter the flour and milk. Corn bread was a food of choice and was cooked in the oven or fried on the stove top (Federal Wroter's Project, *North Carolina: A Guide*, pp. 101–106).

Greens were "dear to the heart and the health of every southerner," reports the *Guide*; these greens or "sallet" may be turnip, mustard, poke "salat" or poke salad, or water cress, often called "creasies." Common vegetables were beans, peas, cabbage, and greens, which the cook usually seasoned with fat meat. If one were to have good luck the whole year, New Year's Day required black-eyed peas and turnip greens, often cooked with fatback, side meat, or hog jowl for seasoning. Cooking two vegetables together — like corn and tomatoes to make succotash, black-eyed peas and rice to make "Hoppin' John,"— and combining corn, limas, tomatoes, and okra to make soup were common practices also (Federal Writer's Project, *North Carolina: A Guide*, pp. 106–108).

Sweet potatoes and molasses — a thick cane syrup often eaten with biscuits and butter — were popular menu items and were sometimes combined to make candied yams. Farmers used the horse-drawn mill to crush the cane cut from the fields; the syrup was boiled down in vats, strained, and stored as molasses for the winter (Federal Writer's Project, *North Carolina: A Guide*, pp. 101–106).

**Soul food.** The African Americans in North Carolina had some distinct recipes. Their fare — called soul food — is "the brilliant masterpiece that derived from want" (Cyber Palate, p. 1). Soul food is epitomized by its use of greens, beans, and parts of the pig, chicken, or cow rejected "at the plantation house"; some of these "rejected parts" include pig feet, pig knuckles, chicken feet, pig ears, pig snouts, hog jaws, tripe, fish heads, and chicken heads. These foods added to corn might constitute the major part of the diet of many African Americans (Cyber Palate, p. 1). Hush puppies, Hoppin' John, blackeyed peas, and cracklin' bread with chitlins or fatback were common menu items. Interestingly enough, much of this diet does not differ greatly from the "white diet" of many Southerners that Kirby scorns in his discussion of the causes of pellagra (Kirby, p. 188).

Soul food usually requires only one pot to make the preparation easier and to prevent a capital outlay for many cooking vessels. In conclusion,

> [s]oul food, like all inspired cuisine, is greater than the sum of its parts. African and West Indian cooks and their offspring were unafraid of hot spices. Chiles figure boldly; Tabasco sauce is as prevalent as salt in soul kitchens. The variety

of soul food is astonishing: chitlins or chitterlings, pig's intestines served boiled or fried in a batter; mess o' greens, or greens (most likely collard or mustard greens) cooked with salt pork until soft and delicious; red beans and rice; barbeque ribs slow-cooked long over an outdoor fire pit; sweet potato and peanut croquettes; cornbread — stuffed turkey with giblet gravy, and corn fritters — an endless feast [Cyber Palate, p. 1].

*Perloo* or *pirlou* is another dish that many African Americans — and other Carolinians — prepared. Rice, meat, and any available vegetables were cooked together in one vessel. Whether its name was *perlou*, *pirlou*, *perloo*, or *perlew*, the dish was the same; one combined shrimp, meats, sausage, game, vegetables, rice, "really anything you have in the pantry" (Grosvenor, p. 1). Harriet Ross Colquitt gives a recipe for perloo in her *Savannah Cook Book*.

> Stew one dozen rice birds [head included] in a quart of water, until thoroughly done, seasoning them to taste with red pepper and salt. When done, remove birds and sprinkle one pint of rice in the water in which they were cooked. Boil fifteen minutes, then drain off water, stir in the birds, and steam until the rice is dry and grainy. And when the pie is opened ... even if the birds don't sing you will have to admit that the dish is fit to set before a King!

Some African Americans — and other Southerners alike — were able to supplement their diets with squirrels, opossums, rabbits, fish, shrimp, crayfish, birds, and oysters (Cyber Palate, p. 1). Getty Davis reports of the custom of some residents of her area of North Carolina of throwing a net — such as a fishing seine — over a bush filled with birds eating berries or corn kernels scattered on the ground below. The hunter would kill, dress, and prepare the birds — regardless of type — for a pie or with gravy.

**Summary.** Images, whether in photographs or memories of the decade, tell it all: the molasses making; the raising of milk cows, chickens, and other animals; the rickets, the pellagra, and other diseases; the vegetables; the tobacco; the poor health and the untidiness of some residents; the pride and the immaculate homes of others; the rows of canned sausages and vegetables; the jeweled jars of jellies and jams on the shelves; the slaughtering of the hogs; the smokehouses filled with cured meat; the peanut snappings and the corn huskings; the country doctor and the health departments; the large families and the smaller families later in the thirties; the varied cookery across the state; and the dignity of the Carolina people — whether rich or poor, young or old, employed or unemployed.

# Chapter Five

# *Housing*

Housing for North Carolina residents varied considerably from one area to another in the 1930s. The type of available housing usually depended both on the region of the state in which one resided and one's occupation.

## *Mill Villages*

At the beginning of the 1930s many textile workers lived in mill villages. Sinclair Lewis had examined the homes of the textile workers in Marion, North Carolina, and reported that they were like a "packing box on stilts." He described the homes as having newspaper for the wall coverings and clapboards that one could pry off with the fingers alone; Lewis noted that there was no running water or indoor toilets (Lewis, pp. 18–19). Other mill villages, however, were clean and pleasing to the residents.

**Advantages of mill villages.** The village houses were sometimes neat, modern residences on paved streets; electricity and running water often characterized the facilities. Rural families often hoped to leave the farms altogether and move to a mill village where the houses had indoor bathrooms and electric lights.

Some paternalistic mill owners were sincere in their day-to-day care of and concern for the workers and their families. For example, Stuart W. Cramer, the owner of Cramerton Mills in Gaston County, provided attractive houses with hedges, lawns, and flowers. A golf course, a community center, increased productivity, and increased pay scales marked employment in his mills (Parramore, *Express Lanes,* p. 32).

One observer remarked that even at their worst, a company home was built better and was far more comfortable than the usual mountain home. Frank Tannenbaum, however, remarked that it was better to have to scratch the soil with one's nails and live on the farm than to live in the mill villages and work in the factories (Tindall, p. 326).

Even in 1926 a survey of the North Carolina villages reported that only 10 plants still lacked the "modern conveniences"; these 10 plants, however, included 1,490 workers. The survey in North Carolina reported that 97 plants with 21,037 workers had lights, water, and inside toilets. Fifteen more plants with 3,789 workers had fully-equipped bathrooms (Tindall, p. 326).

Mill owners professed to give their laborers paternal treatment by providing the workers with electricity, indoor plumbing, low rents, inexpensive coal, credit at the village stores, buildings for schools and churches, and — in one mill village — even toilet paper when the tenants clogged the indoor commodes with the newspapers they had used (Byerly, p. 12). Many mill families were grate-

*A mill village in Gastonia, 1938.*

ful for these benefits, took pride in the village, and helped improve the appearance of their streets and houses (Parramore, *Express Lanes,* p. 32).

**Disadvantages of mill villages.** Other families, however, felt that the company overregulated their lives. For instance, many mill managers influenced strongly the hiring of the mill village preachers, the teachers, the doctors, the storekeepers, and, of course, the mill workers themselves. Employers sometimes set village standards for behavior: required church attendance, purchases only at the village store where the owners set the interest rates, and the employment of the entire family. In some areas the mill village housing was substandard (Stoney and Helfand, *Uprising of '34*). The house rent for most of the mill villages ranged from as low as 25 cents a month per room to as high as 50 cents per room per week. This rent could cut deeply into the average wage of $9.00 per week (Parramore, *Express Lanes*, p. 33).

Many mill villages were not desirable places to live. These inferior mill homes were dully painted or not painted at all. The cottages were often flimsy and even perched on stilts that rested on slanting lots served by roads (Byerly, pp. 11–12). Running water and electricity were not available. High prices in the village store and an undesirable family environment contributed to the dissatisfaction.

**"The passing of the mill village."** After 1934 the mill villages, long a part of the scene around cotton mills in North Carolina, began to disappear (Herring, *Passing of the Mill Villages*, jacket). High maintenance costs, improved roads that allowed workers to travel longer distances to work, and the difficulty in rationalizing the subsidized housing for certain workers and not for others helped some owners make the decision no longer to sponsor the mill village. Minimum wage legislation forced some plant owners to spend more money on pay for the workers than for

*In the community house kitchen of a Gastonia mill village, 1938, a banquet is being prepared for 75 guests.*

housing; many mill owners found they could not pay the required wages and furnish housing at a discount to factory workers.

To cut their losses, the companies began to sell the housing and often to give employees the first option to buy. Selling the houses, which the mills had often provided at a minimum cost, enabled the employers to raise the wages of the mill workers according to law but affected the lives of the workers and their families. Many textile employees now had trouble securing adequate housing at a reasonable price. By 1950, the percentage (21.8 percent) of houses that the mill owners had sold and the number of mills selling houses (83) exceeded that in all the other states in the South (Lefler, 1954 edition, p. 599). When new buyers of the textile industries did not personally know the residents of the villages, the decision to sell the housing was often easier for them to make. Textile owners in North Carolina became some of the first managers in the South to begin selling mill houses (Glass, pp. 84–85). In *The Passing of the Mill Village* Herring describes the selling of these homes as a "death" (Herring, jacket).

At the same time that many mill owners began to sell the houses, Charles A. Cannon clung doggedly to the homes in Kannapolis. In the 1930s he began to rebuild downtown Kannapolis in pseudo–Williamsburg styles (Parramore, *Express Lanes,* p. 32).

## Rural Homes

Rural homes, in contrast to most mill village houses, were often without electricity, running water, or indoor bathrooms. More than half of the 3 million farmhouses surveyed in 1930 in 14 Southern states were unpainted; boards weathered by the elements gave a distinct color to the countryside. More than a third did not have screens; the open windows and doors allowed mosquitoes to enter and increased the chances of malaria and other diseases carried by insects. Only 5.7 percent had running water. The National Emergency Council described these rural homes as being old, of little value, and in need of repair (National Emergency Council, pp. 35).

Some rural homes were small but well-kept; it was evident that their owners took great personal pride in them. By contrast, other rural homes were two-story residences on vast acreage. The building materials varied, but wood, stone, and brick were common on the Carolina countryside.

In remote Appalachia the houses were usually heated by a fireplace, were never painted and typically had no toilets or running water inside; usually at least two people occupied each room. Mountain cabins often had ceilings and inside walls paneled with tongue-and-groove boards (Kirby, pp. 178–179).

"White mud." Certain areas of North Carolina hosted a type of clay that was white in color. By mixing the white clay with water one could make a type of whitewash (Burns). Other rural Carolinians also knew of this feature of the clay and used it to enhance the appearance of their homes.

> I want to tell you about—there used to be a lot of white mud. You'd go to certain banks; it was not just everywhere ... we had a big fireplace. I could stand up in it.
>
> Well, my mother would wash and clean all the ashes out. She'd clean all that up good, get all the soot down and wash it real good with soapy water. And then she'd go to the bank and get white mud.
>
> And she had a big old pot she made up the whitewash in, with cold water to mash it up good in, you know. And it would be just like paint. And she'd whitewash the fireplace all up good inside and outside. And it would dry.
>
> And when that would dry, she'd go and get her some flowers or even honeysuckle or something and make her a big old flower pot and put it in there.
>
> And the fireplace would be so pretty and smell so good [Bertha Norman in Ginns, p. 23].

## *Electrification*

North Carolina felt the upcoming depression long before the rest of the nation.

*This photograph is evidence of the variety of housing in the state—a Southern home in April 1938. Photograph by John Vachon.*

The 1920s brought decreased usage of electrical power with the slowdown of Carolina industries. The year 1925 was particularly devastating.

**1925.** The summer of 1925 brought a record-breaking drought; the dry spell resulted in both a low stream flow and a long duration of the low flow period; these conditions reduced the effectiveness of hydroelectric plants across the state. The drought underlined the importance of bringing the auxiliary steam stations into full service.

Organized as the Southern Power Company in 1904 and developed by James B. Duke (tobacco tycoon from Durham, North Carolina), Duke Power Company had became the largest utility producing and distributing electricity in the state; its 1927 value was $200,000,000 (Lefler, 1963, pp. 548–549). J. B. Duke was not to oversee this full-service use of the steam stations, however. By October of 1925 he was dead.

The plans Duke had started continued, however. The new plants completed soon after Duke's death included the Cedar Creek Plant (1926), the Oxford Plant, the Buck Steam Station, and the Riverbend Steam Station. But even harder times lay ahead (Maynor, p. 49).

**Belt tightening.** With the fall of the stock market in 1929, the demand for more power from increasing industrial and population growth did not come to North Carolina. Duke Power Company, for example, was "forced into belt tightening and austerity programs designed to weather the economic storm."

> [W]hen the Depression struck and times were critical, the progressives put on a strong punch for federal intervention in the things businesses and industries had been operating without extensive governmental influence. Now, the drive for socialization was one, and those who clung to the foundations of American free enterprise traditions found themselves enduring the heat of the political kitchens [Maynor, p. 69].

Power companies began to cut expenditures. For example, Duke Power Company found it necessary to halt some of its building and expansion during the decade of the 1930s.

The other major utilities in the state—the Carolina Power and Light Company, the Tidewater Power Company, and the Virginia Electric and Power Company—also faced hard times and competition also. For example, many towns in the state owned and operated electric plants; only a few of these, however, possessed their own generating plants (Lefler, 1963, pp. 548–549). The industry and power companies faced a slowdown.

**Electricity for the mill villages.** Many textile workers began to request electrical power for the mill villages from the power companies.

> At first, they [Southern Power officials] found requests by textile executives to provide power to the homes in their mill villages more of an irritant than a market.
>
> Then, too, the rural dwellers—those who made most or a great part of their living from the farm—were a hard group to convince that electricity in any form was not a force of the devil himself.... Representatives of Southern Power Company began cultivating the farmer's interest in earnest by the 1920s. But most rural dwellers made their livings from the land just as their fathers and grandfathers before them had done, and they saw little reason to put in some modern paraphernalia that they neither understood nor trusted. Anyway, electricity was a fearful force, and life was hard enough for a farmer without worrying about built-in lightning running loose in his house and barn....
>
> Yet new markets were waiting to be tapped, and after some experience in providing residential power service as a courtesy, Southern Power Company officials began to see where these potential markets were, and they went after them [Maynor, p. 67].

**Targeting the farms, homes, cities, and small businesses by power companies.** With the "vacuum left by the closing or production cutbacks of large industries" (Maynor, p. 71), power companies began to target the farms, the villages, the homes, the cities, and the small businesses of the state that they had not previously "wooed." Consultants from the companies even gave counsel and advice to potential customers on how electricity could help them. The company stressed the affordability of the new energy source in its promotions and advertisements. Duke Power had this quotation in one of its publications:

One typical attitude is reflected in the expression of one housewife who exclaimed, "It's such a relief to not feel that you should turn off the lights behind you every time you leave a room, and to be able to plug in any appliance that you want to use anywhere in the house..." [Maynor, p. 71].

## IV. Increased Housing Problems During the 1930s

John Christoph Blucher Ehringhaus (North Carolina Governor from 1933 until 1937) was quite concerned about the housing situation in the state in 1934.

**Home foreclosures.** On January 10 of that year he asked that those who were in a position to foreclose "exercise all possible forbearance" (Corbitt, *Ehringhaus*, p. 289). On September 17, 1934, in his speech "Better Housing Campaign," Ehringhaus "called upon the citizens and businesses to give the Federal Housing Administration active and vigorous cooperation and support." Ehringhaus's hope was to see the housing program of the federal government perfected so that laborers would be employed and house renters would become homeowners (Corbitt, *Ehringhaus*, p. 78).

**Vying for farms.** Sharecroppers, landless farmers, and tenant farmers often vied for places. They often took whatever was available. One North Carolina landlord used an "innovative and grimly poetic manner." He created one-room shanties from eight-by-fifteen-foot wagons; he anchored the wheels deep in the field dirt for increased stability. With the new federal programs, however, some landlords collected federal subsidies. They had no need for workers; many of these mobile workers were without work during the late 1930s (Kirby, p. 177).

## V. Increasing the Electrification in 1935 and Afterward

By 1935 only 9 states exceeded North Carolina in total kilowatts of electricity; only three states exceeded North Carolina in hydroelectric capacity (Lefler, 1963, pp. 548–549).

**The Rural Electrification Administration (1935).** On August 26, 1935, the President asked that the Administrator of the Rural Electrification Administration (REA) write to him to request bids for direct labor or for construction so that the REA could begin its work. Through the Rural Electrification Administration, work began which ensured that many areas of the state of North Carolina received electricity ("A Letter to Various Government Agencies on Allocation of Work Relief Funds," *The Public Papers and Addresses of Franklin D, Roosevelt*, IV, pp. 344–345; Lefler, 1954 edition, p. 582).

The cost of signing up with REA was just five dollars. To justify running the line, however, there had to be at least three customers per mile. Without identifying the area or individual, an employee reported an unusual event. A farmer came in to pay his five dollars and to sign up for electric service. The farmer, however, was not eligible because "his house was too far from the right of way." A few days later he returned and waved his money. He had moved his house (Harris, p. 1).

**Farms and electricity.** Electricity had been slow in coming to some rural areas. However, as the power companies and the federally sponsored REA brought electricity to the farms, things began to change drastically in the nation and in the state of North Carolina.

> It was about the same everywhere in the Piedmont. Farmers were using electricity for everything from barn curing hay, to warming baby chicks to milking cows. Agricultural productivity increased in direct proportion to the use of electricity, and Duke didn't miss many opportunities to point that out.
>
> The introduction of electric power in the rural areas in general and on the farms in particular, was the beginning of the end of the cotton economy and the first step into what would one day be called agri-business [Maynor, p. 68].

Not all farmers, however, even had access to electricity during the lean years of the 1930s.

**Electrified farms in North Carolina.** In

January of 1935 the percentage of farms electrified in the United States, according to the Report of the Rural Electrification Administration, was 10.9 percent. North Carolina, however, had only 3.2 percent of electrified farms. By July of 1940, 25.9 percent of North Carolina farms were electrified as compared to 30.4 percent of U.S. farms. By the 1950s the percentage of North Carolina farms electrified had surpassed the percentage of U.S. farms electrified (Hobbs, p. 287).

**Electrification amidst economic recovery.** Duke Power and other power companies continued to improve their service — especially as economic conditions recovered. Steam stations began to replace hydroelectric plants at a rapid pace. In 1938 Duke Power, for example, announced its plans to construct a new steam station (Maynor, p. 73).

The new plant, the Cliffside Steam Station, was located at the confluence of the Broad and Second Broad rivers. This largest generating center of the Duke Power System was in Cliffside, North Carolina; it brought two 40,000-kilowatt turbo-generator and boiler units to the state. The new plant began operation in July 1940 and was just ahead of the increased power demands of the World War II era (*Cliffside Station: Duke Power Company*, p. 1).

**Objections to the REA.** Some people objected to the Rural Electrification Administration. For example, L. C. Gifford praised Duke Power's work in North Carolina — particularly in the late 1930s and early 1940s. In the *Hickory Daily Record,* the newspaper he edited, Gifford voiced his comments in one of his articles; he objected to the interference of the federal government into the electrification of the nation and presented Duke Power as a model for other companies.

> If public utility companies generally could see the wisdom of adopting the progressive policies of the Duke Power Company ... there would be little need for the Federal government to subsidize an REA.
>
> The *Record* has just obtained data covering the rural line of the Duke Power Company in the Hickory district, and we believe our readers will be interested in receiving the gratifying information.
>
> During the eight year period from 1937 through 1944, the Duke Power Company constructed more than three hundred twenty nine miles of rural lines in the Hickory area, to serve 2,492 new county customers [Maynor, pp. 67–68].

*The building of the Cliffside Steam Station in July 13, 1939.*

*The new Cliffside Steam Station is operational. The plant brought two 40,000-kilowatt turbo-generator and boiler units to the state just ahead of the increased power demands of the World War II era.*

**Electrification at the end of the Great Depression.** By 1945 the 3 percent of electrified North Carolina farms begun to increase because of the 5,250 miles of power lines the already existing utility companies had strung. By 1939 more than 50 counties had available electricity to 20 percent of their farms; an additional 39 of the Carolina counties had more than 30 percent of their farms electrified. The national average of electrified farms in 1940 was 30 percent. By 1951 the state ranked second in the nation with 85 percent of the farms electrified. By 1954 the percentage had reached 96.9 percent (Lefler, 1963, pp. 614–615). It was in the 1950s and after, however, before some residents of the state saw the coming of the power lines and were able to pack away their kerosene lamps for antique collectors of future decades.

## Government Aid to Housing

It was through the Farm Security Administration (1937) that financial aid was extended to a selected number of tenants in order that they might become landowners (Lefler, 1963 edition, p. 582). Mr. and Mrs. John Lee Davis obtained their North Carolina farm with this financial help from the federal government.

> One day Mr. John Ed Davis, who helped with the Cleveland County office responsible for assisting tenants in securing land, approached us. He told John of some land in Mooresboro, North Carolina, that we could buy. Mr. John Ed helped us arrange the purchase of this land [Mrs. Getty Davis].

John Ed Davis (October 21, 1917–February 9, 2000) worked with the Cleveland County office to help meet the needs of local residents. When John Ed Davis enrolled in Wake Forest College in the early 1930s, he planned to become a doctor; he took his cow with him to college and sold milk to help obtain the money he needed for college. He entered North Carolina State after two years and took up agriculture as his major after he realized his cow would not produce sufficient milk for him to become a doctor. Over 3,000 young couples, through his work, were able to afford home ownership (Bynum, pp. 179–180).

John Ed Davis retired from the Farmers

*A rural home that is being supplied with electricity through the Rural Electrification Administration in Caswell County, October 1940. Photograph by Marion Post Wolcott, Farm Security Administration — Office of War Information Photograph Collection (Library of Congress).*

Home Administration (FmHA) in Cleveland County. The FmHA, established by the Farmers Home Administration Act in 1946, had predecessor agencies: the Subsistence Homesteads Division of the Department of the Interior, the Rural Rehabilitation Division of the Federal Emergency Relief Administration, the Resettlement Administration (RA), and the Farm Security Administration ("Records of the Farmers Home Administration"). John Ed Davis worked with many of these programs from the 1930s until his retirement.

When John Ed came to work in Cleveland County, however, many people were dubious about the new programs. Donnis Curtis recalled:

> Many tenant farmers in the 1930s were not taking advantage of the new programs because they were afraid to borrow money. They had seen others who had borrowed money lose everything they had. Their fear at this time prevented them from using the opportunity.

Getty Davis recalled:

> The farm we bought — with government help — was about 100 acres of fertile land. It contained a creek and some woods, in addition to the fields. We moved on the land just before Thanksgiving of 1941. The big house into which we moved was cold and in poor repair, but we lived there until our new home was complete. We moved in the new house in February of 1942 — just before the birth of our eighth child on February 25, 1942. We were delighted with our purchase and with our home, but I was very lonely after leaving my family and friends.
> 
> I have thanked the Lord many times that we did not buy the land from Mr. Joe, the man for whom we farmed. The land we were considering was inferior to that we bought; the size of the

farm was smaller, and the well was running dry on the land we were considering.

The first African American to receive a federal loan under the United States Tenant Purchase Program was Nat Williamson, a North Carolinian. The Williamson family resided in Guilford County. Federal photographer John Vachon photographed Williamson with Administrator E. H. Anderson in April of 1938 — after substantial changes in the Resettlement Administration. (In 1937 the Farm Security Administration had replaced the RA.)

## Resettlement

In order to move farmers to better land, provide advice, and help with the necessary housing and equipment, President Roosevelt used money from the Emergency Relief Appropriation to create the Resettlement Administration (RA), which was "to administer rehabilitation and resettlement projects for the relief of farm areas." After the abolition of the RA in 1937, the Farm Security Administration completed the remainder of the program.

**Penderlea, a resettlement area in North Carolina.** The Resettlement Administration set up experimental projects (such as agricultural trials) and communities, such as Penderlea near Raleigh. The community in Penderlea was similar to that of Greenbelt, Maryland, the first of three planned towns built and owned by the U.S. Government during the Great Depression. The projects led

*Nat Williams, the first Negro in the United States to receive a loan under the Tenant Purchase Program, and E. H. Anderson, a Farm Security Administration official, Guilford County, April 1938. Photograph by John Vachon, Farm Security Administration.*

to the domino employment theory: engineers to design the layout of the community, skilled and unskilled workers to build the houses, and the opening of necessary local businesses and government activities, which also required employees ("Employment and the Construction of the Greenbelt"). Penderlea provided employment and income for many locals.

In Penderlea the builders used local timber resources, which required workers to fell the timber and sawmill employees to dress the lumber. Many components of the homes used prefabricated materials, often built and transported by local labor. Engineers helped to design the layout of the proposed project; both skilled and unskilled workers helped to build the dwellings—which were to be improvements on the housing of the new residents ("Employment and the Construction of the Greenbelt"). The usual payments were $100 a year for 30 years (McGlohon). Many of the homes were still standing more than 60 years later.

**Residents of Penderlea.** Joe McGlohon lived in a Penderlea home for six decades. In 1936 he was nine when he moved into the home with his parents. The house had a fireplace of brick and masonry, a ceiling of fiber panels, indoor plumbing, the foundation above the ground, and a porch — screened in on some of the houses. Each family had 20 acres of land, a house, a pump house, a wash house, a smoke house, a storage house, a barn, a chicken house, a corn crib, a hog house, a mule, a cow, a hog, and some chickens. The government subsidized the family of four for $6 a month. Joe's dad worked the farm, but he hired out when he could; for instance, he helped clear the land for 25 cents an hour. Later some residents got jobs at the shipyard and in building Camp Davis and Camp Lejeune.

Another government resettlement proj-

*A homesteader washes clothes in the yard at her home at Penderlea Resettlement in August 1936. Photograph by Carl Mydans, Farm Security Administration — Office of War Information Photograph Collection (Library of Congress.*

ect in North Carolina. The government began another resettlement project near Penderlea. The quality of these homes was, however, inferior to those at Penderlea. These houses were cheaper. They had no indoor plumbing, a tin outbuilding, and outdoor privies; these homes did not survive 60 years as did the Penderlea homes (McGlohon). The city-farm encouraged community activities—like Sunday School and picnics.

**Federal photographers and the Resettlement Administration.** Rexford Tugwell, the director of the Resettlement Administration (RA), realized that the organization was a tempting target for conservative critics. To help alleviate the anticipated criticism and to make a permanent record, Tugwell brought to the historical section of the RA a group of photographers headed by Roy Stryker; some of these photographers would later become a part of the Farm Security Administration. Using filmed images, the professionals would publicize both rural and urban life, conditions during the Depression, and America itself. Six of the photographers traveled through North Carolina and depicted the rural life, migrant camps, the mill villages, the city life, and the resettlement housing.

The resettlement areas in Enfield, in Roanoke Farms, and in Johnston County, North Carolina, were the subjects of photographs by Mydans, Vachon, Rothstein, and Shahn. Many times the photographs tell the complete story of the farm; for instance, a photograph of a sign orients the viewer to the area and other photographs record such events as clearing the land with tractors and by hand, loading trees on trucks, cutting and stacking lumber, constructing prefabricated portions of homes, building houses, and moving into the finished structures.

**Results of the Resettlement Administration.** Of the 500,000 families in America the Resettlement Administration intended to aid, less than 1 percent actually received help (McElvaine, *The Great Depression*, p. 301). In North Carolina the actual number of families resettled through the RA was small. Badger estimates the number to be 751 at most, largely because of the attacks on the RA by Harold Cooley and others; the RA, in their opinion, reversed traditional land policy and gave excessive supervision to the clients. Some units failed before the RA "died" because of their small size, the formidable cost, and the many cooperative activities for individualistic families (Badger, p. 208).

## IX. Housing for the Migrant Worker

Migrant workers in North Carolina—as in other states—faced a different housing problem. In each of the places where they worked, migrant workers had to find their own housing, live in their own vehicles or tents, or use the housing their employer provided. The provided dwellings were often

> ...built of a single thickness of rough boards, without window sash or screens. The galvanized iron roof epitomizes the South's place in the nation [Raper, p. 21].

Sometimes as many as thirty-five people slept in a "warehouse." These landless workers moved from one area to another with the maturation of the crops. The families sought better dwellings and better working conditions (Roy Stryker Papers, I).

Federal photographer Jack Delano's many images of the migrant workers in North Carolina depict the complete story of the migrants—from their arrival until their departure. He displayed the entire institution of migrant workers in the Belcross area of North Carolina. His photographs show the young and old alike; the family groups and the individual worker; and the various settings—the tents, the warehouses, the sleeping accommodations, the eating facilities, and the shacks.

Delano's letter to Roy Stryker (received July 2, 1940) describes the housing problems of the migrants.

> Housing for the transients is the chief problem. Some of the farmers have been able to furnish the migrants with warehouses or barns to stay in, but most of the negroes [sic] just have no place to stay at all. So at night you find them

*Five: Housing* 173

*Eight migratory agricultural workers stay in this shack in Belcross, July 1940. Photograph by Jack Delano, Farm Security Administration — Office of War Information Photograph Collection (Library of Congress).*

asleep in box cars, on potato sacks, in the potato graders, or out in the open….

Last night I tried to get some pictures of the boxcar sleepers. If you had been here at 2 A.M. you would have seen 3 scared figures in the darkness—(myself and two boys carrying flashbulbs)—quietly opening the door of a box car and seeing exactly this ■, me pointing the camera in the general direction of loud snoring, setting off the flash then running like hell!

Tomorrow, I am going out to a house occupied by some transients about eleven miles from here. They're lucky to have a house but there are thirty seven of them staying in 3 rooms and an attic! I gave one of them a five the other day to get to talk to him and went up to the house. They think I'm a "pretty right guy" so I ought to be able to get some pictures there [Roy Stryker Papers, I].

**Summary.** The housing across the state of North Carolina during the 1930s is best described as varied. The mill villages, the fine Southern homes, the rural homes with electricity, the growing cities with their crowded houses and multi-family dwellings, and the shacks in both urban and rural areas are indicative of the many types of dwellings in North Carolina during the Great Depression.

## CHAPTER SIX

# Labor

Even though the general public is most familiar with labor stirrings during the Great Depression, the North Carolina labor movement actually had its origin long before the 1930s.

## I. The Labor Movement Before the 1880s

With the rapid increase of both industrial and agricultural workers in the state of North Carolina after 1880, some controversies were inevitable. By the end of the nineteenth century, however, many Carolina workers seemed ready to unionize.

Employers in the state had typically resisted collective bargaining, the establishment of labor unions, wage controls, and increases in wages—which they often paternally insisted were high enough for the workers and enabled the businesses to compete successfully nationally. The rigid anti-union views of most North Carolina employers, the hostility of management, the indifference of state government and the general public, the inconsistency of federal support, and the large number of unskilled workers in the state resulted in the slow development of a labor movement in the Tar Heel State despite the seemingly strong beginnings that labor presented.

The employees recognized that the power of many of the companies was extended far beyond the walls of the business. The textile workers in the isolated villages and in the company-owned homes had little "room" to complain. Mill owners sometimes built the stores in which their employees shopped, usually supplied the churches in which their workers worshipped, and occasionally helped provide the schools in which the children of their staff learned—if the youth were not themselves members of the workplace. Some owners helped to pay the ministers, the teachers, the merchants, the sheriffs, the guards, and even the company spies who reported back to them on the words and actions of their workforce.

The Knights of Labor had tried to achieve a toehold in the textile industry in North Carolina in the 1880s. The organization was, however, unsuccessful (Draper, p. 5).

## II. Unionization from 1900 Until the End of World War I

Skilled printers, railway workers, carpenters, engineers, and machinists were the first workers in North Carolina to organize unions successfully. In North Carolina eighty-two labor unions—including 16 textile unions—were evident by 1900. Textile strikes in Gibsonville, Durham, Raleigh, and Fayetteville were unsuccessful, however, and union activity in the state declined for more than a decade. By 1908 the United States Department of Labor reported union activity in only one locale in North Carolina. The United Textile Workers did not even attempt to extend its activities to North Carolina because of the general anti-union feeling in the state (Lefler, 1963 edition, pp. 550–551).

With the advent of World War I, the focus of the nation veered from labor and toward the threat from beyond. The United States was no longer an island; cooperation with other nations had become a necessity. This preoccupation continued throughout the period of the war (Lefler, 1963 edition, p. 551).

## III. Labor Immediately After World War I and Through 1919

North Carolina in 1919 was a magnet to outside industrialists. Like most of the South, the state had the best and the cheapest labor market in the United States. Women and children who commanded lower wages were available for employment. In addition, North Carolina had hydroelectric power and enterprising power companies (Tindall, p. 318).

**Low wages for the Southern laborer.** The laborers in the South received wages that were below that of most of the rest of the nation. The National Industrial Conference Board estimated that the cost of living for Charlotte in 1919 was $1,438 a year. In 1919, however, the average textile worker in North Carolina earned only about $730; by 1921 this wage had dropped throughout the state to an average of $624. The average annual wage in the South was 73.9 percent of that in the rest of the nation in the postwar boom of 1919; the average annual wage in the South for the other years in the first three decades of the 1900s was only 60 to 70 percent (Tindall, pp. 318–319).

**The employment of North Carolina youth.** Unfortunately for the youth and the state, all North Carolina young people had not been able to take advantage of an education. In North Carolina in 1914 the proportion of students under 16 who were wage earners was 13.3 percent; by 1919 the number had dropped — but only to 6 percent. Many of these young people worked in the mills. An investigator in the late 1920s in Gaston County found few children over fourteen who were not working or caring for younger children. This disadvantage for the youth of the state was a boon to employers intent on profits (Tindall, p. 322).

**Labor unions.** After the end of World War I, craft unions and other groups of American workers across the nation began to renew their recruiting activities and to organize for improved working conditions. North Carolina was a site for the activities of these organizations, which involved many different Carolina industries (Draper, pp. 5–6).

**The Tobacco Workers International Union.** In 1919 organizers for the Tobacco Workers International Union had set up six strong locals in Winston-Salem; prior to this time the Tobacco Workers International Union had been visible in the South mainly in Louisville, Kentucky. In August the locals signed an agreement for a 47-hour workweek, a 20 percent wage increase, and pay for overtime work. The movement spread to Durham and Reidsville; the workers did not meet with success, however. The membership drifted away; the agreement lapsed. By 1922 the membership for the Tobacco Workers International Union was sparse. Tobacco companies breathed a sigh of relief (Tindall, p. 336).

**United Textile Workers.** By 1919 the center of the strength of the United Textile Workers (UTW) was in North Carolina. During a strike in Charlotte, for example, 1,500 striking textile workers achieved bonuses, a shortened work week, re-employment of union members, and even free house rent; twelve similar strikes occurred in the state. September of that year was one of the most active years of strife in America's labor history (Lefler, 1963 edition, p. 551). The UTW chartered 43 locals and enrolled 40,000 members in North Carolina (Tindall, p. 333).

There followed a series of disputes in the

Piedmont area of the states. One of its strikes was at the Loray Mill in Gastonia in October of that year. For several weeks 750 textile workers stayed out of work to protest the discharge of some union members. The work of the union was to no avail. The UTW retreated (Draper, pp. 5–6).

**A strike at White Furniture Factory.** Governor Thomas W. Bickett arbitrated a brief strike attempt in 1919 at White Furniture Company, the oldest maker of fine furniture in the state and in the South. Not a single whole day was lost and not a single violent act occurred. The factory never organized — not even in the 1940s when the United Furniture Workers of America had its highest membership (Bamberger and Davidson, 32).

Bamberger and Davidson explained that the workers were not docile or passive. Most of them made a conscious choice to work at White's. These employees believed that they had job security, and they ranked this higher than wages. Management purported that African Americans had the same treatment as whites and were able to secure jobs in the 1930s. However, most of the superintendents remained "white" for many years (Bamberger and Davidson, pp. 32, 40).

## IV. Unionization in the Early 1920s

In January of 1920, a mass meeting in Charlotte began the union campaign of the decade. New locals began to spring up in North Carolina and other Southern states.

**1921.** By 1921 the economy began to falter. Although all parts of the nation and all occupations did not foresee the retreat of prosperity, the recession immediately affected unionism, the workers, the textile industry of the South, and the state of North Carolina. Union recruitment slowed. Only 30 additional unions began in the entire South over the next 12 months (Tindall, pp. 330–339).

**Textile workers in 1921.** Textile owners felt the lack of prosperity. As the demand for their textile products declined, many owners and managers began to shorten employees' hours and reduce their workers' wages. Morale was low for North Carolina textile workers.

**Textile unions from the end of 1921 until the end of 1926.** By the end of 1921 most textile strikes in the state ended, but dissatisfaction remained. The gap between textile owners and textile workers widened. Mill owners often maintained the reduced wages for the workers. A male loom fixer, for example, who had made $32.50 a week in 1920 made only $21.41 in 1922 (Tindall, pp. 334–339).

**Changes in mill ownership.** Entrepreneurs in other parts of the country began to buy many of the Southern textile mills. Because these new owners often did not change their residence to be near the mills, they did not know their employees as individual people and frequently did not take a personal interest in the workers. The new owners chose often to sell the houses in the mill villages. While such distance and separation had a downside, a positive consequence was that the paternalism that many textile workers disdained began to decline.

**Efficiency experts and stretch-outs.** Owners, seeking to get the most from their employees, brought in efficiency experts. Frank and Lillian Evelyn Gilbreth, who lived in Charleston, South Carolina, and who told of their experiences in *Cheaper By the Dozen*, were a frequently sought team. Often the textile employees saw these consultants as hastening the pace of their jobs, increasing the work, and reducing the number of workers—actions the workers dubbed "a stretch-out."

**North Carolina strikes in 1921.** The mills began to "cut back" even further; managers lowered wages—often as much as 50 percent. Workers became even more bitter. Even though the union officials promptly advised against a walkout, on June 1, 1921, approximately 9,000 textile workers left their jobs. Because there was little need to re-open in a depressed economy, the mill managers merely waited for the union efforts to collapse (Tindall, pp. 330–339).

The North Carolina State Militia came to Kannapolis and Concord to protect the "scabs"—those who returned to work while fellow workers, family, and friends tried to continue the protests. Returning workers continued their employment even though wage cuts remained in effect and even though management did not guarantee union members a job (Tindall, pp. 330–339).

> By the end of 1921 the upthrust of unionism was over. In not a single case had it brought an important union recognition, and the feeble locals soon disappeared. Failure of a railroad shopmen's strike in 1922 left that group largely unorganized. The other craft unions, which had shared in the growth, felt the severe impact of open-shop organizations that proliferated across the country after the war [Tindall, p. 338].

The union effort in the State of North Carolina collapsed. Postwar prosperity had built the unions; the slump of 1920 and 1921 destroyed the unions in the state and nation. Dissatisfaction with working conditions and with wages festered among the workers (Tindall, pp. 333–334).

## V. Labor and Unionization in 1927

In 1927 the average earnings for workers in the South were $571 for workers in cotton, $747 for timber and lumber workers, and $823 for Southern industries (Tindall, p. 320). The South was experiencing "a bad time" long in advance of the Great Depression.

In 1927 unions renewed their activity across the state in an attempt to reduce the inequities. Union officials tried to help their members become more efficient. In Burnsville, the American Federation of Labor (AFL) conducted classes for women textile workers. In Henderson, North Carolina, on August 4, 300 workers demanded their former wages and walked out. Although some families faced eviction from their mill village homes and from the plants themselves after the strike, the union still gained some members (Tindall, pp. 340–341).

## VI. Wages, Working Conditions, and the Labor Movement in 1928

The highest-paid mill worker was the loom fixer—always a male. In the South he earned weekly in 1928 only $22.20, a reduction from the $32.50 of 1920. Because full-time work was not always available, he usually took home only $18.38. The female weaver with only part-time work usually earned $12.05. The male frame spinner usually earned only $6.76 with the reduced hours. Five other standard workers in 1928 earned less than $10 a week (Tindall, p. 339).

The average hourly earning in cotton goods ranged from 20 cents an hour to 39.9 cents per hour, depending on the skills of the worker. Salaries for workers in hosiery and underwear production were the highest: 22.6 cents per hour to 65.5 cents per hour. Sawmills paid 21.9 cents to 83.1 cents. Foundries and machine shops paid from 28.5 cents per hour to 79.4 cents per hour. Regional differentials tended to decrease at the higher levels of skilled labor; the differences disappeared altogether for blacksmiths, machinists, and bricklayers (Tindall, p. 320).

**The workweek in the textile industry.** In 1928 the textile industry hired more workers than any other industry. The average workweek for a textile worker was usually ten or eleven hours per day for five days with a five-hour day on Saturday; the workweek, then, was fifty-five to sixty hours per week (Tindall, p. 30). Despite these low wages and long hours, managers began to increase the work even further for the employees—when the mills were running.

**The class structure in Carolina.** A social hierarchy—long implied—began to solidify in the state. Those outside the mill environment began to increase their scorn of the "Lintheads." To increase the hierarchy even more, the mill managers tended to alienate themselves from the workers whose wages they cut, whose hours they managed, whose work they increased in the stretch-out, and whose jobs they controlled (Tindall, p. 340).

**The Piedmont Organizing Council.**

Distressed workers began to turn to the unions. The Piedmont Organizing Council, formed in 1927, launched a series of monthly meetings in the state in January. Such union activities led to strikes across the state. As a result of these organized, statewide activities, workers became more confident, and strikes began to spring up across Carolina (Tindall, pp. 340–344).

**Gastonia.** Gastonia, at the time, was the largest town in Gaston County and called itself "the South's City of Spindles." Gastonia was important for several reasons. Loray Mill, built in 1900, was the largest mill in the county. Only a few miles from the mill was the town proper, a typical mill village of the period.

**Loray Mill.** Local interests had originally controlled Loray Mill, but in 1919 the owners had sold it to Jenckes Spinning Company of Rhode Island; Jenckes Spinning merged with Manville Company, also of Rhode Island, to form the Manville-Jenckes Company in 1923 (Draper, pp. 4–5). The paternalism of many mills was not strong here.

The Loray Mill in Gastonia had long been the subject of severe "stretch-outs." In 1927 the company had sent G. A. Johnstone to serve as the new superintendent. He began to increase the workloads—sometimes doubling them. He did not bother with explanations to his employees or with time studies. He brought in cheaper help and discharged workers (Tindall, pp. 343–344). Johnstone cut the 3,500 workers down to 2,200; although this increased the work, he still reduced wages on two occasions by 10 cents an hour (Draper, pp. 6–7).

The President of Manville-Jenckes Company and owner of the Loray Mill wrote in November of 1927 to Johnstone to encourage him to continue his "good work." President Jenckes congratulated the resident agent on cutting $500,000 from the payroll without decreasing production. Jenckes told him to try to cut twice as much and still maintain the

*Exterior of a mill in Gastonia in 1938.*

same production (Draper, pp. 6–7). Employee morale was at an all-time low; workers seethed with resentment.

**The Gastonia strike of 1928.** At the Loray Mill, workers struck briefly in March of 1928 in response to the stretch-outs and other grievances. Later, the workers assembled a parade which included a casket carried by eight pallbearers. At brief periods a "superintendent" would appear and shout that "six could do the work" and to "lay off two." The owners realized the dissatisfaction and removed Johnstone in November (Tindall, p. 344).

## VII. North Carolina Labor in 1929

Communism publicly reared its head in the state on January 1, 1929, when Fred Beal arrived in Charlotte. The new National Textile Workers Union (NTWU) linked Communism with the unions. Whereas many Carolinians saw the NTWU as a form of revolution, managers voiced their view that the organization gave the state a "bad" name (Tindall, p. 353).

William Green, President of the American Federation of Labor and a professed enemy of Communism, explained astutely the reason why Gastonia gave the Communists an opportunity to act. He said,

> These southern workers know nothing about the philosophy of communism; they do not know what it means. It is all Greek to them, but in their hour of distress, when they are rebelling against conditions they accept support and help of anyone who extends the friendly hand [Draper, pp. 28–29].

**Gastonia, the 1929 pivot.** Gastonia was

*An outdoor meeting during the Gastonia strike in 1928.*

the "in" that the Communists and the labor unions wanted. George Pershing, a Communist labor advocate, emphasized the importance of Gastonia:

> North Carolina is the key to the South. Gaston County is the key to North Carolina. And the Loray Mill is the key to Gaston County [Parramore, *Carolina Quest*, p. 369; Tindall, p. 345].

After his arrival in Charlotte on January 1, 1929, Fred Beal worked for two months organizing workers. He went to Gastonia in mid–March of the same year, and in his work attempted to enroll African Americans—a group long excluded from even the meager textile wages. On March 25 the mill discharged five members of the union. At an open meeting on March 30, one thousand employees voted for a strike; on April 1 a majority of the employees on both shifts refused to work.

The demands of the employees were implausible: $20 a week as minimum wage, equal pay for women and children, discontinuance of stretch-outs, screens and bathtubs, cheaper rents, electricity, and union recognition. Superintendent J. A. Baugh provoked the workers further when he suggested that they go elsewhere or put up their own 7 million dollar mill. Agitation increased.

On April 4 when workers began coming back to work, the state militia arrived. Deputies replaced the militia on April 20. By the end of the month only about 200 strikers were in evidence (Tindall, p. 345). Bad times continued. On May 7, 1929, Gaston managers at the Loray Mills evicted 62 families. The union formed a tent company and worked together to survive and plan their strategy (Draper, pp. 16–17).

**Increased dissatisfaction across the state.** Workers continued to demonstrate their dissatisfaction across the state of North Carolina. Marion displayed its labor unrest as mill workers protested substandard housing, the lack of running water, filthy privies, wages below $10 per week, and no salary for workers in training. In Asheville, police wounded seriously 25 protesters and killed another six—whom fellow employees claimed were retreating. Pineville, Lexington, Bessemer City, Charlotte, and Leakesville also experienced their share of strikes and unrest. Although the neighboring state of South Carolina also experienced strikes, there was a difference: North Carolina workers used outside organizers while South Carolina workers organized themselves (Tindall, p. 349).

**Further unrest in Gastonia.** On June 7, exactly one month after the eviction of the mill workers in Gastonia and the setting up of the tent colony, the union held a parade as a symbol of another walkout; deputies broke up the parade in accordance with an ordinance prohibiting demonstrations. Later the same night police officers came to investigate a complaint about trouble. The end results of the confrontation and the violence that erupted were the mortal wounding of Chief of Police O. F. Aderholt, the serious wounding of a unionist, and the slight injuries to three or four police officers (Draper, pp. 16–17; Tindall, p. 347). Later that same night, a mob raided the tent city (Tindall, pp. 346–347).

**Mob rule.** The September 9 trial of the sixteen unionists accused of the murder of the Chief of Police ended in a mistrial. Disappointed by the outcome of the trial, there was an outburst of mob activities. A parade of more than 100 cars led by police officers on motorcycles drove through Gaston County and neighboring areas. The participants wrecked union property and terrorized organizers (Tindall, p. 353). The band of anti-unionists seized three of the NTWU leaders, beat them, carried them into another area, and released them (Parramore, *Carolina Quest*, p. 374).

**Ella May Wiggins.** One of the Gastonia workers seeking to better her life and that of her children was a woman. Willing to face the dangers of union membership, Ella May Wiggins, a twenty-nine-year-old mother of nine, attended the union meetings. At the gatherings and in the tent colony, she often sang the verses and tunes she had written about the strikes. Ella called her ballads her "Song Ballets." The workers heard them seriously.

Ella May did not have much education

*Women struggling to get past a National Guardsman during a textile strike in Gastonia in 1928.*

because she had gone to work in the factories at an early age. She did possess, however, a heritage of song in the mountain ballads of her family; these mountain songs had their roots in the English ballads. With her "native intelligence and feeling which is so common among these Southern workers," Ella May was able to put into words the feelings of many of her fellow North Carolina laborers (Larkin, p. 382). Like many of her Carolina companions,

> ...she understood little of what the Communists or other speakers said, but they talked of better days ahead for the workers. Ella May knew she agreed with that [Parramore, *Carolina Quest,* p. 372].

On the eve of the Great Depression, Ella May Wiggins had long felt "lean times." In an interview just three weeks before her death, Ella May talked of her plight as a textile worker with nine children and with a husband who had deserted her.

"I'm the mother of nine.... Four of them died with whooping cough, all at once. I was working nights and nobody to do for them only Myrtle. She's eleven and a sight of help. I asked the super to put me on day shift so's I could tend 'em, but he wouldn't. I don't know why. So I had to quit my job and then there wasn't any money for medicine, so they just died. I never could do anything for my children, not even to keep 'em alive, it seems. That's why I'm for the union, so's I can do better for them" [Larkin, p. 382].

Some of her ballads mentioned the tent colony and the names of George Pershing and Fred Beal, Communist leaders who had supported the workers:

Up in old Loray, on the sixth floor so high,
Where Beal and Pershing found us, ready to die.
Let me sleep in your tent tonight, Beal,
For it's cold lying out on the ground [Larkin, p. 383].

Some of her ballads reminded the workers why they were supporting the union:

> We leave our home in the morning,
> We kiss our children goodby,

While we slave for the bosses
Our children scream and cry.

And when we draw our money
Our grocery bills to pay,
Not a cent to spend for clothing,
Not a cent to lay away....

But understand, all workers,
Our union they do fear,
Let's stand together, workers,
And have a union here [Larkin, p. 383].

**The death of Ella May.** The Communists called a meeting on Saturday, September 14, after the abuse of their leaders on September 9. Gastonia's anti-unionist "Committee of One Hundred" began to make plans to stop the meeting. Ella May and fourteen workers climbed on a truck at Bessemer City, fourteen miles west of Gastonia, and began their ride to the meeting. The union members understood that there was some risk in their attending. *The Gastonia Gazette* on September 11 had stated that the Communists had received warning to stay away from the area; if they come to Gastonia, the article stated, they would do so at their own risk.

As the truck approached Gastonia, a roadblock halted their progress. The driver turned and headed down Route 10. Several cars pursued the truck loaded with the workers. At the Southern Railway, one of the cars raced past and braked to a stop in front of the truck. The driver could not stop in time and slammed into the car. At the point of impact, a shot rang out, followed by Ella May's scream. "'Lord a'mercy, they done shot and killed me.'" She died at the scene (Parramore, *Carolina Quest*, p. 374–376).

The crash threw some workers from the truck. More shots rang out, and the workers on the ground fled the scene. The anti-unionists chased them across a field. The police were able to restore order before more deaths occurred.

The burial of Ella May Wiggins was a quiet Methodist service on a muddy hillside. Her five children were in attendance. No one was ever punished for her death because there was no proof of who fired the shot.

Beal and three others received a sentence of 17 to 20 years in prison for the death of Chief Aderholt. They fled to the Soviet Union when they received a release on bond. By fall of 1929 the mill managers were again in control (Parramore, *Carolina Quest*, pp. 374–376).

One North Carolina editor noted that

> In every case where strikers were put on trial, strikers were convicted; in not one case where anti-unionists or officers were accused has there been a conviction [Weimar Jones, p. 16, as cited by Tindall, p. 351].

**Writings about North Carolina labor.** North Carolina labor intrigued many writers. Articles and books on the subject appeared in abundance. One document was particularly important to the rights of laborers.

The "Statement of North Carolina Industry," written by University of North Carolina Professor Frank Graham (who became President of the University of North Carolina in 1930) and signed by 415 North Carolina citizens who supported the right of laborers to bargain, called for tougher child labor laws and the reduction of night work and hours per week. O. Max Gardner (North Carolina Governor from 1929 until 1933), a textile manufacturer before his gubernatorial election, supported increased wages, shorter workweeks, and the elimination of child labor.

Howard Odum of the University of North Carolina wrote of the labor situation in the state. In addition to his books exploring the textile industry, Odum edited *Social Forces*, a labor periodical. The University of North Carolina Press regularly produced up-to-date information on the State of North Carolina and its laborers (Tindall, p. 353). By 1929 the organization of workers displayed itself significantly in these writings, meetings, and the increased numbers of union members (Lefler, 1963 edition, p. 551). The Communist *Daily Worker*, American publications like *The Nation* and *Social Research*, and newspapers across the country covered the North Carolina strikes and analyzed the actions in this Southern state.

## VIII. North Carolina Unionization in the 1930s

The 1930s echoed with worker dissatisfaction, hostile management, reduced wages, decreased workers, and increased duties ("the stretch-out"). As in 1928, Communists sought to exert their influence on Carolina locals. Although some Communists enrolled in the University of North Carolina in 1931–1932, they did not re-enroll the following year (Tindall, p. 390). Frank Porter Graham, the President of the University of North Carolina, received much criticism for allowing the Communists to enroll in the first place; their failure to re-enroll, however, seemed to hush the uproar temporarily. Later, Senator McCarthy would interrogate Frank Porter Graham (Parramore, *Carolina Quest*, pp. 409–410).

**Satisfaction among textile workers in 1934.** There were two sides to the labor controversy of 1934. Many workers favored the family environment of the mill village and liked the fact that if a family moved to the provided housing, there would normally be a job for everyone. They liked the fact that the mill owners sometimes distributed "free" coal and "free" electricity to those in the mill village. Renters in the villages usually considered the cost of their housing — 25¢ to 50¢ a room per week or per month — to be reasonable. Some residents were pleased with the many rules of conduct: no drinking, no gambling, required church attendance, and no fights. They saw the rules as keeping their community safe and pleasant for them and their families (Lefler, 1963 edition, p. 551; Parramore, *Carolina Quest*, pp. 409–410). Some textile employees believed that if things became too bad in one plant, they could seek employment elsewhere (Tindall, pp. 326–327).

**Dissatisfaction among textile workers in 1934.** Other workers expressed dissatisfaction. Their gripes were many. Stretch-outs, discrimination, reduced wages, and long hours heightened unhappiness. The whole city — often even the doctor's office and the company store — seemed to belong to the mill owners. Disgruntled workers viewed the mill owners' "paternalism" as excessive control (Stoney and Helfand, *Uprising of '34*).

**Women textile workers.** Laws to protect women workers in the South lagged behind other parts of the country, and the women comprised more than a third of the work force. All those who worked in the mills faced a building filled with dust and cotton fibers; this atmosphere made the workers prone to respiratory ailments. The machinery needed constant attention, and during the stretch-outs the number of machines for which one was responsible became more and more. Few women could muster strength for work at home after a long day in the mill. By 1931 North Carolina had set limits for the number of hours per day that women could work, but that limit was nine to twelve hours a day for the labor of women in manufacturing; there was no law against night work for women in the mills (Tindall, pp. 323–324).

These textile workers needed courage to "buck the system," but some did so. This time before the proposed strike was "an even of hope — and despair" (Stoney and Helfand, *Uprising of '34*).

**African Americans in the unions.** African Americans worked as operatives in North Carolina tobacco factories, occasionally in hosiery mills, but less often in furniture and textile manufacturing plants. The only African American establishments on most main streets were cleaners, tailoring shops, an occasional restaurant, and barber shops. Plumbers, painters, brick masons, and other skilled trades in which African Americans worked were not usually unionized occupations (Federal Writer's Project, *North Carolina: A Guide*, pp. 54–55).

Generally, no African American women or men could work in the textile plants as spinners, weavers, or loom fixers. African American women could work only as domestics, and African American men could work only outside the mill or as custodians within the building (Stoney and Helfand, *Uprising of '34*). African American women across the nation fared much worse than other women.

"Nine out of ten agricultural laborers, and two-thirds of domestic servants were black" (Hapke, pp. 7–8). These occupations were not usually represented by labor unions.

**The Labor Day strike of 1934.** On Labor Day in 1934 the closest thing to a revolution in North Carolina in the 1930s occurred. The site was Gastonia. Those who remember report that it was "a hush thing," never mentioned in school and only discussed in whispers in the community after it was over.

**The uprising of '34.** Flying squadrons of outsiders went from mill to mill in North Carolina to help with union organization. On Labor Day of 1934 the strikes began. Thousands lined the streets in Gastonia to witness the Labor Day parade of striking United Textile Workers. It is estimated that from 2,500 to 5,000 persons joined the parade, which was the high spot of the celebration (*Charlotte Observer*, September 1934).

For the first few days some strikers—many of whom were women—reported the activities as "fun." By the end of the week the activities became less joyful. There were no paychecks, and there was little backing from the union or the governor. Workers began to fear for their jobs, their homes, their families, and their lives. When six or seven workers died in the sister strike at Honea Path, South Carolina, no church would house the funerals. Many textile workers from North Carolina showed their support of their sibling workers by joining the 10,000 people who attended the services (Stoney and Helfand, *Uprising of '34*).

Frances Biggerstaff, born in 1929, had just turned 5 when her hometown of Avondale experienced the Textile Uprising of 1934.

> The weather was pleasant, and I was sitting on the front porch of our home near Haynes Mill in Avondale, North Carolina. I remember how happy I was sitting there. I was rocking in my little green chair that my father had handmade for me. It had a slatted seat and to me was the most wonderful chair in the world. I was alone on my front porch, but I did not care. I was very happy.
>
> And then something happened! Some grown men who were not working—strikers—came down my street. They saw me sitting there and threw a rock at me—hard!
>
> I remember screaming and running into the house. My mother grabbed me in her arms, and we ran one street over to Mrs. Linnie Bailey's home. Other women and children had gathered there. They, too, had been frightened by the strikers who were roaming the streets and targeting the homes of those employees who were not striking. We waited there until my father returned home from work.
>
> My father's job during the strike was a very dangerous one. Because he had remained loyal to the company, management had positioned him as a guard to prevent the strikers from entering the mill. The management of Haynes Mill was afraid of what the strikers might do to the workplace and the workers if they re-entered the mill. My father had been brave enough to serve, and the strikers had attacked his wife and me—his only child.
>
> The strike had caused hard feelings among long-time friends, neighbors, and families across the state.

**The end of the strike of '34.** On September 23, the unions and the members called off the strikes in response to President Roosevelt's appeal to them (Lefler, 1963 edition, p. 607). The broken backbone of the textile union in North Carolina was evident after 1934 as the activities throughout the state as the activities dissipated.

Many union members believed that in the uprising of '34 they had received no support

*Badge of a member of the United Textile Workers Union, 1930s.*

Top: *A. W. Hinson, President of the Textile Union Local No. 8115 of Ranlo, is shown getting a unanimous "Yes" answer from striking workers here after he had asked them whether they wanted the Parkdale Mill in Gastonia closed.* Bottom: *Bristling rifles and machine guns ensured security to these textile workers, who are seen entering the Gibson Mill, a plant of the Cannon Mills here. As the workers repaired to their looms and machines, strikers and pickets outside the protected zone held to their vigil.*

from Section 7-a of the National Industrial Recovery Act (NIRA). Section 7-a should have granted them the right to bargain collectively, prevented discrimination against union members, ensured union rights within the companies, and prevented the discharge of workers for union activity. It had not (Stoney and Helfand, *Uprising of '34*).

**Tobacco Workers.** Tobacco workers, likewise, scored only temporary advances with the unions in the early 1930s. Although Winston-Salem, Durham, and Reidsville had some success initially, unionization became a passing fad for the tobacco industry in the 1930s. With abundant workers in the state, laborers found it difficult to negotiate for better working conditions, increased salaries, and shorter hours. It was, however, these many workers, low wages, and long working hours that drew many industries to the South — and to North Carolina in particular (Tindall, p. 336).

**State government.** State government, however, began to be more responsive to the demands of both labor and management. The North Carolina Department of Labor began to collect labor statistics, settle labor-management conflicts, assist with employment, minister to the disabled and the young, enforce labor legislation, and inspect places of employment. Of great importance was the administration of the Workmen's Compensation Act through the North Carolina Industrial Commission (Lefler, 1963 edition, p. 607).

**New Deal Legislation and the Wagner Act.** Many North Carolina workers were grateful for this governmental help. Union members generally welcomed the passage of the New Deal Legislation (1933–1945) and particularly the Wagner Act (1935), which had some of the same purposes as 7-a (Lefler, 1963 edition, p. 607). Workers believed that the Wagner Act might help them in ways that 7-a had not.

**1937.** New Deal legislation foreshadowed what was to come: more effective communication with labor in North Carolina, the discontinuation of using state troops in strikes, employing collective bargaining instead of violent strikes, less open strife, and the decline of "paternalism" in Southern industry. Carolinians, however, were not unanimous in their opinions on unionization and New Deal legislation.

While many employers believed that unionization, collective bargaining, and New Deal legislation would help improve relations between labor and management, others viewed the legislation as government intrusion. Some employers tried to disregard the new legislation and found themselves in violation of federal law and in danger of disciplinary action (Lefler, 1963 edition, pp. 606–609).

In 1937 John L. Lewis and the Committee on Industrial Organization (CIO) sought to increase the unionization of the South, particularly its textile industry. His work was not, however, highly successful in North Carolina at this time (Lefler, 1963 edition, pp. 606–609).

**Summary.** The first three decades of the 1900s in North Carolina mirrors a rapidly fluctuating unionization. The number of agricultural laborers increased and exhibited little unionization; there was a perpetuation of the "Big Three": tobacco, cotton, and corn. Photographs from Stryker's collections and from the newspapers of the time reflect these directions in labor in the state of North Carolina.

# Chapter Seven

# *Popular Entertainment*

The health education books of the 1930s particularly emphasized the importance of mental hygiene for the citizenry. Witty and Skinner defined *mental hygiene* as "the way in which the individual accepts and responds to the requirements and opportunities of society and the cultural patterns transmitted to him...." The goal of adulthood is "wholesome, sane, co-operative living, with adequate release through aesthetic experience and creative activities..." (Witty and Skinner, p. 291).

With the hard work, disappointments, "stretch-outs," limited budgets, strikes, unemployment, poor health, inadequate diets, and education and housing problems, the recreational activities that cost a great deal in time or money were prohibitive for many families and individuals. Yet some relaxation from the stresses of the decade was advisable. Exactly which aesthetic experiences and creative activities were meaningful and possible for an individual varied from area to area and from time to time.

## I. Family Entertainment

Many families, because of finances, limited time, social customs of the area, and even religious beliefs, engaged in few leisure time activities. Often they spent any "off" time sleeping and resting for the next workday—if it were to come.

**Parlor games.** Some families could afford parlor games. A game of dominoes, Parcheesi, Chinese Checkers, Chutes and Ladders, Pick Up Sticks, Tiddlywinks, or Backgammon challenged young and old alike. Even the families that could not afford a "store bought" game might still be able to play checkers. A board made of cardboard or wood with squares carefully drawn and shaded with a pencil or colored with crayons and checkers made from bottle caps—label up for red, label down for black—were the only materials needed for an evening of entertainment. This homemade board became a treasured part of many homes even after the family was able to buy a manufactured board.

Some children had their own games, like Brilliant Mosaic, to enjoy. Other children had no such playthings and may have been too tired to use them after a day in the field or at work if even available. Some expensive board games like The Wizard of Oz beckoned, often in vain, from the windows and shelves to child consumers of the 1930s. Other games—such as The Treasure of Little Orphan Annie—were available upon the submission of "the thin aluminum seal from inside the lid of a can of Ovaltine" (Louise Hunt).

In 1934 Charles B. Darrow presented a game called Monopoly to the executives at Parker Brothers; they rejected his game. Darrow produced 5,000 copies on his own and sold them promptly to a Philadelphia depart-

The Treasure of Little Orphan Annie, *a game made in 1934, was available upon the submission of "the thin aluminum seal from inside the lid of a can of Ovaltine."*

ment store. He had to go back to Parker Brothers for help. In 1935, the first year it was marketed nationally, Monopoly became the best-selling game in America (Monopoly Companion). It is interesting that the public was intrigued with a financial game during the Great Depression.

During the 1930s Parker Brothers released another board game called Sorry! to a "game-hungry public." During the same decade View Master created the picture wheels to allow the public to see the world from their living room ("Yesterdayland: Toys"). A major appeal of the parlor games is that after the one-time cost of purchase, the family had an entertaining way to spend many evenings together.

**Card games.** Card games like Rook, Canasta, Hearts, and Rummy were popular — except in those families which considered games with cards and dice to be evil. The card game Old Maid for children, more than 100 years old, was still popular. A 1930s edition included "speakeasy" characters like "Da Cops," "Da Mall," and "Da Entertainers"; the Old Maid in this version dressed in a '30s-style gown with a fan and flowers pinned to her bodice; she wore rouge and long, dangling earrings (Retro).

**Handcrafts.** Embroidery, quilting, tatting, knitting, darning, and stitchery of all kinds were necessary tasks in many households. The women and girls often included friends and relatives in the quilting and other handwork activities. Some women entered their crafts in the county fair to exhibit their proficiency — and in hopes of getting a ribbon and the accompanying monetary award.

**Toys in the 1930s.** The 1929 Stock Market Crash made toys a luxury to most children of the 1930s, but through their imagination most still enjoyed their free time. Those who had access to toys found several available construction toys: erector sets, Lincoln Logs, Tootsie Toys, and Tinker Toys. The Great Depression hit the electric train industry very hard. Many Carolina children would receive no new toys, puzzles, or games in the hard times of the 1930s.

**Homemade toys.** Threading and twirling buttons on a string, projecting silhouettes on the wall, making string designs, assembling and playing with rag dolls, making dolls from twigs and leaves, and constructing "tea sets" from acorn caps and bits of broken dishes were activities that could be played inside — and outdoors. The amount of cash outlay for the paraphernalia associated with these leisure activities was minimal, but the fun was optimal and enduring through the years.

**Oral games, riddles, stories, and ballads.** Many of the oral games, riddles, ballads and rhymes for the diversion of children in North Carolina had their origins in an earlier time and place.

Nell Burns (1923–1998) learned the riddle-rhyme "As I Was Going to St. Ives" and the riddle "Two Legs" from her mother Ella Turner Daves (1887–1980). Ella Turner Daves had learned these poems from her grandfather William Washington Black, born in 1853. He had learned the rhymes from his parents and grandparents of an earlier time (The Opies date the first rhyme from the 1700s [Opie, p. 377]; their version is similar to the one Nell Burns taught her daughter. The Opies date the second rhyme from the 1600s [Opie, p. 268]; their version is somewhat different from the one below that the author learned from her mother.).

*This is a photograph of a rare 1933 portrait puzzle of President Franklin D. Roosevelt. The puzzle, in its original red, white, and blue striped box reads, "New Deal Picture Puzzle of President Roosevelt."*

### "As I Was Going to St. Ives"

As I was going to St. Ives,
I met a man with seven wives.
Each wife had seven sacks.
Each sack had seven cats.
Each cat had seven kits.
Kits, cats, sacks, and wives.
How many were going to St. Ives? (Answer: one).

### "Two Legs"

Two legs sat upon three legs; up jumps two legs.
Picks up three legs, and throws it after four legs.

Answer: A milkmaid is sitting on a stool; she jumps up, picks up the stool, and throws it after the four-legged cow (Davis, *Children's Literature Essentials*, pp. 130–131). Thomas explains that Jenny Giles, a Presbyterian, hurls her stool at the Four Tables, which required the reading of Archbishop Laud's Church Service Book (Thomas, p. 214).

Many of the other games and rhymes for the diversion of the children of Carolina had their origins in an earlier time. One of these finger plays that Nell Burns learned from her mother, Ella Turner Daves, was a handstack or club-fist rhyme game.

### Handstack or Club-Fist Game

**Directions:** The two or three or more players make a "handstack." The players achieve this tower by the first making a fist with the thumb extended. The second player grasps the first player's thumb with his or her fist and extends a thumb for the next player. The stack continues with all the players alternating hands. The last player to have a remaining hand asks the question, "Knock it off, take it off, or let the crows peck it off?" The player whose hand is on the top makes a choice as to how he or she prefers the questioning player to remove the hand. Once the questioning player removes the fist, the questioning player gives the choice to the next person with a fist on the stack. The play continues until only one fist remains. The questioning person asks of the person with a fist remaining, "Whatcha Got There?"

### "Whatcha Got There?"

**Questioning player:** Whatcha got there? (The player is addressing the last person remaining.).
**Remaining player:** Bread and cheese.

**Questioning player:** Where's my share?
**Remaining player:** In the woods.

**Questioning player:** Where are the woods?
**Remaining player:** The fire burned them.

**Questioning player:** Where's the fire?
**Remaining player:** Water quenched it.

**Questioning player:** Where's the water?
**Remaining player:** Ox drank it.

**Questioning player:** Where's the ox?
**Remaining player:** Butcher killed it.

**Questioning player:** Where's the butcher?
**Remaining player:** Rope hung him.

**Questioning player:** Where's the rope?
**Remaining player:** Rat gnawed it.

**Questioning player:** Where's the rat?
**Remaining player:** Hammer killed it

**Questioning player:** Where's the hammer?
**Remaining player:** Behind the kitchen door cracking walnuts. The first person who shows teeth gets a _____.

(The remaining player decides the punishment for smiling and showing teeth. Usually the "punishment" is physical: a pinch, a hair pull, or a slap. The game continues with a different person on the bottom of the stack.).

Most readers can envision an earlier time in a cottage in England or Scotland with young siblings sitting before the fireplace after evening chores playing the game with its repetitive lines. *Folklore in America* includes a similar game (Coffin and Cohen, pp. 180–181; Davis, *Children's Literature Essentials,* pp. 130–133).

Nell Burns remembered a game taught to her by her mother. She played the game by tapping a person's back while reciting the rhyme "Higgledy, Haggledy, Hornie, Cup."

### Higgledy, Haggledy, Hornie, Cup

Higgledy, Haggledy, Hornie, Cup.
How many fingers do I hold up?
(The player with a back turned makes a guess.).
A-two (or three, or whatever the guess was) you said,
And a-four (or whatever the number was) I had.
Higgledy, Haggledy, Hornie, Cup.

(If the player guesses correctly, the riddler must attempt to guess the number of fingers that the other player holds up after reciting the rhyme.) Brewster and others call this game "Hickety hack on your poor back." They collected this game in 1927 (Brewster and others, Vol. 1, p. 59; Davis, *Children's Literature Essentials,* pp. 134–135).

Other games like "I Spy," jokes, and riddles were important diversions as a family sat around the fireplace, rested on a cotton sheet in the field at midday, made a long trip, or sat on a porch in the cool of the evening.

In addition to the oral games, rhymes, and riddles, many Carolina families had their own storyteller who could capture the attention of an audience. This storyteller often told parables (stories which are realistic and have morals), fables (stories with morals which are not realistic and often have animals as main characters), fairy tales (stories which always have the element of magic—but not necessarily fairies), folktales (stories told in the language of the people), myths (stories to explain things which the teller does not understand), and legends (stories—usually exaggerated—about real people, places, and things) (Davis, *Children's Literature Essentials,* pp. 83–84).

An important purpose of the Appalachian mountain folklore was entertainment and the "practical application" of keeping the children working. As Chase observes, these tales reinforce

> ..."keeping the kids on the job" for such community tasks as stringing beans for canning, or threading them up to make the dried pods called "leather britches." Mrs. R. M. Ward tells us: "We would all get down around a sheet full of dry beans and start in to shelling 'em. Monroe would tell the kids one of them tales and they'd work for life!" [Chase, p. VIII].

The oral tales could make the drudgery of many tasks more enjoyable.

The author remembers her grandfather singing "I Gave My Love an Apple" as he peeled an apple for her with his Barlow pocketknife. Years later she found the riddle-song in her college English Literature book. She was amazed that her grandfather, who had no formal education, knew this ballad. His parents, grandparents, and great-grandparents had recited and sung the same riddle in their North Carolina mountains and in their mother country of England. The family had preserved through frequent telling and singing these tales and songs of long ago. Some of the lines differed somewhat from that in the literature book, but the gist of the riddle-song was intact. These are the lines as sung by the author's grandfather P. R. Price:

> "I Gave My Love an Apple"
>
> I gave my love an apple
> Without a core.
> I gave my love a house
> Without a door.
> I gave my love a story
> Without an end.
> I gave my love a baby
> With no crying.
>
> How can there be an apple
> Which has no core?
> How can there be a house
> Without a door?
> How can there be a story
> Without an end?
> How can there be a baby
> With no crying?
>
> An apple in the blossom
> It has no core.
> An apple, which is uncut,
> It has no door.
> My love is a story,
> Which has no end.
> A baby, who is sleeping,
> Has no crying.

**Music in the parlor.** The voices of a family lifted in song around a piano or a pump organ were a part of many Sunday afternoons—particularly in those families which did not approve of the sinful games of cards or Parcheesi with the dice. Other families taking their Sunday afternoon constitutional could hear these songs through open windows. Hymns and ballads were popular.

> [T]here are many similarities between the ballad sung by a native of Scotland, the ballad sung by a native North Carolinian whose parents and grandparents and great-grandparents also lived in North Carolina, and the versions recorded by Francis Child, collector of traditional literature (Davis, *Children's Literature Essentials*, p. 132).

Many families sang their hymns from memory or from a hymnbook with shaped notes; shape note singing is an early American form of notation for untrained choirs and singers. The shape indicates a note's position on the scale.

Singing schools and traveling teachers of the shape note system promoted the method. William Walker's *Southern Harmony* songbook, with his 1835 preface from Spartanburg, South Carolina, sold 600,000 copies; it was perhaps the most popular songbook ever printed. Through the WPA, a photo-reproduction of the 1854 edition appeared (Wilcox). Many depression-era families used a copy of the hymnal handed down from an earlier generation.

Some family members might pull out a harmonica, a Jew's harp, a fiddle, or a banjo and join the group at the piano; in other families the musician might take the harmonica, fiddle, or other instrument to the porch and play the music there for all to hear. "Playing the spoons" or "beating ham bone" was another rhythmic activity that some family members might demonstrate on the porch.

Music through a Victrola—hand-cranked for those without electricity—or from a radio, which might be operated by batteries or by electricity, was entertainment not all families could enjoy. Those who possessed the spring-wound Victrola or were favored with a radio no longer had to provide their own entertainment.

**Music through the radio.** On April 10, 1922, the Department of Commerce issued a license for the first commercial radio station in the Southeast. That license went to WBT in Charlotte, North Carolina. In the beginning the station did not operate 24 hours per day, but the radio and what it meant were very important to the citizenry. By 1931 in North Carolina one family out of seven had a radio ("WBT History").

*The Sears Roebuck Catalog of the Thirties* indicates that the cost of a radio "for the home" could be as inexpensive as $19.95; for $24.95 one could purchase a model on which the user could "push a button and there's your station." A table model that was vertical or

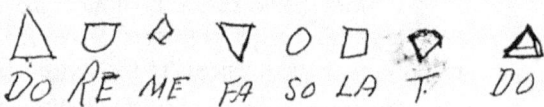

Top: *A handwritten sample of shaped notes. This explanation is by an unidentified scholar of the singing schools.* Bottom: *A 1930s photograph of Bethel Baptist Church and its singing school. The participants ranged in age from the very young to senior adults. Susan Daves McGee's father, Fay Daves, is the fourth from the left on the first row. Zeb Daves is the third from left on the first row.*

horizontal was $24.95; a console was $29.95 (*The Sears Roebuck Catalog of the Thirties*, p. 702). The prices—$19.95, 24.95, and $29.94—must, however, be compared to other items. On a "Depression Shopping List for 1932 to 1934" a wing chair was $39.00, a '29 Ford automobile was $57.50, and a mahogany coffee table was $10.75 (Time-Life, *This Fabulous Century*, p. 27). It is not surprising, then, that 6 people out of every 7 did not have a radio.

Donnis Curtis tells of the day her rural family without electricity received its first radio.

> One Saturday my father said he was going to town to buy something very special for us. He would not tell us what it was.
> All day my two older brothers, younger sister, and I watched and waited for him to come home. Later in the afternoon we saw him coming toward us, and we ran as fast as we could to see him and find out what he had. It was a battery-operated radio.

**Radio music.** Music was an important part of the listening of many families that had a radio. *The Grand Ole Opry* became the longest continuously running radio show in the nation; begun in 1925, the Saturday night program entered the homes of many families across the country ("Grand Ole Opry").

Music from the radio filled many homes. Some of the "hit" songs of the 1930s included songs about money. These tunes included "I Found a Million Dollar Baby," "Pennies from Heaven," "With Plenty of Money and You," and—the song many associated with the decade—"Brother, Can You Spare a Dime?" (McCutcheon, pp. 238–241).

Popular musical shows from the 1930s included *Your Hit Parade, Paul Whiteman, Kate Smith,* and *Benny Goodman.* A North Carolinian became known across the nation with his *Kay Kyser's Musical Class and Dance.*

**Kay Kyser.** Born in Rocky Mount, North Carolina, in 1906, Kay Kyser graduated from the University of North Carolina in 1928. Kyser led the college band while in school and first appeared professionally in Chicago at the Blackhawk Restaurant ("Kay Kyser," *Compton's Encyclopedia Online*).

His radio show, *Kay Kyser's Kampus Klass* (1937), became the network show *Kay Kyser's Kollege of Musical Knowledge* in 1938. During his career Kyser had 11 number one records and 35 top ten recordings. His number one songs during the 1930s included "The Umbrella Man" and "Three Little Fishies," upbeat songs that helped a nation forget its problems. Many of his songs encouraged the nation during World War II; the songs on everyone's lips during the 1940s included his "The White Cliffs of Dover," "He Wears a Pair of Silver Wings," "Praise the Lord and Pass the Ammunition," and "Till Reveille" ("Kay Kyser, the Ol' Professor of Swing!").

**Radio drama.** Although electricity and radio were not a part of everyone's life, radio was a source of entertainment and discussion throughout the week for many. Charley McCarthy seemed like a real person—not a dummy—to Sunday night listeners across the nation. Many wondered if Our Gal Sunday "from a mining town in the West" would be able to "find happiness as the wife of a wealthy and titled Englishman." *The Green Hornet, The Shadow,* and *One Man's Family* were other characters—and programs—that were popular with the radio audience.

Radio shows for children included *Little Orphan Annie.* Annie advocated capitalism; she herself proved capable of selling products as she pitched the drink called Ovaltine to her listeners (Time-Life, *This Fabulous Century*, pp. 30, 76). She encouraged young children in the radio audience to "send in the thin aluminum seal from under the lid of a can of Ovaltine" for free premiums (Louise Hunt). Little Orphan Annie had many "gifts" available with the seals from the can. Perhaps the most popular was the decoder pin; at the end of each radio show Annie gave a secret message that listeners could decipher—if they had the decoder (Time-Life, *This Fabulous Century*, p. 76). However, her board game, equipped with its own spinner, must have brought fun to the lives of those fortunate enough to be able to afford the can of Ovaltine and the radio, which carried details of how to order. Although Annie and her dog Sandy were popular, the most popular radio

*James Kern (Kay) Kyser (1906–1985) was born in Rocky Mount, in 1906, and graduated from the University of North Carolina in 1928. His radio show,* Kay Kyser's Kampus Klass *(1937), became the network show* Kay Kyser's Kollege of Musical Knowledge *in 1938. During his career Kyser had 11 number one records and 35 top ten recordings. His number one songs included "The Umbrella Man" and "Three Little Fishies."*

characters were two men whom everyone knew by first name.

**Amos 'n' Andy.** In 1925 Freeman Gosden and Charles Correll broadcast on WBT as "The Two Black Crows"; they moved to Chicago and broadcast there as the team of *Amos 'n' Andy* ("WBT History"). After they began their program,

> [e]very weekday evening from 7:00 to 7:15 p.m., telephone use all over the country dropped 50 percent, car thieves had an easy time on empty streets, and many movie theaters shut off their projectors to pipe in our radio while some 30 million Americans—including President Roosevelt—tuned in to *Amos 'n' Andy*.... Such devotion to a comedy serial—created in blackvoice by a pair of white vaudevillians, Freeman Gosden and Charles Correll—was typical of radio audiences in the '30s. The big box in the living room was everybody's ticket to adventure, laughter, sweet music and romance.
> 
> People listened for the openers of their favorite shows the way little children listened for the sound of father's car in the driveway [Time-Life, *This Fabulous Century*, p. 30].

Donnis Curtis remembers how much fun the program *Amos 'n' Andy* was for her family.

> It was the 1930s, and we—like most of the rural farmers—did not have electricity. My daddy placed the battery-operated radio in the bedroom that he and my mother shared. He put the radio on a table in front of the window. He explained to us that we would be very saving of our battery. We would listen to *Amos 'n' Andy* at 7:00 p.m. each night, but we would not be listening to the radio at many other times.

In the summer when we raised the window and turned the radio on for the *Amos 'n' Andy Show*, we would often see our yard and porch full of friends and neighbors who had walked over to share with us our radio and everyone's favorite radio program.

**Grady Cole.** Grady Cole, who came to work at WBT in 1929, became a household word to many people in the state. His morning radio show filled kitchens across the state. Nell Burns reports that on a trip to Kentucky when she could no longer find Grady Cole on the radio in the morning, "I felt I was in a foreign country! I knew I was very far indeed from the North Carolina soil."

**The Briarhoppers.** The musical group called the Briarhoppers began their career in 1935 on WBT in Charlotte. In 2001—more than six decades after their start—the group is still performing country music.

The Briarhoppers originally opened their shows with their trademark: Orvan A. Hogan (1911– ) would ask, "Do y'all know what time it is?" The standard reply across the state was a resounding, "It's Briarhopper Time!" The group would then break into their theme song, "Wait Till the Sun Shines Nellie," a song that most families loudly sang from their kitchens along with the group ("Briarhoppers Publicity Sheet").

Don White (1905– ) was an original member of the Briarhoppers in 1935. Roy "Whitey" Grant (1916– ) has also been playing with Hogan since 1935. The Grand Ole Opry Archives place them in the Country Music Hall of Fame as the oldest performing duet in country music today. The current members of the group include Dwight Moody (1929– ) and David Deese (1941– ) ("Briarhoppers Publicity Sheet").

Some radio programs of the time, however, were not strictly entertaining.

**Fireside Chats.** Through the radio, the President of the United States Franklin Delano Roosevelt entered the homes of the American people. Getty Davis recalls:

> The radio programs that I remember most when John and I were first married were the occasional "Fireside Chats" that President Roosevelt gave. It seemed as if when things were worse, he always took time to talk with us. His chats were at night as if he recognized that working people only had time to listen after the work in the fields was over for the day.
>
> The President had a soothing voice and spoke so that all of us could understand what he was saying. He talked about the banks, new programs, and important news. He reminded us that "All you have to fear is fear itself."
>
> I always felt optimistic after his talks. It was a special time in our house when he visited with us by radio. We talked about it for days afterward.

*Photograph of Grady Cole, who broadcast on WBT, the first radio station in North Carolina.*

President Roosevelt recognized that few things could calm the American people; he elected to speak directly to them during the worst economic slump in history. He gave the first of his talks—about the bank holiday—when the people were the most discouraged. Because the people who trusted Roosevelt began to use the banks again, Roosevelt recognized the success of the radio and decided to employ it again and again (Bryon).

Roosevelt gave a total of fourteen "Fireside Chats" during the 1930s. He spoke

1. On the Bank Crisis on Sunday, March 12, 1933

*The Briarhoppers were still performing in 2001. The Grand Ole Opry acknowledged their length of performance and gave some members of the group an award for being the longest performing group in the nation. The group began their career in 1935 on WBT in Charlotte, North Carolina. Left to right: Dwight Moody (1930– ); David Deese (1943– ); Roy "Whitey" Grant (1916– ); Arvil Hogan (1912– ); Don White (1910– ).*

2. Outlining the New Deal Program on Sunday, May 7, 1933

3. On the Purposes and Foundations of the Recovery Program, on Monday, July 24, 1933

4. On the Currency Situation on Sunday, October 22, 1933

5. Review of the Achievements of the Seventy-third Congress, June 28, 1934

6. On Moving Forward to Greater Freedom and Greater Security on Sunday, September 30, 1934

7. On the Works Relief Program on Sunday, April 28, 1935

8. On Drought Conditions on Sunday, September 6, 1936

9. On the Reorganization of the Judiciary on Tuesday, March 9, 1937

10. On Legislation to be Recommended to the Extraordinary Session of the Congress on Tuesday, October 12, 1937

11. On the Unemployment of the Census on Sunday, November 14, 1937

12. On Economic Conditions on Thursday, April 14, 1938

13. On Party Primaries on Friday, June 24, 1939

14. On the European War on Sunday, September 3, 1939 ["Fireside Chats of Franklin D. Roosevelt"].

**Sports on the radio.** Through radio broadcasts, North Carolina families could participate in sports events across the nation. Many listeners were able to

> ...hear Lou Gehrig when the great ballplayer, dying of amyotrophic lateral sclerosis, said in a low, clear voice before 60,000 at Yankee Stadium, "I consider myself the luckiest man on the face of the earth." [Time-Life, *This Fabulous Century*, p. 30].

They also participated in the boxing rematch between Joe Louis—"The Brown Bomber"—and Max Schmeling, a German heavyweight who had taken the title of Heavyweight Champion from him in 1936. Adolf Hitler had used this outcome as evidence of both Aryan supremacy and German supremacy over Americans ("Joe Louis"). President Roosevelt had told Louis in 1938,

"Joe, we're depending on those muscles for America." In 1938 Joe won the match. "Never has any fight carried more symbolic weight than Louis-Schmeling on June 22, 1928," reported *The Sporting News* (Kindred).

More and more different sports were broadcast as time passed. Sports events became a part of the listening activities of families across the state.

**Outdoor games.** Just as today's parents do, parents in the 1930s encouraged their children to "Go outside and play." Tag, kick-the-can, and stickball (softball with a stick) were important games to the young — whether rural or urban — during the 1930s; none of these outdoor games required any expensive equipment.

After "laying by" the crops, rural children often had more free time for play than before and enjoyed, like their urban counterparts, a game of hide-and-seek. Although the rules were the same, the poem used to give the ones hiding the chance to seek shelter varied slightly across the state. The following rhyme was a part of the culture of children in Rutherford County, North Carolina, during the 1930s, but the rhyme itself dates back much earlier. Nell Burns recalls:

Hide and Seek Rhyme

A bushel of wheat, a bushel of rye.
All not ready, holler "I."
A bushel of wheat, a bushel of clover.
All not ready, can't hide over.

Paul G. Brewster collected a similar rhyme in 1928 in Durham (Brewster, Vol. I, pp. 38–39).

Most rural children had their own slingshots made from a forked stick, equipped with some rubber from an old tire, and loaded with an acorn. Horseshoes removed from an animal were set aside and saved from year to year for the game of horseshoes.

Although bicycles, skates, scooters, and wagons might be a part of many children's lives during the 1930s, all children did not have these possessions. Many children attempted to construct their own stilts, sleds, and wagons when time and materials permitted. Other children might receive a Radio Flyer Wagon or a cap gun for a birthday or Christmas gift.

Open fields and woods formed the playgrounds for many rural children and adults. The creek, haymows, and barn rafters became their playground equipment. Fishing and hunting for sport and necessity were a part of the lives of young and old in rural areas across the state.

**Publications of the 1930s for children.** All the publications of the 1930s were not great literature; some were merely designed to sell. The comic strips in the newspapers, the comic books, and the Big Little Books — though popular — may not become classics, but they were certainly popular and may become collectibles.

The Whitman Publishing Company of Racine, Wisconsin, introduced Big Little Books (BLB) in 1932. The squat, 400-page cubes of print and pictures called Big Little Books sold for a dime. These books — popular with adults and children alike — usually had the standard dimensions of $3\frac{5}{8}" \times 4\frac{1}{2}" \times 1\frac{1}{2}"$. The first BLB was *The Adventures of Dick Tracy* (1932). It preceded the first true comic book by one whole year. Bill Hillman, however, is quick to note that Whitman set the standards for similar books by other publishers, such as Dell, Fawcett, and Goldsmith (Hillman).

Little Orphan Annie in comic strips, in weekly radio shows, in paper dolls, on watches, and in Big Little Books encouraged the children and the "Depression-ridden" adults with her faith in "good old capitalism." Her standard "Leapin' Lizards" amused her reading and radio audience (Time-Life, *This Fabulous Century*, p. 76). Her optimistic comments about the economy encouraged.

An interesting series similar to the Big Little Books appeared in the 1930s. The Engel van Wiseman Book Corporation of New York produced 23 titles under the trademark Five Star Library series. The series began in the last half of 1934 and ended near the end of 1935. The 160-page books came entirely from motion pictures; a black-and-white photograph from the motion picture alternated with a page of text. The covers were hardboard and the spines were soft. One of these books was *The Fighting President*; the life of

Franklin Delano Roosevelt formed the basis of the book ("Five Star Library Series: Engel van Wiseman Publishing"; van Wiseman).

By the end of the 1930s, Edgar Rice Burroughs's character of Tarzan had become the hero "of 21 fast-selling novels, a deftly drawn comic strip, a 15-minute daily radio serial and 16 movies" (Time-Life, *This Fabulous Century*, p. 84). Johnny Weismuller, in the title role:

> ...enlarged the American vocabulary with the line "Me Tarzan, you Jane" and also introduced his fearful jungle yodel, a mixture of five sounds that included his own scream, a soprano singing high C and a recording of a hyena's howl played backwards [Time-Life, *This Fabulous Century*, p. 84].

In addition to Tarzan, the characters of Dick Tracy, Flash Gordon, Jack Armstrong, Buck Rogers, the Green Hornet, the Lone Ranger, and Tom Mix appeared in the Big Little Books, in some radio programs, and even in movies of the decade.

Participation books — pop-up books, cut-out books, and paper dolls of Shirley Temple, Buck Rogers, and even President Roosevelt — were popular and still remain. Some Carolina children who could afford them even amused themselves with paper dolls featuring English royalty. The overseas idols of Princess Elizabeth and Princess Margaret Rose were important to the toy chests of some American girls whose families could afford the purchase. Those without paper dolls might make their own by folding newspapers or using Crayola crayons to color their own.

**Bestsellers of the 1930s for adults.** An interesting feature of the decade of the 1930s was the repetition of the authors and titles on the best-selling lists of fiction for each year of the decade. Authors who repeatedly appeared were Edna Ferber, Pearl Buck, Lloyd C. Douglas, A. J. Cronin, Hervey Allen, Margaret Mitchell, James Hilton, Charles Morgan, Walter D. Edmonds, Daphne du Maurier, Ellen Glasgow, John Steinbeck, Warwick Deeping, Mazo de la Roche, Sinclair Lewis, Rachel Field, Louis Bromfield, and Marjorie Kinnan Rawlings. Thomas Wolfe, an important North Carolina writer who resided in Asheville, added his name to the notable books of 1935 with *Of Time and the River*. His earlier *Look Homeward Angel* had brought the wrath of local citizens who did not like his portrayal of his hometown — and the residents there.

*The Good Earth, Anthony Adverse, Rebecca,* and *Gone With the Wind* appeared as the number one bestsellers two years in a row ("1930s Bestsellers"). Nonfiction writers who wrote about the State of North Carolina in

*Thomas Wolfe, author of the book* Of Time and the River *(1935), and his mother in Asheville; Wolfe's mother took in boarders in this home. His earlier work* Look Homeward Angel *had brought the wrath of local citizens who did not like his portrayal of his hometown and the residents there.*

the 1930s were plentiful. Their names included Howard Odum, Harriet Herring, Margaret Jarman Hagood, and others.

## II. Community Entertainment

Interestingly enough, some of the same books that were bestsellers appeared also in the movies of the decade. *The Good Earth, Anthony Adverse, Rebecca,* and *Gone With the Wind* were among those bestsellers that also became movies shown in the local communities.

**Theater.** The community movie house was a popular place for people to forget their own problems; most movie theatres in the 1930s were changing from projecting silent films only to offering movies with sound. In some areas of the country where no movie houses existed, entrepreneurs set up tents and chairs for their audience.

For 25 cents a ticket (10 cents for children), one could temporarily forget troubles and cares in a theater—if one had the money. Some movie houses even began to offer premiums to moviegoers; by giving one item of dinnerware per person per movie, some theaters secured repeat viewers as families tried to get a "whole set" of dishes.

David Niven, a star of the 1930s and afterwards, describes a visit to the theatre during the era of the Great Depression:

> In the late Thirties the twice-weekly program presented by most theatres consisted of a newsreel, a cartoon, a short, the second feature, and the first feature. The whole show lasted for a bun-numbing four hours, but as a result, Hollywood was booming.

**The serial.** To many moviegoers, the selected short subject or serial was as important as the main feature; this twenty-minute adventure appeared on the screen between the cartoons and the feature film. A serial had from ten to fifteen weekly chapters; each chapter ended as a cliffhanger. The captured audience would return the next week to see what would happen. Some of the stars of the serials of the 1930s were Rin-Tin-Tin, Buster Crabbe, Mickey Rooney, Dick Tracy, Tom Mix, Zorro, The Green Hornet, Flash Gordon, Jackie Cooper, Mandrake the Magician, The Shadow, Terry and the Pirates, Red Ryder, the Lone Ranger, Bela Lugosi, and Clyde Beatty (McCutcheon, pp. 252–254).

**Academy Awards.** The Academy Awards that began in the 1920s continued into the 1930s. The 1939 Academy Award Ceremony was significant. Hattie McDaniel was the first African American to receive an award; hers was for the Best Supporting Actress in *Gone With the Wind*. This movie, based on the book about the South that had been the bestseller two years running, received the award for Best Picture; other awards associated with the movie were Best Actress and Best Director (*New York Times* on the Web). A surprise to viewers of the still popular film was that the leading man—Clark Gable—received no award although his leading woman did. Vivin Leigh, the leading actress, depicted the working woman of the Civil War era as a cold, scheming person. The female in this film produced during the thirties was not an endorsement of a working woman.

*Kitty Foyle*, on the best-selling list in 1939, also depicted a working woman. The movie won an Academy Award in 1940. Ginger Rogers won an Academy Award in 1940 for her portrayal of the "white collar" female employee. The image of the working woman was changing.

Walt Disney produced *The Three Little Pigs* in 1932. The cartoon impacted the public extraordinarily. Many people saw this film as Walt Disney's comment on the Great Depression. Its hit tune was "Who's Afraid of the Big Bad Wolf?" The song and the movie itself seemed to be a symbol of all Americans had to fear: fear itself (Finch, p. 72).

**First feature-length cartoon.** In 1934 Disney began work on *Snow White*. The musical score—like the song "Who's Afraid of the Big Bad Wolf?" from *The Three Little Pigs*—encouraged Americans, suggested the joy of working, and predicted a bright future: "Some Day My Prince Will Come," "Heigh Ho, Heigh Ho, It's Off to Work We Go," and "Whistle While You Work" (Time-Life, *This Fabulous Century*, p. 203). The photographers

*By the 1930s most of the North Carolina theatres had begun to install audio equipment and were no longer showing only silent pictures. This Carolina theater in Cliffside was unusual because upon entering the theater, the screen is toward one's back; the patron finds a row and must turn around to face the screen.*

from the Farm Security Administration recorded the advertisements for the feature in the Carolina movie houses.

Radio City Music Hall—far from the Carolina countryside—showed the movie also. One legend reports that after the engagement of the movie, the management re-upholstered all the seats because "so many children were terrified by Snow White's wicked stepmother that the seats were thoroughly drenched after each performance" (Time-Life, *This Fabulous Century*, p. 203).

Walt Disney's name and productions appeared eleven times on the list of Academy Award winners during the decade of the 1930s (Finch, p. 451). The entertainment he provided was popular during the Great Depression—for those who could "spare a dime."

Disney's success surprised many. Financiers had been reluctant to lend Disney the two million dollars he had needed to produce the 80-minute animated feature *Snow White*. The prediction of these sponsors had been that the public would not pay to sit through an animated fairy tale. Their predictions were in error. The movie broke all previous attendance records, was translated into ten languages, and grossed over eight million dollars at the time (Time-Life, *This Fabulous Century*, p. 203).

**School events.** The schools—one room or larger—formed another place to gather, socialize, and enjoy certain events that the school sponsored. Basketball, baseball, football, plays, elocution programs, suppers, exhibits, spelling bees, graduations, honors recognition events, glee club programs, and debate exhibits were some of the popular events that the community flocked to see.

**Churches.** Although the schools were important, very often it was the churches that served as the centers of the community. In Ellenboro in 1934, the Home Demonstration Club helped to ensure a community facility at the local church by their donations toward an outdoor fireplace placed under a cover (Public Records from Rutherford County Cooperative Extension Office).

> All through the South, of course, the church is an important social and cultural force, its sociability running the gamut of church-going, baptizings, funeralizings, brush-arbor revivals, all-day singings with dinner on the grounds, church suppers, singing schools and conventions [Botkin, p. 93].

G. C. Waldrep, too, notes that church was important, "the social reality, uncontested at the institutional center of mill village life" (Waldrep, p. 26).

Nell Burns remembers that her minister at Hopewell Methodist Church asked her to attend a training session at Lake Junaluska. She would learn how to set up a Methodist Youth Fellowship (MYF) in her church; Nell would also be responsible for training churches throughout the county on how to set up a MYF in their church.

> I was thrilled! I had never been to the mountain retreat and had never spent a week away from home. As a high school student, I considered it quite an honor to be asked to take the training and assume a leadership position for the Methodist churches throughout the county.
>
> My church provided me with education, socialization, and spiritual training.

In times of celebration like weddings and christenings, the people of the area congregated in the church. Likewise, in times of trouble the church was the center of the community where the people came for comfort and for prayer. During times of drought or times of flooding, for instance, it was not unusual to find the people of a community gathering to pray with others about their problems.

Ewart Burns (1904–1984) always laughed when he recounted a humorous story of the drought of 1930. Mr. Pritchard (not his real name) was repairing the roof on his house; Ewart and some of the other neighbors were helping him with the work. Mrs. Pritchard came out of the house with her parasol.

> "John," Mrs. Pritchard called. "I am going to meet the other women at the church to pray for rain. I will be right back."
>
> "Darn it, Jane!" Mr. Pritchard exploded loudly from the hot roof. "Can't you at least wait until we get the darn roof on our house?"

The list of social events sponsored by the church included revivals (sometimes held in

*Ellenboro School had a portion of its building completed through the WPA. The school was a cultural center of the community.*

Top: *A baptismal service held in a river in North Carolina in the 1930s.* Right: *Frances Logan photographed this unidentified country church in North Carolina before her death. The photograph was a gift to Nell Burns.*

tents), hayrides, ice cream socials, schools for children, choir practices, chicken pie dinners, bazaars, watermelon slicings, and even church softball games, which might pit one denomination against another.

**Revivals.** Although annual revivals at one's own church were events to anticipate, many families attended the revivals and socials at other churches also. Men, women and children mingled with family, friends, and acquaintances; women exhibited their culinary skills at the dinner that usually followed

*Lake Junaluska, the site of the Methodist Youth Fellowship Retreat in the 1930s.*

the service. In addition to the revivals held in the churches, there were "tent meetings" across the state during the months when outside services were feasible.

One of the revival preachers to visit the state was the Reverend Mordecai Ham. Accompanied by his music director, W. J. Ramsey, the team of "Ham and Ram" traveled across North Carolina. Although Reverend Ham criticized all "these feminine movements today trying to throw off [the] headship of man," an important member of his evangelical team was a woman (Parramore, *Carolina Quest*, p. 354).

Rosamonde Ramsey — later to become a 1943 graduate of the doctoral program in sociology from Duke University — was a member of the traveling band of "Ham and Ram." In an interview for the archives of Converse College, Rosamonde told of her work with the evangelist and her father, W. J. Ramsey.

My father served as the business manager and music director of Dr. Mordecai Ham. Dr. Ham

*Avondale Methodist Church, circa 1924. T. M. McMichaels architect, Avondale.*

Top: *Built in 1881, this wooden church building of Bethel Baptist Church replaced a log structure completed in 1847. The white landmark for the community remained a facility in use until 1978 — almost a century.* Left: *This Memorial Day Remembrance with "Dinner on the Grounds" was at Shiloh Church in Rutherford County in the 1930s.*

was a well-known evangelist of the 1920s and 1930s. As the business manger for Reverend Ham, my father always made sure that the operation remained solvent. We often built a wooden tabernacle in the place we visited, or we paid rent for the facility we used.

My father did not approve of soliciting money as many of the evangelists do today. All the monies for our operation were raised through the collection that was taken at the nightly service.

At times I traveled with them, and I often conducted the noonday prayer services. It was not unusual at this time (before I went to the University of South Carolina to study) for women to speak from the pulpit and to hold important positions. Despite the more conservative views of others, my father encouraged me to pursue a profession. Since the 1930s, I think that there have been times that women have lost some of the responsibility that they once had.

I remember the spring of 1934 before I enrolled in college in the late summer. [Parramore says the year was 1937 in his *Carolina Quest*; Cornwell says the season was spring of 1934 on page 55; Pollock says on page 14 that the date was September of 1934; Bishop gives fall of 1934 on page 5 as the occasion; Frady on page 84 identifies the time as the summer of 1934; Mitchell on page 108 says merely 1934; High explains on page 34 that Mordecai Ham "had opened a three-month assault on sin in the Graham home town of Charlotte, North Carolina."] We were visiting in Charlotte and were conducting our services in a wooden tabernacle constructed especially for our use. On this particular day I had been asked by Dr. Ham and my father to conduct the noonday service. After the service was over, a young, blonde, good-looking man with two friends came up and expressed a desire to live closer to the Lord and to do His work. The young man stated that the meetings had brought him to a new commitment. My father told them that they should make a public profession at the night services when Reverend Ham could receive them.

The three men came to the tabernacle that night. When Dr. Ham extended the invitation and my father was leading the hymn "Just As I Am (Without One Plea)," two of the young men came forward. The two men were Billy Graham and Grady Wilson. I actually had led the service after which Billy Graham had discussed becoming a Christian, but because I was not the head of the revival, I was unable to take him as a convert. The third man, I remember, did not come forward at the evening service. I found out later that the man was T. W. Wilson, a brother to Grady Wilson [Dr. Rosamonde Ramsey Boyd].

An account by Curtis Mitchell continues T. W. Wilson's story:

Several services later, Grady's big brother, the terrible-tempered T. W., began to feel pangs of conscience.

Describing his personal struggle, T. W. says, "I was sick of religion and puritanical ideas. That night a man sitting two rows away looked as if he was coming over to speak to me about my soul. I said, 'If he comes any nearer, I'm going to get out of here.' He started toward me, and I left. I ran out into a big open field behind the Charlotte bus terminal. But I was so miserable, I felt I'd rather die than go through another night like this one."

"Well, the Spirit of God started to work. I

*Rosamonde Ramsey Boyd led the midday prayer service in Charlotte in 1934 when Billy Graham decided to be baptized. Because Dr. Boyd was not an ordained minister, she asked him to come back that night. Her father, W. J. Ramsey, served as the business manager and music director for Dr. Mordechai Ham, the well-known evangelist of the 1920s and 1930s. Dr. Boyd obtained a doctorate from Duke University in sociology.*

called on the Lord to forgive my sin. Kneeling, white trousers and all, in the dirt, I forgot all about everything, and I took Christ for my savior. Then I went home. Next morning I was so happy, I couldn't sleep, so I came downstairs and began to read my Bible. Mother came in quietly and discovered me. She said, 'Son, have you been converted?' and I said, 'Yes, Mother, I have.' I don't know whether she started laughing or crying, but of all the prayer meetings I've been privileged to attend, that was the greatest, at 5:30 in the morning, with just my mother and me" [Mitchell, pp. 115–116].

All three boys—Billy, T. W., and Grady—became ministers.

**Community socials.** In rural areas the community often banded together to achieve things that would not always have been possible for a family alone. Barn raisings, corn shuckings (sometimes called corn huskings), house buildings, and quilting parties brought

*Billy Graham holding his sister Jean in their backyard in Charlotte. The friend in the picture is Paul Fellers, who was one of Billy's Sunday School classmates.*

adults and children together for work — and play.

Donnis Curtis remembers her parents participating in and hosting one yearly social event not related to church or school.

> My parents were known throughout the community for their delicious molasses. They made the rich syrup in the fall of the year after they harvested the sugar cane that they grew.
>
> Usually on a Saturday evening they would invite couples throughout the community for a taffy-pulling. Although many of the men and women had to bring their children with them, the candy pull was for adults — not children. We were instructed to stay out of the way of the hot fire. We children watched quietly as our parents laughed, stretched, and pulled the candy. I remember watching the adults pulling the molasses that had been boiled until it had become a thick consistency.
>
> Although many people think of a taffy pull as a pastime for children, the party was for adults only in our community.

Although many families might not have more materially than the family that they were assisting, the camaraderie in times of trouble strengthened community ties and provided aid to those with problems. Ewart Burns always told proudly the story of how neighbors came to help when their family home burned.

> Neighbors flocked to the site in the days to come. They helped to fell the timber from the woods on our family land, set up a sawmill on our place, brought in food for the workers, and actually helped in the construction of the home. Within a few weeks a new house, built from our own lumber — green though it was — was standing where the old one had been. Homes today take months to construct. Our two-story, thirteen room house was built through friendship in record time.

Selma Best remembers families going to a neighbor's home and helping with shelling peas, breaking beans, or husking corn during an abundant harvest. With many hands working, the task moved quickly — plus the neighbors were able to socialize, something that they were unable to do during the regular workday. A bonus was that the neighbors would come to your home to assist you on a future evening.

**Civic groups.** There were some civic groups that were important to individuals with special interests. The Farm Bureau attempted to organize those in agriculture. Insurance groups, like the Woodmen of the World, met periodically and provided some social events for their members, as well as insurance coverage. Fraternal orders, country clubs, Home Demonstration Clubs, and other church and civic groups provided social occasions and a means to achieve common goals for community members. The veterans of World War I also met and planned events— like memorial events and parades.

**Parades.** Parades usually included people the observers knew were important in the community. The civic groups, schools, churches, and local merchants often worked together to make the parade possible. Many times the planners scheduled the event on a holiday when most people would attend. Rich and poor alike lined the streets to enjoy the sights and sounds of the decorated trucks, cars, flatbeds, and marchers.

**Community centers.** Some towns and cities had community centers or clubhouses available for family reunions, community events, and socials. Some mill villages also had a room or small building available to the residents for their social events. Sometimes the tables and chairs would be pushed aside for music and dancing. All areas, however, did not condone this activity.

**Food.** Much of the community entertainment centered around food. Church bazaars and dinners, ice cream socials, community watermelon feasts, oyster roasts,

*A parade in Rutherfordton, circa 1930. Inexpensive leisure activities were often the most popular during the 1930s.*

potluck socials, club luncheons and teas, kudzu and ramp festivals, and barbecues were occasions that the whole family could enjoy.

The decade of the 1930s is often depicted as the era of "fake food:"

> Radish roses, sugar cubes painted with flowers, topiary salads and citrus baskets added flair to plates.

The crowning glory of the club luncheon was the sandwich loaf, made with at least two types of breads and fillings, then "frosted" to look like a cake. Food disguises were a hallmark of the period. The 1934 edition of the *Boston Cooking-School Cook Book* told cooks how to form mushrooms out of cream cheese, to make an Indian salad that resembled a feather headdress and to fashion a bunny salad from a canned pear half.

It also was the era of the Mystery Cake, which contained canned tomato soup; pigs in blankets (made with Bisquick [introduced in 1931]); and Burning Bush, an appetizer of cream cheese balls wrapped in chipped dried beef and stuck into a whole eggplant with toothpicks [Dawson].

Marshmallows were a popular food during the 1930s; a recipe that combined the marshmallows in a "food disguise" was sure to be a hit. Such a recipe was "Sweet Potato-Marshmallow Surprise." The cook wrapped cooked, mashed sweet potatoes around a marshmallow; after rolling the balls in crushed Post Toasties, the chef baked the balls until browned but not long enough to melt the marshmallows ("Cioppino").

Food companies were hard at work during the Great Depression developing food products that would tempt the consumer. Some of the new products were Hormel's Spam (1937), Bird's Eye's "frosted" (frozen) foods (1930), the Good Humor Bar (1930), Bisquick (1931), Ritz Crackers (1934), Campbell's Cream of Mushroom Soup (1933), Gallo's wines (1933), Girl Scout Cookies (1934), Pepperidge Farm Loaf (1935), and Nestle's Chocolate Chips (1939). The Toll House Inn developed a new recipe: Toll House Cookies (1937) (Dawson). The Divan Parisien Restaurant in New York City also created a new dish: Chicken Divan ("Cioppino"). Food was important to those who did not have it and to those who did.

**Dances.** Many in the religious community opposed dancing, but it was very much a part of the culture of some Carolina areas. At the eleventh annual Mountain Dance and Music Festival at Asheville, North Carolina, August 5, 1938, the Asheville *Citizen* reported on page 3 that one judge "was more than on the defensive against church criticism" of the event:

> We say these folk dances, next only to our church meetings and religious songs in this section, God's country, typify our Scottish traditions, our local sufficiency within ourselves, our love for and desire to be with each other in happiness, in exultation; it's the all for each and each for all spirit within us, which is our heritage, our raising, so to speak.
>
> The fervor and pathos of mountain music, the community exuberances of these dances, the full, physical, spirited outpourings of the folks into them: the snap, the zest, the go-git in them, are entirely unhurtful expressions of wholehearted mountainerishness [Botkin, p. 702].

The types of dancing varied. In addition to the folk-dancing and the square dancing of the rural communities, many of the areas continued the 1920s dances, like the Charleston. Some "modern thinking" areas began the swing dance that quickly became a national craze: the Big Apple. Created in 1937 by Lee David and John Redmond, the dance was unique:

> Danced in a circle by a group, the Big Apple is led by one who calls the steps, as in a Virginia reel. Fundamental step is a hop similar to the Lindy Hop. In the words of "Variety," "it requires a lot of floating power and fannying." In groups or singly, the dancers follow the caller and combine such steps as the Black Bottom, "shag," Suzi-Q, Charleston, "truckin'," as well as old square-dance turns like London Bridge, and a formation which resembles an Indian Rain Dance. The Big Apple invariably ends upon a somewhat reverent note, with everybody leaning back and raising his arms heavenward. This movement is called "Praise Allah." Through it all, the "caller" shouts continuously—"Truck to the right.... Reverse it.... To the left.... Stomp that right foot.... Swing it" [Time-Life, *This Fabulous Century*, p. 237].

**Dance marathons.** One of the fads of the 1930s was the dance marathon. The object of the event was to determine which dance couple could remain on the floor the longest.

*Square dancers.*

At a time when money was scarce, many young people were eager to compete for the prize money.

One hungry vagrant, Jan van Heé, aged 16, told of leaving his parents' farm to ride the rails. When he saw an advertisement of a dance marathon, he was eager to enroll to try to earn some money. He reports seeing a table with sandwiches, soft drinks, and doughnuts for the dancers and remembers

> ...being so doggone hungry that I went over to the table even before we started to dance, but the girl stopped me. I could only eat during my first break. I had to stagger around for four hours before I could get to those doughnuts [Uys, p. 197].

To get some rest, one of the partners would try to keep his or her feet moving enough for the judge to consider the dancer to still be dancing; the other dancer would lean against the slightly moving dancer in order to get a short break. Heé and his partner

> ...lasted four days and nights until only one other couple remained. We'd slap each other to keep awake but finally she just slid down in front of me onto the floor. The other couple won the contest [Uys, p. 198].

Heé reports that he and his dance companion won $15 for their performance.

**Café society.** Even though most of the country and state were foundering in the Great Depression, the Café Society was trying to keep up appearances. Others tried to copy their fashions and their dances, like the Lambeth Walk, which originated in England in 1938 and ended in shouts of "Oy!" Americans in New York and small towns alike adopted the dance (Time-Life, pp. 244–245).

**The general store.** The local general

store often provided a gathering place for the men after they had finished a day in the field or textile mill. Women, too, visited at the store. A pot-bellied stove in winter or a spreading chinaberry tree in summer might provide the focal point for the grouping. Discussions centered about the New Deal, political candidates, federal legislation, local regulations, crops, prices and wages, recipes, child-rearing, and other pertinent topics.

The stores of the southern countryside quickly became the heartbeat and pulse of a good portion of American business. In their own community, they were centers of every sort of neighborhood activity. Everything of importance that ever happened either occurred at the store or was reported there immediately.... When he wished to "cuss" the government or to complain to the Lord because of the perfidy of politics and weather conditions, there was no place like ... the store....

As one old-timer boasted, his store was where we put clothes on anything that had a back to wear them between the cradle and the grave, crowded their feet into something to keep them off the ground, and rammed food down everything that had a gullet to swallow it [Clark, p. 16].

Jessie Gibbs can attest personally to the place of Price's Store in her community:

P. R. Price's General Store was a favorite gathering place for residents near the Rutherford County–Cleveland County line. "Pop," as we all called the owner, allowed no profanity from his friends and neighbors who gathered regularly at the end of the day and enjoyed a "Three Center" or a "sody dope" as they talked. Most of the time the women did not come to the store; they were busy preparing — or cleaning up after — the evening meal.

Things took a different turn during cotton picking season. The owner of the field often loaded the "hands" on the back of the truck after he paid them and took them to Price's Store. While he talked, workers could purchase their

*Farmers' wives gather at Mrs. Clement's grocery store to exchange information in Stem, Granville County, May 1940.*

*P. R. Price waters the chinaberry trees in front of his dry goods store in North Carolina. The store was at the Rutherford County–Cleveland County line and served as a gathering place for the community.*

essentials and might even splurge for a "Moon Pie" or a can of Spam.

Some families regularly went to the nearest town on Saturday. The entire family looked forward to several hours socializing, window-shopping, and getting away for a little while. Price's Store, however, had everything most families needed, and many people gathered there.

Outside the local drug store the retirees in our little town always kept a game of dominoes going. On some days the players came and went; on other days the same players who had started that morning were there in the afternoon.

**Local baseball and softball.** Textile mills often had their own baseball teams. Their games against other mill teams were important local events for workers and for management. Harriet L. Herring surveyed 322 North Carolina mills. Although only 20 of the companies provided insurance coverage, 127 of the mills sponsored and supported baseball teams (Herring, *Welfare Work*, pp. 352–352).

Mill officials saw the teams as in no way threatening the power relationships between employee and employer. The team provided release and achievement for the worker and immersed the village into the mill system. Some companies rewarded players generously for their efforts. "Baseball was the biggest thing — next to the churches" (Waldrep, pp. 24–25).

Yandle reports on the textile games played in Charlotte in the 1930s.

> Blacks and whites played each other here, and according to the *Washington Post* one game was known as the first mixed game in the South. An old newspaper clipping from the *Charlotte News* of July 8, 1933, billed it as the first game in Charlotte between black and white teams.

Woodrow "Woody" Austin played in this game. He said that Grady Cole, the famous WBT Radio personality of the Charlotte area, was the announcer and people from all over Charlotte filled the stands, while many others stood or were seated on the ground. Woodrow said the blacks out numbered whites that night, and the excitement was high for the game ... there were many games between the blacks and whites played in North Charlotte using the larger of the two fields mentioned above. "We would just meet up out at the field in the afternoon. We would have mixed teams. We didn't care, so long as we could play," said [Charlotte second baseman Lester "Zeke"] Henderson [Yandle, p. 109].

Women's softball teams also were a part of the recreation in many textile villages. Church teams and civic teams increased the competition in the local areas. Local residents discussed the winner of the games for weeks.

Native Americans had their sports and games also. These events were important for spectator and participant alike. Sunday afternoons on the grounds of the residential school in the Qualla Reserve or in an unused field was a typical setting for the outdoor events. Dancing was another popular recreational event. Both men and women often displayed their talents at ceremonial occasions.

**College and high school sports.** The selection of a college team in the state to support was common; even high school dropouts sometimes chose a college team and identified with its wins—and losses. The high school or college team an individual boosted was usually that in their immediate geographical area. The important high school and local teams provided much pleasure to their fans; much good-natured "ribbing" occurred among the supporters.

**Fairs, circuses, recreation parks, and traveling entertainment.** Seasonal entertainment in North Carolina included the fairs and circuses, which made their yearly visits to

*A ballgame among members of the Cherokee tribe.*

Top: *Cherokee dancers led by Will West Long, 1937.* Bottom: *A fan in Durham who "Bet on Carolina" and lost pays off the wager by pushing a Duke fan in a wheelbarrow so all can see, November, 1939.*

the state. Posters heralded the upcoming events that were popular occasions for young and old alike.

Usually the traveling trains or trucks arrived in rural communities in the fall after the laborers had picked the cotton and harvested the tobacco. The amusement owners wanted to be sure that their arrival came when the people had some money to spend. For visitors who did not have a great deal of pocket money, the joy of visiting the exhibit halls — usually free — and walking the midway was a treat to those whose lives had recently been filled with only work. The advertisements and the anticipation of the upcoming fair or traveling circus brought happiness to many hearts.

Midway shows were available to those who had the necessary coins to enter. Those who could not afford to "step inside" contented themselves with looking at the billboards and enjoying the free preview given outside just before the "show inside began." Odd animals and people — either real or contrived — were a feature of some of these sideshows.

Rides and the smells of cotton candy and frying potatoes reached the nostrils of those who arrived. The sounds of screams from the rides, the enticements of workers inviting fairgoers to try their luck at the booths, and the calls of "B-6" from the bingo booths filled the air. The actual sights would not be lasting, however, for the travelers would remove their displays and would be gone within a few days.

The exhibit halls of the fairs featured the products of the farms, the food preparation and conservation of the families, and the other displays and handiwork of the residents. Usually there was no charge for this exhibit.

On the last night of some of the fairs and circuses was a fireworks display. The exhibit marked the end of the fair or circus until the next season — and ensured that the audience would stay until the last possible moment and increase the profits of the sponsors.

A diary entry of Ewart Burns describes the fair through his eyes as a teen-ager:

My Trip to the Fair

On October the fifth, at two o'clock, I arrived at the Rutherford County Fair Ground.

The first thing I did after arriving was to go through the exhibit hall. In this place they had automobiles, radios, fancy needle work, farm products of all kinds, and numerous other things on exhibits.

When I had finished going through the exhibit hall, the next thing that attracted my attention was the horse races, which had already started. When the race ended, there was an acrobat performance in front of the grandstand. While this act was in progress, a cloud came up and it started to rain. Believe me, it was some rain! Everyone ran to the exhibit hall for cover. There I met more people that I knew during this shower than I have ever had the privilege of seeing in one place.

That night there was a display of fireworks; the cannon-like reports as the rockets shot skyward, the sudden bursting of them in the sky, and the brilliance of the stars that poured forth their lights made the fair at night something to be remembered.

Some cities had permanent recreation parks. Asheville, for instance, had a recreational facility, which often featured some carnival rides. Traveling exhibits — which included "crime shows," agricultural exhibits, and "freak shows" (genuine and fake) — toured the state. Some people took advantage of these traveling shows as a form of amusement. In some areas the rivers, lakes, and ponds were "free" to the user. Developed local lakes and pools for swimming and fishing provided inexpensive fun for Carolina residents.

**Holidays.** North Carolina residents observed holidays, such as Christmas, the Fourth of July, Thanksgiving, and New Year's Day, even during the hard times. Donnis Curtis recalls:

A family event that was annual in our area was the Fourth of July fish fry. The men would go to the river and clean off an area where the families could spread out blankets and picnics when they arrived later in the day.

The men would fish all day and in the late afternoon they would prepare the catfish that came from the river. The children, however, would have to eat only the food brought from home because the parents feared that a child might swallow a tiny bone from the fish.

*Asheville Recreation Park.*

Many children would be allowed to wade and swim in the river. However, swimming was not a favorite activity of mine, and I often did not participate.

In Cleveland and Gaston counties during the 1930s the New Year's Shoot was a still-celebrated custom that the German-speaking settlers brought to the New World. At the stroke of midnight residents of Cherryville came to the downtown, brought their weapons, and would begin firing. A town crier would read a speech as a part of the ceremony. The blasts from the guns would sound for 18 continuous hours (Botkin, pp.621–62). Getty Davis's husband also celebrated the custom on his farm in Cleveland County by firing his shotgun at the stroke of midnight to welcome the New Year.

If one were to have good luck the whole year, New Year's Day required black-eyed peas and turnip greens, often cooked with fatback, side meat, or hog jowl for seasoning. Cooking two or more vegetables together — like corn and tomatoes to make succotash, black-eyed peas and rice to make "Hoppin' John," and corn, limas, tomatoes and okra to make soup — was a common, Carolina practice (Federal Writer's Project, *A Guide to the Old North State*, pp. 106–108). Charles Kuralt, former Charlotte resident, tells of a Carolina tradition of placing a dime in the Hoppin' John on New Year's Day; whoever got the dime was in for the best luck of all during the coming year (Kuralt, *American Moments*).

Gifts were few and far between for most family members; homemade presents or none

*Opposite: The Colfax Free Fair in Ellenboro was ranked the "Best in State" in 1936. Professor A. B. Bushong, the director of the fair, noted that the Colfax Fair placed its emphasis on the purpose and the aims of a community fair, rather than on the amusement phase. The exhibit hall was always free to fairgoers and was a popular part of the fair. A baby show, a professsional stock company performing in the auditorium, livestock, and athletic events were some of the important events (Forest City Courier, September 3, 1936).*

*Between the Methodist Youth Training sessions at Lake Junaluska, Nell Burns took time to don a swimsuit and visit the Carolina lake.*

at all was the rule in most households during the Great Depression. Nell Burns remembers her usual Christmas stocking with "an orange, a nut, and an apple." One Christmas morning she arose before daylight and before anyone else had stirred; she ate her fruit and nut and went back to bed. Much later family members came to arouse her to "come and check your stocking." Nell turned over in bed and said, "I have already eaten mine; I will just sleep a little longer." Jessie Gibbs's family was able to enjoy apples at Christmas because of their packing the apples in cotton seed. Some families stored the fruit in a cellar.

Homemade valentines made from paper colored with crayons and pasted with flour-and-water glue marked Valentine's Day; Nell Burns recalled that the smell of the homemade paste filled the classroom on Valentine's Day. Easter was typically celebrated with eggs colored with homemade dye; Nell remembered that the class sometimes had an "egg cracking" contest to see who would have the strongest egg. "Usually someone boiled a guinea egg to make things interesting," she laughed.

**Cultural events in North Carolina.** In the 1920s critic H. L. Mencken referred to the South as a "Sahara of the fine arts." He went on to explain that the literature, the painting, the music, the sculpture, and the drama came from other sections of the nation. Mencken neglected, however, to consider the fine arts in the Cherokee Indian Reservation (Parramore, *Carolina Quest*, p. 464).

Mencken also neglected to stress the claim to fame of Anna McNeill Whistler, a native of Wilmington; Anna was the mother of James McNeill Whistler and the subject of his most famous work. Mencken did not mention Thomas Wolfe of Asheville or Boiling Springs author W.J. Cash, who wrote *Mind of the South* (Parramore, *Carolina Quest*, p. 481).

Things began to change in the Tar Heel State. The North Carolina Art Society, begun in 1925, was beginning to acquire several small collections by 1929. The General Assembly, which had agreed to take control of the society, to provide annual funds, and to furnish some space in state buildings, was beginning to contribute to the visual arts of the state. The North Carolina Symphony began in 1933. It is the oldest state symphony in the United States (Parramore, *Carolina Quest*, pp. 481–485).

The federal government, through its work programs, was also subsidizing some artists during the Great Depression. For instance, artists painted murals in post offices

*The residence of Thomas Wolfe in Asheville.*

and federal buildings. Federal photographers began recording images of the population and the resources of the United States. Federal work legislation brought drama and other programs to auditoriums and schools across the nation.

**Plays and programs.** Many towns and communities took advantage of the seating of school, church, and civic to present and host plays and programs for the enjoyment and edification of the community. Some of the local communities set up their own "little theatre groups," but other communities had little time, money, or facilities for these cultural events. Visitors to the Outer Banks attended *The Lost Colony* in the new amphitheater. The program was the work of Paul Green, another North Carolinian forgotten by Mencken.

**Paul Green.** A native of Harnett County and educated at Buies Creek Academy, Paul Green was a pitcher for Lillington, a professional baseball team, after his graduation from Buies Creek in 1914. After serving in World War I, Green entered the University of North Carolina and graduated in 1921 with a philosophy major. After going to Cornell University, Green returned to UNC to become an Assistant Professor of Philosophy until 1939 when he resigned to write full-time. Green earned the Pulitzer Prize in 1927 for his drama *In Abraham's Bosom*; produced at the Garrick Theater in New York City, the play was not his only one. His other Broadway plays included *The House of Connelly, Roll Sweet Chariot, Johnny Johnson,* and *Native Son.*

North Carolinians probably remember him most for his 1937 "symphonic drama" *The Lost Colony.* Performed in an outdoor theater developed largely with federal labor on Roanoke Island, the site of the 1587 colony, the play was a success. Paul went on to produce 15 other outdoor dramas performed in North Carolina, Florida, Virginia, Texas, Kentucky, and elsewhere. His play brought many visitors to the coast of North Carolina even during the Great Depression.

*A scene from* The Lost Colony *by Paul Green. The drama is being performed in the amphitheater — partially made possible through federal funds — on the Outer Banks.*

## III. Tourism

A rich variety of sights and cultural programs dotted the state, including many annual events, such as the fiddler's convention at Union Grove (Parramore, *Carolina Quest*, p. 481–485).

**The Ole Time Fiddlers and Bluegrass Festival.** Union Grove's Ole Time Fiddlers and Bluegrass Festival began in the 1920s. Still held today, it bills itself as "the oldest continuous ole time fiddler's contest in North America." Each year traditional bands in old time and bluegrass divisions vie for championships ("Fiddler's Grove").

**The Singing on the Mountain at Grandfather Mountain.** The Singing on the Mountain at Grandfather Mountain began in 1924. This annual event in June includes gospel singing, preaching, picnic lunches, and entertainers (Pacher and Richard).

**Other annual events.** Other annual events in the 1930s that brought visitors to various areas in the state included the Tulip Festival at Washington, North Carolina, the Dahlia Show at Durham, the Cotton Festival at Gastonia, and the Rhododendron Festival at Asheville (Botkin, p. 43).

**Tourist attractions.** The Cape Hatteras Lighthouse and the Carolina beaches attracted some vacationers and area residents seeking a day trip for recreation. The work of the CCC made beaches even more attractive. Chimney Rock, the Blue Ridge Parkway, the Grove Park Inn, the Biltmore Estate, Grandfather Mountain, Lake Lure, Blowing Rock, the Bottomless Pools, and Linville Caverns were only a few of the attractions that drew visitors to the mountains of the state.

Even those who had no money for long vacations or overnight trips might sometimes take a day trip. Depending on location, these trips might take families and individuals to a nearby city, the coast, the rivers, mountains,

## Seven: Popular Entertainment

*This scene is from the coast of North Carolina.*

or streams; some people were able, therefore, to enjoy a brief respite from the problems of the Great Depression. Many city dwellers sought the rivers, lakes, ocean, and woods for a retreat from a busy urban life. Some farmers allowed out-of-state hunters the use of their land and even their dogs—for a fee.

**The Grove Park Inn.** In the summer of 1896 Edwin Grove went to Asheville from St. Louis to get help with his attacks of hiccoughs.

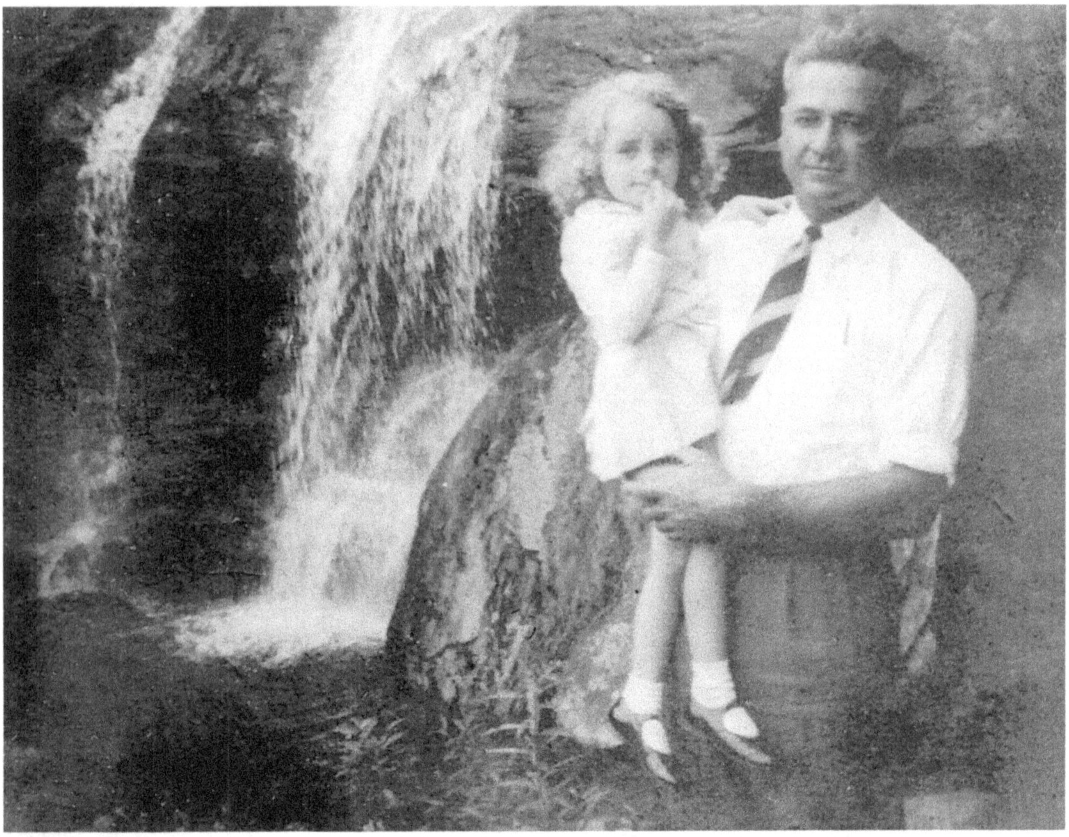

COURTESY NELL BURNS

COURTESY LISA GOSNELL

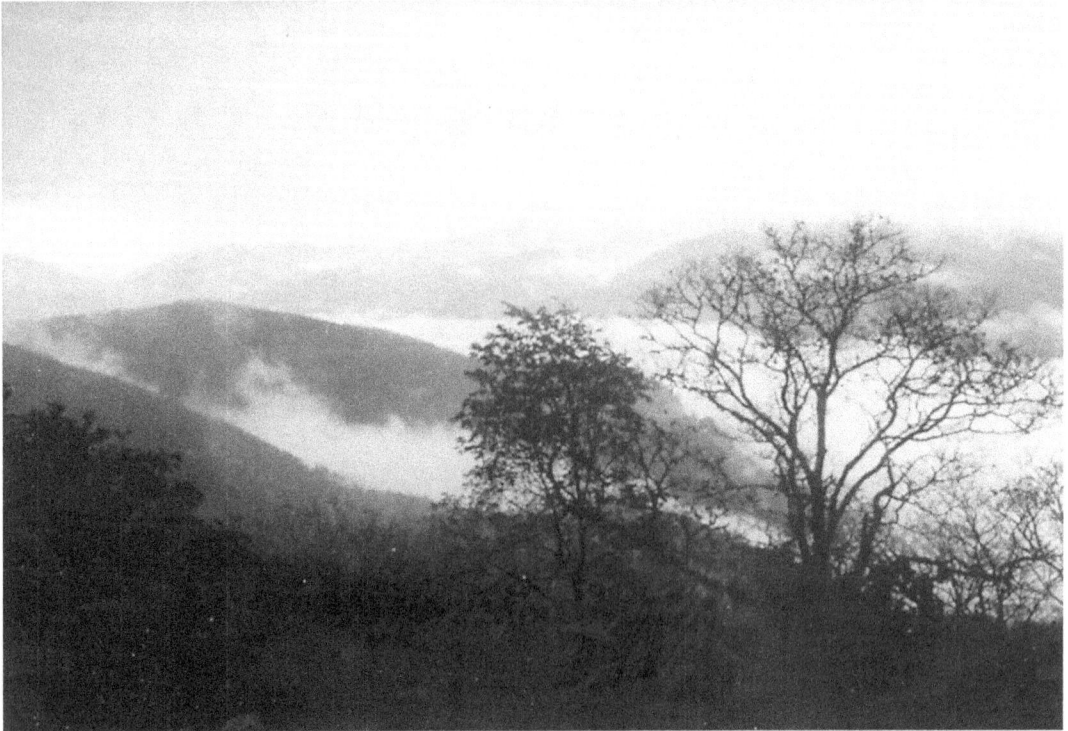

*Hunters with bear and turkey in 1935.*

This trip to North Carolina proved eventful: his daughter met Fred Seely, and the two married in 1898. On this trip, Grove thought of starting an inn in Asheville. Because he feared the tuberculosis sanitariums might limit those who came to his inn, Grove bought the sanitariums in Asheville and closed them. In May of 1912 he selected the site for his resort. This inn, built with funds secured from the Grove's Tasteless Chill Tonic, would serve as a historic lodging during the 1930s and in the coming years.

**The construction of the Grove Park Inn to serve the emotional health needs of the population.** Edwin Grove easily secured the construction workers he needed because he paid the area's highest wages—10 cents an hour. People from all over the South came to work in Asheville for this excellent pay. Grove approved the erection of a huge circus tent to house those who had traveled great distances and who had no other place to sleep.

The workers used mules for most of the construction, but they did use a Packard truck to pull 14 wagons loaded with 40 tons of granite up the mountain on each trip. The original Grove Park Inn was 6 stories tall with walls 4 feet thick. Grove prescribed that no cut edges of the stone show. He wanted the workers to lay the stones with the weathered, "time-eaten face" from "thousands of years of sun and rain" to the front; he believed the lichens and moss would enhance the appearance. To make sure that there were no seams in the concrete roof, workers poured the 5-inch thick roof weighing 90,000 pounds day and night without stop; the steel rods that strengthened the roof added another 90,000 pounds.

Inside the Grove Park Inn was a 120-foot entrance with two 36-foot-wide fireplaces. The workers used 120 tons of stone on each fireplace; logs that were 12 feet long could fit inside the structure. Hidden within a fire-

Opposite, top: *This scene is from Linville.* Bottom: *The mountains of North Carolina.*

place was the elevator; Grove did not want the elevator to take away from the beauty of the entrance of the Inn.

The Grove Park Inn was ready for opening almost one year to the day that the construction had begun. The 156 guestrooms held 400 male guests on Saturday, July 12, 1913. The visitors found running water that was piped 17 miles to the Inn and 400 French rugs gracing the floors.

The Grove Park Inn was to be an up-to-date inn that was convenient, clean, and quiet. Grove saw the Inn as a place for tired people who were not ill but who wanted sanitary surroundings, good food, luxurious rooms, and peace. He requested that all guests speak in hushed tones and that all employees wear rubber soled shoes. Patrons who spoke in loud voices received notes asking them to lower their voices. Grove required employees to wash all coins before giving them to the guests; employees could give only new bills when they made change. Grove required employees to boil all silverware, glasses, and dishes two times before the guests used them (Johnson, pp. 50–52).

The Grove Park was an important resort to the state, the nation, and the world. By the end of the 1920s the Grove Park Inn had become the most popular resort for wealthy Americans in the nation. To stay at the Inn, one had to secure reservations months in advance. Fred Seely had to approve any new guests. Certain traditions became a feature at the Inn; for instance after performances, the guests received washed apples and a sheet of thin gray paper for the core. It was truly, as Seely said, a place where guests could get away and rest.

The Great Depression brought problems to even this nationally-known fixture:

> ...the Grove Park Inn could not escape the repercussions of the stock market crash of 1929.

The Great Depression paralyzed the nation, including the two groups of people on whom the Grove Park Inn had come to depend: the established wealthy class and a growing business class.... On January 15, 1932 ... the First National Bank and Trust Company of Asheville... [was] receiver for the resort.... Albert Barnett was to become general manager of the inn....

Under Barnett's leadership, the Grove Park Inn maintained a steady course for the remainder of the decade (Johnson, pp. 50–52).

**Out-of-state events of the 1930s.** Even during the hard times of the 1930s, many Carolinians were able to travel outside the perimeters of the state for memorable occasions of the decade. Two such events were the Chicago World's Fair of 1933 and the New York World's Fair of 1939 — "the biggest, costliest, and most elaborate international event" ever held up to that time (Time-Life, *This Fabulous Century*, p. 2687). Ewart Burns was among those who traveled to Chicago:

> When I was in my twenties, my friend Grover Hamrick and I decided to attend the Chicago World's Fair in 1933. Neither he nor I had ever been on such a trip before, but we filled the car with gasoline and gathered all the "Indian Head Pennies" that they could find. The local rumor was that admittance to the fair was free with an Indian Head Penny. We two entrepreneurs planned to sell our pennies for ½ of what the admission price was; we would make money and the buyers would save money. We planned to come home rich and cosmopolitan. Unfortunately, the tale was untrue, and we had to spend the pennies for food and lodging. We used the last of their pennies at the last stop we made for gasoline. The memories lasted, but our money did not.

**Summary.** Although times were lean during the 1930s, many Carolinians were able to draw on their inner strength and provide for their mental health through entertainment — as simple as a walk to the river or as elaborate as a cross-state trip to one of the state's resorts.

# Appendix I

# *Important Federal Photographers in North Carolina During the Great Depression*

When the federal government created the Agricultural Adjustment Administration (AAA) in 1933, Rexford Tugwell came to Washington as Assistant Secretary of Agriculture. Tugwell, a teacher at Columbia University, drew Roy E. Stryker, one of his students, with him. Stryker's fascination with the pictorial images captured by the federal government began, and his work with the federal government in building the collection would continue for a decade.

Through the years, Roy Stryker would meet and work with many photographers at the Agricultural Adjustment Administration (AAA), the Resettlement Administration (RA), the Farm Security Administration (FSA), and the Office of War Information (OWI). This chapter focuses on the eight federal photographers who came to the Tar Heel State during the Great Depression.

## I. Arthur Rothstein (1914–1983)

On July 10, 1935, when Roy Stryker assumed his position of Chief of the Historical Section in the Division of Information of the Resettlement Administration (Contract of July 1, 1935, Stryker Papers, Series I), twenty-one-year-old Arthur Rothstein worked with him as a photographer. Rothstein, one of Stryker's students at Columbia University, had originally wanted to go to medical school, but "it didn't break right for him" (Interview, p. 4, Stryker Papers, Series II. B). He would serve five years with Stryker.

**1935 assignment.** Rothstein had had no professional photographic experience and spent his first weeks with the Resettlement Administration trying to prepare for his work. He practiced using the camera and studied intently the photographs on file.

Stryker noted the scarcity of photographs of tenant farmers; he asked Rothstein to record on film any evicted farmers who would relocate through the Resettlement Administration. Rothstein traveled to North Carolina and recorded people and scenes in August and September of 1935. His work ably filled the gap and produced remarkable photographs of these impoverished farmers (Interview, p. 4, Stryker Papers, Series II. B).

**Controversy in South Dakota.** In May of 1936 Rothstein went to South Dakota to document the drought there. In the southwest corner, Rothstein came upon a scene that was compelling to him as a photographer. The skull from a steer lay bleaching on the parched land. No shade was in sight on the alkali flats. Rothstein began to photograph the skull from several angles; he moved the skull to achieve just the shadowing he wanted. Next, Rothstein placed the skull on a knoll near scrubgrass and a cactus. The result was a photograph suggesting that overgrazing had created a desolate environment.

The photographs of the "drought" received much public acclaim. President Roosevelt decided to make a trip to the area to see the situation firsthand. While he was on the train, however, copies of the August 27, 1936, Fargo *Evening Forum* appeared throughout the cars. In the *Forum* (p. 6) was an article charging Rothstein and the RA with fakery and fabrication. The Republican party leaped with enthusiasm upon the article and charged that the whole resettlement program was a sham. Stryker was on vacation, and his assistant Edward Locke answered the press "hesitantly and meekly" (J. Curtis, pp. 69–78).

The stories escalated, but meanwhile, Stryker and others tried internally to add some levity to the somber situation. On August 29, 1936, Ed Locke wrote to Stryker:

> They will probably try to get in touch with you if this matter goes any further, so if you still have that ... skull hide it for ... sake. Stick close to my story [Letter from Ed Locke to Roy Stryker, August 29, 1936, Stryker Papers, Series I].

**Levity concerning South Dakota.** On October 23, 1936, C. B. Baldwin, Assistant Administrator of the Resettlement Administration, jokingly completed a requisition for a skull with "teeth in article as mandatory requirement of acceptance of included article." The fictitious requisition form number 1,895,553,144,378,222 (with the fictitious stock number 111,111,222,222, and the fictitious price of $4 billion) contained the added description that the teeth in the skull must contain "no dental work" (Requisition form from C. B. Baldwin to Roy Stryker, October 23, 1936, Stryker Papers, Series I).

With the requisition, C. B. Baldwin sent Roy Stryker an accompanying memorandum with the following comments:

> It is felt by officials of the RA that, because of the value from the publicity angle which has accrued from the article requisitioned, every effort should be made to have as many of them available as possible. I shall appreciate your cooperation in making it possible for me to have one of them.
> 
> I should prefer one with the weathered surface so that no question of its authenticity could possibly arise. May I also request that teeth be included.
> 
> It is not felt that the alkali background is essential, since from all reports these backgrounds have been more than plentiful this season, and again I do not want the manufactured effect [Memo from C. B. Baldwin to Roy Stryker, October 23, 1936, Stryker Papers, Series I].

The memorandum from the Finance and Control Division in reply stated:

> The Finance and Control Division has fully considered the advisability of encumbering the attached requisition against the allotment of AD Staff. Possible objections were: that the furnishing of such material, setting it up artistically on desks, etc., might be considered more properly as a project of the Special Skulls Division; that since the Information Division has publicly acquired such a reputation in the handling of such material, and a precedent has already been established for purchasing such items from allotments of the Information Division, the encumbrance should be made against the Division.
> 
> However, it was finally decided to make the charge to AD-1 on the ground that the possession of such items have a future value to the AD Staff in that hollow skulls provide an appropriate reminder and a lasting memorial to the accomplishments of the Information Division [Memorandum from Finance and Control Division to C. B. Baldwin, in reply to requisition of October 23, 1936, Stryker Papers, Series I].

**Rothstein's reputation.** Rothstein's popularity dropped. Opponents criticized him also for taking county agents and administrators with him on his tours of an area. They suggested that this tactic created cooperation from his subjects that might not have already been there. His opponents, then, believed that he set up many unrealistic settings with both people and places (Evory, *Contemporary Authors*, NR, pp. 437–438). While some photographers criticized him for not photographing literal truths and for modifying the scenes he filmed, other photographers understood his zeal to capture the ideal picture and to perfect his craft (Walsh, p. 646). Rothstein admitted that he did sometimes direct his subjects much as a motion picture director moves and directs the actions of the players (J. Curtis, pp. 69–78).

**Tugwell's resignation.** The public scrutinized the work of Rothstein, Tugwell, and the RA. Tugwell resigned shortly after the re-election of Franklin Roosevelt. Following Tugwell's resignation late in 1936, the Resettlement Administration quietly became a part of the Farm Security Administration (J. Curtis, p. 122).

Despite the controversy surrounding him, Rothstein continued with his work. He kept his eye for balance and mood. He sought to give his subjects dignity while he captured them in their everyday duties; he did not portray them as victims. The components of his pictures give even the most uncomfortable, squalid homes a certain attractiveness (Fleischhauer, pp. 146–149).

**Rothstein and North Carolina.** Rothstein visited North Carolina for purposes of photography in 1935, 1936, 1937, 1938, 1939, and even as late as 1942. The perceptive viewer of photographs of North Carolina taken during the Great Depression may be able to identify Rothstein's photographs of people — particularly children. His signature is evident in the poignant pictures of the poor who project dignity, of mothers and children seemingly deliberately posed, and of agents and administrators with the "little people." Though controversial, these subjects often bolstered support for the works of the Farm Security Administration. His photographic collection from North Carolina includes not only people but interesting objects: wash boards, slaughtered hogs, hams, wash tubs, pitchers, cotton bales, and other significant articles.

After his federal work, Rothstein, a New York native, entered the United States Army from 1943 through 1946. He served in the China-Burma theater and received the Army Commendation Medal. Upon his discharge he went to work at *Look*, where he served until 1971 as technical director of photography and as director of photography. In 1947 he married Grace Goodman. They had four children. Rothstein also served on the faculty of the Graduate School of Journalism, Columbia University, from 1961 to 1971, and wrote ten books. He worked for one year with *Infinity* magazine before serving as photographer and administrator with *Parade* (Evory, *Contemporary Authors*, NR, pp. 437–438). Rothstein died in 1985 at the age of 71.

## II. Carl Mydans (1907– )

Before turning to photography, Carl Mydans studied journalism at Boston University and worked for the *American Banker* as a reporter. When his photographic work brought him to the attention of the Suburban Resettlement Administration, twenty-eight-year-old Mydans went to work with the federal government in 1935. Later, Tugwell's Resettlement Administration subsumed the Suburban Resettlement Administration, and Stryker headed the photographic project (*Encyclopedia of Photography*, pp. 351–352).

**Mydans and North Carolina.** In March 1936, Carl Mydans traveled to North Carolina to record its scenes and people. Mydans returned to the state in August of 1936 to record more about Carolina and its people — from convicts to settlers in Penderlea. Shortly after his trip to North Carolina Mydans left the Resettlement Administration.

**Paramount, World War II, and prisoners of war.** On November 21, 1936, Stryker reported in a letter to Dorothea Lange, another photographer in his division, that Mydans "has left us to go to Hollywood to do candid photographs for the Paramount Company." (Stryker Papers, Series I) Later Mydans went to work with three other photographers to launch *Life*. He remained there until 1972, when the magazine temporarily closed (*Encyclopedia of Photography*, p. 351).

During his tenure at *Life*, Mydans covered major news events throughout the world. He photographed England preparing for attack, the Finnish campaign against Russia, France at war, and General Patton. Mydans and his wife Shelley — a former researcher with *Life*— were both captives of the Japanese in the Philippines; after 21 months in prison, their captors released them in exchange for Japanese prisoners (*Encyclopedia of Photography*, p. 351).

The couple wrote of this experience in *The Open City*,

> ...a novelized account of life in Manila (Santo Tomas camp). The author and her husband, photographers for *Life* magazine, were imprisoned at Santo Tomas for ... months, before they were repatriated... [James, *Book Review Digest*, p. 514].

**Achievements and awards.** Carl Mydans's achievements have included his receiving the *U. S. Camera* Gold Achievement Award. He has completed photojournalistic assignments with *Time, Fortune, Smithsonian Magazine*, and many other recognizable journals (*Encyclopedia of Photography*, p. 351). He returned to *Life* for assignments when the magazine reopened.

*Life* reported at a celebration of Mydans's birthday in May of 1997 that Mydans and *Life* had been linked for six decades. The article noted that Carl had even met his wife Shelley at the office Christmas party. In 1997 Mydans, at ninety, was still regularly coming to the *Life* offices, was working on his memoirs, and was still married to Shelley ("May," *Life*). Of all the FSA photographers to have visited North Carolina on assignment during the Great Depression, Mydans was the last surviving.

## III. Ben Shahn (1898–1969)

Ben Shahn was born in Lithuania in 1898 and came to New York with his family when he was six. Shahn became an apprentice to a lithographer when he was 15 and continued in that role until age 18. In 1919 he enrolled at New York University and completed his studies in 1924 at New York City College. In 1922 he married Tillie Goldstein; they had two children. After studying at the National Academy of Design, he traveled in North Africa and in Europe. His first one-exhibitor show was in 1929. After the death of his wife Tillie, he married Bernarda Bryson in 1935 (Kronenberger, *Atlantic Brief Lives*, p. 697).

**Shahn's early murals.** Shahn's style and his attention to social themes led to his 23 gouaches and 2 mural panels in 1931–1932. In 1932–1933 he completed 15 gouache studies of Tom Mooney, a prominent labor leader. Shahn became assistant to the Mexican mural painter Diego Rivera; they painted the murals for the RCA Building in Rockefeller Center, New York City.

**Murals for the federal government.** Various federal agencies commissioned Shahn for murals and panels. He did eight paintings on the theme of prohibition for the Public Works Arts Project, for example. A mural for the Federal Housing Development Commission in Roosevelt, New Jersey (1957–1988), is typical of his work; representations from anti–Semitism to unfair labor practices are in the images ("Ben Shahn," *Encyclopedia of World Biography*, p. 1).

The Federal Emergency Relief Administration commissioned him to prepare a mural in 1934. In the following year he accepted Rexford Tugwell's invitation to join the Resettlement Administration as an artist and part-time photographer (Fleischauer, pp. 76–79). He served there from 1935 to 1938 (Kronenberger, *Atlantic Brief Lives*, pp. 697–698).

Shahn was meticulous with detail, but he was also aware of the feeling the viewer would have upon seeing his work—and the work of the others. During his visits to North Carolina, he photographed—among other things—scenes from the settlement of Penderlea. His pictures of the children in Sunday School there touch the heart. Shahn puts a human face on the issue of resettlement.

Shahn executed large murals for the garment workers' resettlement project, for the Bronx Post Office (1939), and for the Social Security Building (1942). He contributed posters for the war effort and after the war for the Congress (formerly Committees) of Industrial Organizations (CIO); his *Register, Vote*, an employment poster for the CIO in 1944, demonstrates his concern for social equality and his coherent design which integrates language and visual form. He held many shows and served as Charles Eliot Norton Professor of Poetry at Harvard University from 1956 to 1957.

In his later years much of Shahn's work became more abstract. His *Lucky Dragon* series (1960–1962) demonstrates the tragedy of the Japanese fishing vessel that entered an atomic testing area in 1954. He created a series of three works, which illustrated religious themes such as *Ecclesiastes* (1967); he illustrated, wrote, and co-authored more than 15 books, including *Shape of Content* (1957) and *Love and Joy about Letters* (1963). Just before his death in 1969 in Roosevelt, New Jersey, Shahn executed a large mural for Syracuse University (Kronenberger, *Atlantic Brief Lives,* pp. 697–698).

## IV. Dorothea Lange (1895–1965)

Dorothea Lange was born in New Jersey in 1895. Her childhood was not easy. Dorothea's father left the family when she was just a child, and at the age of seven Dorothea had polio, which left her with a limp. Dorothea, however, caused some of her own problems because she often cut school. She spent stolen days wandering through the city and making notes on what she saw. By the time she was 18, she knew she wanted to record with a camera (Anita Davis, *Focus on Women*, p. 62).

**Using the camera.** Dorothea went to California and set up a studio in 1919. She became well-known in the area as a portrait photographer because of her interest in people and in preserving their images (Anita Davis, *Focus on Women*, p. 62).

**Lange and social issues.** During the Depression Lange became increasingly interested in social issues and exhibited her photographs of unemployment, hunger, and despair in San Francisco in 1934. Even though her photographs were not always appealing, they told of true life. Paul Taylor, a sociologist and economist, was impressed with her work. The two began to document the living conditions of the migrant worker on film for books, magazine articles, and exhibits. As a result of the work of this team (who had become husband and wife), Americans demanded improvements in the lives of the migrants (Anita Davis, *Focus on Women*, p. 62).

**Lange and the Resettlement Administration.** Lange took a job with the Resettlement Administration on September 19, 1935. Preferring to work out of her Berkeley home, however, she did not move to Washington (Anita Davis, *Focus on Women*, p. 62).

A careful observer can easily identify many of the works of the portrait photographer, whom Stryker dubbed the matriarch of the unit. Lange's photographs create a mood rather than a description of events. Many of her images are really character studies, and her sympathy for the people is apparent. Her photographs helped to bolster support for the work of the federal government (Fleischhauer, pp. 115–117, 160–163).

Lange's best-known work was Migrant Mother; indeed it is the best-known photographic work of all the Depression years. This image of the migrant woman holding her infant inside a tent in California is a documentary masterpiece; a print from her work is on display at the Museum of Modern Art (J. Curtis, p. 67).

**Lange and North Carolina.** Lange, however, photographed many other scenes and many other people of the Depression era. She successfully captured with her camera both North Carolinians and Carolina scenes in 1939. In North Carolina, the sharecroppers with the crops to their door creates a character study and at the same time evokes strong emotion.

**Stryker's termination of Lange.** Stryker found it necessary to terminate Lange; he later explained that

> Last July the budget committee presented me with the cold facts of how much money I would have to spend on personnel.... I am sure that I did what anyone in my place would have done. I selected for termination the person who would give me the least cooperation in the job that is laid before me... [Roy Stryker Papers, I].

Jonathan Garst wrote to Stryker on November 21, 1939, to suggest that Stryker "retain her on a W.A.E. basis. This will give her an official relationship and occasionally you can use her to great advantage." Garst explained, "Paul Taylor is apparently still violently in love with Dorothea Lange and takes her problems very much to heart." Garst also stated that "the Taylors are hard up" (Roy Stryker Papers, I).

Stryker responded on November 30, 1939, that he appreciated "the spirit in which you and Walter Packard have presented your feelings in the matter of Dorothea's termination...." Stryker went on to say that he did not

> ...believe that there is much that can be done regarding the situation now.... I think I appreciate as fully as anyone, perhaps more so, the contribution which Dorothea has made to the photographic file of the FSA, and certainly to the presentation of the migrant problem to the people of this country. I know that judgments of art are highly subjective. And yet subjective or not, I had a decision to make. I made it to the best of my ability [Roy Stryker Papers, I].

**Lange and the War Relocation Authorities.** In the early 1940s the War Relocation Authority hired Dorothea Lange to document the lives of the Japanese aliens and the Japanese Americans whom the United States government forced to live in relocation camps. Because her photographs show the difficult life of these prisoners, the public did not see many of her photographs until after the war.

**Lange's illness, final contributions, and death.** Lange stopped her next project — photographing the United Nations Conference of 1945 — when she became ill. Her illness lasted several years.

By 1951 Dorothea was able to work again. Her photographs now focused on family life; several of her assignments were for *Life*. In 1964 Dorothea found she had cancer, but she did not stop her work. She designed an exhibit of her photographs, planned for a center for documentary photography, and recorded a study of the country women of America. Dorothea died in 1965, but her photographs remain. They are a reminder of how she helped others by depicting their conditions (Anita Davis, *Focus on Women*, p. 62).

## V. Walker Evans (1903–1975)

Walker Evans was born in 1903 to a prosperous St. Louis family. Shortly after his birth, the family moved to an exclusive suburb on Chicago's North Shore where his father worked as an advertising copywriter. Walker attended private schools. In 1915 his family moved to Ohio.

After attending the Loomis School, Phillips academy, and Williams College in Williamston, Massachusetts, he worked for several years at night in the map room of the New York Public Library. After spending a year in Paris where he used a vest-pocket camera, Walker arrived in New York in 1927. He took odd jobs, and in 1928 he began photography. Some of his photographs appeared in the poetry book *The Bridge* (1930) by Hart Crane. Other collaborations followed (Trachtenberg, "Walker, Evans," p. 235).

**Evans's federal appointment.** Evans's federal appointment began on September 24, 1935, shortly after Lange's September 19, 1935, appointment. Evans's position was "an emergency appointment for such period of time as your services may be required on emergency work and funds are available therefor, but not to extend beyond June 30, 1937" (Contract of September 16, 1935, Stryker Papers, Series I).

Evans's duties were:

> Under the general supervision of the Chief of the Historical Section with wide latitude for the exercise of independent judgment and decision of Senior Information Specialist to carry out special assignments in the field; collect, compile and create photographic material to illustrate factual and interpretive news releases and other informational material upon all problems, progress and activities of the Resettlement Administration. To supervise a small group of assistants from time to time depending on the importance and size of the assignment, and other related tasks [September 16, 1935, letter to Miss McKinney of the Division of Information, Stryker Papers, Series I].

Stryker seemed very pleased to have Evans. In his letter to Professor Carman at Columbia University on October 11, 1935, Stryker explains:

Mr. Walker Evans, who is soon to join our staff as a special photographer, will be in New York some time next week. I would very much like to have him call and talk to you. In my mind Mr. Evans is one of the best photographers in this country for the job of photographically documenting American history. It is very likely that we might get him to work for us for a year. I am very anxious that he talk with you to give you some conception of his ideas for the use of the camera as a device for recording American history. I wish to goodness that we had money enough to hire him this year and let him devote his entire time to making a photographic record of the agricultural material. Incidentally, he will do some of this anyway, but I wish we could put him on that job and nothing else [Letter of October 11, 1935, Stryker Papers, Series I].

Evans's request for letter of authorization on February 7, 1936, indicates that he is planning a trip by common carrier from Washington to New Orleans and that he will return to Washington. His travel would carry him to various points within the states of Louisiana, Mississippi, Alabama, Georgia, South Carolina, North Carolina, Virginia, West Virginia, Kentucky, and Tennessee. The dates of the planned trip were from February 8, 1936, to April 8, 1936 (Request for letter of Authorization, February 7, 1936, Stryker Papers, Series I). Evans's voucher shows that he visited in North Carolina — particularly in the Winston-Salem area — on April 8–9, 1936 (Public Voucher for Reimbursement of Travel and Other Expenses Including Per Diem, May 6, 1936, Stryker Papers, Series I).

**Working on *Let Us Now Praise Famous Men*.** In the summer of 1936 Evans left Stryker and the federal government to join James Agee of *Fortune* to photograph tenant farming in the South. *Fortune* rejected their collaborative effort. Their work appeared in print as the book *Let Us Now Praise Famous Men* (1941), reissued in 1962. The work is "a classic work of the 1930s" (Trachtenberg, *Dictionary of American Biography*, p. 2). The Museum of Modern Art held its first one-man show devoted to photography in his honor in 1938.

**Evans's life and accomplishments continue.** After several conflicts with Stryker, Evans left Stryker and the federal government in 1938. For several years he used a hidden camera to photograph subway riders in New York. These photographs appear in *Many Are Called* (1966).

In 1941 he married Jane Ninas. He held a Guggenheim Fellowship for the years 1940, 1941, and 1959; he was staff writer at *Time* from 1943 until 1945. He moved to *Fortune* as staff photographer and assistant editor. Evans remained there for 20 years; he published 40 portfolios and photographic essays during that time. After his divorce from Jane Ninas in 1955, he married Isabella Boeschenstein von Steiger in 1960. They divorced in 1972.

Evans retired from *Fortune* in 1965, but he remained active. He joined Yale University School of Art and Architecture as the first professor of graphic arts. After his 1972 retirement, he spent years as artist-in-residence at Dartmouth College. The Museum of Modern Art in 1971 held a major retrospective of his work as an original artist.

**Accolades.** Evans continued to work quite actively with photography until a fall in 1974 resulted in a break in his collarbone. His death came on April 10, 1975, in New Haven, Connecticut.

Evans is best known as a master of black-and-white photography. However, throughout his career he worked with color film also. While living in Old Lyme, Connecticut, in his later years, he used polychromatic images. When he became intrigued with the SX-70 Polaroid Color Camera, he used it constantly. His work with photographs spanned almost half a century.

## VI. Marion Post Wolcott (1910–1990)

Marion Post was born in 1910. From 1925 until 1927 she attended the Edgewood School in Greenwich, Connecticut; from 1928 until 1929, the New School for Social Research in New York; from 1929 until 1930, New York University; and from 1930 until 1932, the University of Vienna — from which she took her bachelor of arts ("Marion Post Wolcott," *Contemporary Photographers*, p. 2).

Post's association with the camera. In 1932 and 1933 she visited abroad. Marion took her first roll of film just before returning to America. After her return to the United States, she studied photography informally with Ralph Steiner in New York in 1935. Marion began to serve as a freelance photographer in New York in 1935. She agreed to make photographs for the book *People of the Cumberlands* (1937) and the *Philadelphia Evening Bulletin* (1937).

Her work with the federal government and in North Carolina (1938–1940). On July 14, 1938, Stryker wrote to tell Marion of her employment with the FSA. Her photographic scenes in North Carolina still remain. A letter from Raleigh on the Saturday before Christmas of the same year explained her work in the state of North Carolina and presented her impressions of the people and their lifestyle.

> I ... just received S...'s letter about the Wadesboro P.H. [Public Health] job last night. (I was in Durham yesterday & didn't return until late.) The Dr. Reynolds he asked me to see here had to go out of town last evening, but I talked with his secretary and some other doctor at the board of health. We made arrangements for me to photograph the Traveling clinics in Wadesboro Monday (if good weather, otherwise Tuesday.) ... I'm leaving for Pembroke now, do what little I can there tomorrow (Sunday) and then come back by there for another day after Wadesboro. I'll also look over the soil erosion near Wadesboro.... Wait till I write you a description of what it was like at Duke yesterday, then you'll understand what we run into ... on these jobs. They were cooperative and helpful enough — it's just that sometimes there are all kinds of unavoidable disturbing circumstances and problems — especially when you can't see what you've got to photograph first and the other people haven't the faintest idea what you want until you arrive.... It's amazing even tho this isn't the deep south the pace is entirely different. It takes so much longer to get anything done, buy anything, have extra keys made or get something fixed, or pack the car. Their whole attitude is different and you'd think the "Xmas rush" might stimulate them a little, but not a chance [Roy Stryker Papers, I].

After her visit to North Carolina, Marion wrote about the locale and the people from her post in Columbia, South Carolina, on December 25, 1938.

> You should see all these Southern towns, decked out fit to kill, with more lights and decorations and junk than you could find in the 5th Avenue big 5 & 10 cent store. The houses too. But ... all the fire crackers, everywhere, all the time, day & nite.
> Especially every time I'm ready to check the camera. I jump like I'd been shot, time after time. Can't get used to it, especially if I'm concentrating on something. I wish that they'd celebrate and have a decent meal in one of the restaurants, just for a change....
> So far I've been mostly dashing around from one tenant purchase farm to another, with one idiot or another (in their own way, of course), and from cancer to syphilis — my malaria jobs haven't come thru yet. Today I hoped to get some interesting places & people, but spent the whole morning waiting around for Mr. D..., who finally was ready to leave here with me at noon and *then* we had to pick up his wife and drag her along, and spent the remaining couple of hours mostly admiring holly trees, etc. The days are so short now that I get impatient. This afternoon it got very cloudy, I'm hoping it won't last and will be clear again tomorrow so that I can get some of the same, & also do a little color work [Roy Stryker Papers, I].

On July 5, 1939, Marion wrote again to Roy on her way from Savannah to New York:

> The P.H. [Public Health] jobs are cleaned up as well as possible. They certainly are a pain in the neck, and I don't mean neck either. I still haven't recovered from the mass of Savannah mosquito and red bug bites I got. The ... mosquitoes we were trying to photograph in the insectary wouldn't feed off anyone else so I had to pose and the next morning my arm was so swollen and blue I couldn't use it. I was actually sick from it, among other things, for days.
> No need to tell you I'll be glad to get back — if only to get rid of my athlete's foot — no it's really not bad, and at least not as *extensive* as S...'s was (according to Arthur's report to me last fall) — if S... makes any complaints about these jobs we'll just ask him how his athlete's foot is!
> I'll also be glad of a rest from the daily and eternal questions whether I'm Emily Post or Margaret Bourke-White, followed by disappointed looks — or what that "thing" around my neck is, and how I ever learned to be a photographer, if I'm all alone, not frightened and if my mother doesn't worry about me, and *how* I find my way. In general, I'm most tired of the strain of continually adjusting to new people, making conversation, getting acquainted, being polite and diplomatic when necessary.
> In particular I'm sick of people telling me that

the cabin or room costs the same for one as it does for two, of listening to people, or the "call" girl make love in the adjoining room. Or of hearing every one's bath room habits, hangovers, and fights thru the ventilator. And even the sight of hotel bedroom furniture, the feel of clean sheets, the nuisance of digging into the bottom of a suitcase, of choosing a restaurant and food to eat.

I'm not going to try to do textile towns on the way up — it's absolutely the wrong time of year, much too pretty and everything covered with much trees and shrubbery and gardens, etc. And it can't be rushed thru too fast... [Roy Stryker Papers, I].

On October 2, 1939, Marion had comments about North Carolina for Roy Stryker, her employer.

I'm afraid I was an unwanted child these days in C.H. [Chapel Hill]. The beginning of the school term — they all teach, too— trying to get students settled, etc., their offices and laboratories temporarily arranged and organized until their new building is finished — all requires much time now.... Mrs. Hagood [author of the 1939 book *Mothers of the South*] had an awful cold, a sick child (daughter) and was trying to rush the proof reading of her book which is to be published very soon. She went out with me one day and we came across a very interesting settlement of negro [sic] owners with well equipped large farms, some of the "grown" children going to college, etc. We want to do much more photography around there and Dr. Odum was particularly interested and may set up a special project to concentrate and work on just that group. At least spend a good deal more time and make a more thorough study of that situation.

Didn't see a great deal of Miss Herring [author of *The Passing of the Mill Village*, 1949] what little time we were out together, was consumed mostly by our efforts to get the car out of the mud — got on a new road right after a heavy rain. I liked her, and am inclined to think she may work out better than Mrs. Hagood in spite of certain characteristics. She's surprisingly good with people and in talking with them knows their lingo *so* well — doesn't interfere and is patient. When I return, it will be possible to arrange for several of their graduate students to go around with me, take notes, etc....

I think it a good place for us to try to work on the use of photography in social research. Good territory because it has several aspects—from the very rural farm land and crops all the way thru the processing and industry. A variety of types of land and terrain, crops and industries. We will be able to get some things which we ordinarily might not feel justified or able to go into.

Here it ties into the whole picture and we still have their cooperation and help.

All the families I spoke to seemed very friendly, quite reasonable about being photographed and working with us. Some of them both work in the mills and run and tend a farm at the same time. None of it is very dramatic or startling or stark. Not easy to do. The country in particular seems sort of straggly, not definitely one thing or another. There was very little activity of any kind going on anywhere while I was there. Mostly due to the closing down of the tobacco markets and auctions.... Everything was stopped at home, and there was no money to do anything, go anywhere, not even to town on Saturday. (I was held up for a long time in a rural country — couldn't get gas because I couldn't get anyone or any store to change a $10 bill — [sic].)

In that section of No. Car. there isn't as much preparation for winter as in New England. Canning time comes just when they're busiest in the tobacco crop and all hands are needed in the fields, topping and stripping tobacco, etc. What little they do was finished by the time I got there.

Marion sometimes found it difficult to photograph Southerners and to empathize with them. Her January 12, 1939, letter about her trip from North Carolina to Columbia, South Carolina, to Florida read:

During those few short days in that part of the swampy lowlands, I found most of the people very suspicious, quite unfriendly. It was practically impossible to do anything about it, especially because of the cold weather. To them very cold and unusually windy. They just get in their huts or shacks, and build a little fire, and close the wooden window and door and hug their arms close to them, waiting till it gets warm again. And they won't let a stranger inside. Often they wouldn't even let me photograph the outside of the house. I tried every different line I could think of. And carried small bribes and food along with me. Along the bigger roads, they were very commercialized — immediately asked for money, and no nickels or dimes, or food either, real money. And, even then they'd just stand up in front like stiffs and not move until you snapped it and left. Well — it's worth doing and I now know a lot of roads and places not to go up, and a few I'd like to go back to.... Most of the people who would talk at all, said more or less the same thing — that they didn't like for us strangers to come bothering around because they mostly played "dirty tricks" on them or brought bad luck. They never would say specifically what or how, but several said got things "tookin' from them"—but what? They haven't got anything! And many times, a neighbor or relative from nearby, who had seen the car stop, would come over—I thought only out of curiosity—but they said whenever a strange car or person comes by and stops "too long" they come around to see if their friends needs any help—"that's the onliest ways we could get along." "We don't ask for nothin' and times is hard but as long as we're not abothered none we're satisfied." Some said they didn't understand why I was riding around in that kind of country and roads all alone: A couple thought I was a gypsy—(maybe others did too) because my hair was so "long and heavy" and I had a bandanna-scarf on my head and bright colored dress and coat. All of which I remedied immediately, but it didn't seem to help. All the things in the car seemed to awe them, too.... Suddenly, when I was going quite fast on a not too wide road, the rubber casing on one of my tires (a new one) just ripped almost completely off and for a couple of seconds, it sounded and looked as if me and my little Leica and ... Plymouth full of all that junk were going straight, or rather cockeyed, to.... But the car finally decided to stay right end up and on the road and we got stopped. It was worse than any blowout I've ever had, and almost caused a very serious accident with another car. For once I was very lucky [Roy Stryker Papers, I].

Stryker responded on January 13, 1939, to Marion's letter.

What a ... of a time you are having! I am certainly glad that your mix-up with the bad tire didn't end more disastrously. It is particularly upsetting to know that this happened with a practically brand-new tire. Those of us who drive on old, slick tires can expect such things, but with new material, you feel safe.

I am glad that you have now learned that you can't depend on the wiles of femininity when you are in the wilds of the South. Colorful bandannas and brightly colored dresses, etc. aren't part of our photographers' equipment. The closer you keep to what the great back-country recognizes as the normal dress for women, the better you are going to succeed as a photographer.... I know this will probably make you mad, but I can tell you another thing—that slacks aren't part of your attire when you are in the back-country. You are a woman, and "a woman," and "a woman can't never be a man"! [Roy Stryker Papers, I].

**Marriage.** Marion married Lee Wolcott, a government official, in 1941, reared four children, and traveled with her husband to Virginia, New Mexico, Iran, and California. Marion Post Wolcott died in Santa Barbara in 1990 (Rosenblum, p. 326).

**Technique.** Marion Post Wolcott often made her photographs from a distance of from 10 to 12 feet. This aspect of her art can be observed in the photograph of the child with symptoms of rickets, the women making molasses, and African American children walking home from school.

**Awards.** Before her death in California on November 24, 1990, Marion exhibited yearly—except for 1989—in individual exhibits. Her awards include the Dorothea Lange Award in 1986; the Lifetime Achievement Award, the California Museum of Photography, Riverside, California, 1990; the Lifetime Achievement Award, Society of Photographic Educators, 1991; and the 1990 Sprague Award from the National Press Photographers' Association.

## VII. John Vachon (1914–1975)

Vachon was born in Minnesota in 1914. After his wife Penny died, Vachon had responsibility for their three children: Brian, Ann, and Gale. He later married Francoise Fourestier, and they had two children: Christine and Michael.

**Vachon and the Farm Security Administration.** The Farm Security Administration hired Vachon as a messenger in 1936–1937. Later during his employment (1937) he began to write captions on, mount, and file the photographs by such federal photographers as Walker Evans, Dorothea Lange, Ben Shahn, and Carl Mydans ("John Vachon" in *Walsh*, p. 1).

Vachon said that as he worked with the files, he "became captivated by the images."

About that time Roy Stryker decided he would like to mold a photographer in his own image. He put a camera in my hand, breathed upon me, and told me to see what I could do (but only on weekends, of course) ["John Vachon" in *Walsh*, p. 2].

Roy Stryker, Walker Evans, and Arthur Rothstein trained him well. He soon became a junior photographer. After traveling with

Rothstein, he at last took his first solo trip as a photographer.

**Vachon and North Carolina.** Vachon visited the State of North Carolina in April of 1938. He was aware of social conditions and documented them. On the courthouse lawn in Halifax County he photographed drinking fountains labeled "colored" and "white." He photographed Nat Williamson, the first African American to benefit from programs of the federal government. His photographs of North Carolina include a Southern home and the sign outside a fish market.

**Office of War Information (OWI) and other employment.** Vachon went with Stryker to the Office of War Information in 1942–43 and to Standard Oil Company in 1943. He served on the *Jersey Standard* from 1945 to 1947.

In 1947 Vachon went to *Life*. Vachon worked one year as staff photographer with *Life* before going to *Look* (1948–1971). In 1968 Vachon worked with Stryker and Rothstein to produce the book *Just Before the War*. His next work was as a freelance photographer from 1971 until 1975; in 1973 he was the recipient of the Guggenheim Fellowship (Walsh, pp. 179–180). In 1975 John Vachon served as Visiting Lecturer of Photography, Minneapolis Art Institute.

**Lasting memories.** John Vachon's death came on April 20, 1975, in New York. This was 10 days after the death of his friend and federal photographer Walker Evans.

The New York Public Library, the Museum of Modern Art in New York, the George Eastman House in Rochester, and the Library of Congress in Washington — to name only a few repositories — hold his collections (Walsh, pp. 179–180).

## VIII. Jack Delano (1914–1997)

Delano had been born Jack Ovcharov in Kiev, Russia, in 1914. He received his education at the Settlement Music School in Philadelphia from 1925 to 1933. Delano attended the Pennsylvania Academy of Fine Arts until 1937 (Walsh, pp. 189–190). While traveling in Europe in 1936–37, he took his first photographs.

**Work as a federal photographer, particularly in North Carolina.** In 1937 Delano went to work with the federal government and remained there until 1939 (Walsh, pp. 189–190). He made many of his photographs of North Carolina in 1940 and 1941. He shows a wide array of people in a variety of roles. Delano's many photographs of the migratory workers in Carolina depict the complete story of the migrants—from their arrival until their departure. He captured the entire institution of workers in the Belcross area of the state. He shows the young and old; the family groups; the terrain; the shacks, the sleeping accommodations, the eating facilities; and the work.

In 1940 Delano married Irene Esser, and they had two children. He was serving as a freelance photographer at the time. On May 6, 1940, he returned to the federal staff of Roy Stryker ("Letter from Stryker to Delano," 3-28-30, Roy Stryker Papers, I).

After he left North Carolina (July 2, 1940) and his work with the migrants, Delano and his wife wrote to Stryker on March 28, 1941, from South Carolina. He described their reactions to the South and Southerners.

> Haya! This is greetings from two would-be southerners. What a place the "south" is—it's got us ga-ga but we like it....
> 
> Both Irene and I are finding it pretty easy to get along with people down here and to get accustomed to Southern ways. Our technique of not trying to be southerners but acting like naive Yankees seems to work quite well and people become friendly out of sheer sympathy for our ignorance.... Although we wouldn't like to spend the rest of our lives here, what we have seen of the South so far fascinates us and I sure hope to be able to do some intensive work here. This sure seems like the most tortured, primitive, poverty stricken (economically and socially) and wasted area I've ever seen. Yet the potentialities are so great that one doesn't leave disgusted with it but feels rather that the South must come out of it even tho it has so many strikes against it... [Roy Stryker Papers, I].

Delano's comments about the University of North Carolina were apparent in the letter: "Incidentally — on relationship with the university: I've found it a great help" (Roy Stryker Papers, I).

**Delano, the military, Puerto Rico, and other professions.** In 1943 Delano began serving with the United States Army Corps of Engineers. In 1946 he received his discharge with the rank of captain, moved to Puerto Rico, and served as photographer for the Puerto Rican Government. He became Director of Motion Picture Services (1947–1953); an independent film maker (1953–1957); Director of Programming for Puerto Rican Educational Television (1957–1964); General Manager of the Puerto Rican Government Radio and Television Service; an independent photographer, filmmaker, book illustrator, and graphics consultant; and a music teacher (1969–1979) (Walsh, pp. 189–190).

**Memorial to Delano.** Delano died in 1997 as an octogenarian. The Library of Congress, the New York Public Library, the George Eastman House, the University of Kentucky, and the Institute of Puerto Rican Culture in San Juan house his works (Walsh, pp. 189–190).

## VIII. Summary

In summary, the works of the eight federal photographers—Arthur Rothstein, Carl Mydans, Ben Shahn, Dorothea Lange, Walker Evans, Marion Post Wolcott, John Vachon, and John Delano—who came to North Carolina during the Great Depression remain priceless. They form a record of the state and its people during an important decade in the nation's past—the decade of the Great Depression.

# Appendix II

# Roy Stryker (1903–1975) and His Work with the Federal Government

Roy Stryker was born on November 5, 1893, in Great Bend, Kansas. He spent his early years on a farm in Montrose, Colorado, and served in the infantry in World War I. Stryker studied economics at Columbia University. At the request of Rexford Tugwell, his mentor, he remained at Columbia to teach.

**Stryker's interest in photography begins.** Tugwell was preparing a book titled *American Economic Life*; he gave Stryker a choice of illustrating the book for pay or of serving as joint author. Stryker selected the option of becoming a joint author (Hurley, p. 12).

It was during this period that Stryker worked with selecting photographs for the upcoming book; during this process he became familiar with the work of photographers of the time. He found that most contemporary photographers were not depicting social movements or economic problems. They were, instead, searching for "abstract beauty" (Hurley, p. 13). Stryker found two notable exceptions: Lewis Hine and Jacob August Riis.

**Lewis Hine.** Lewis Hine advertised as a social photographer offering "graphic representation of conditions and methods of work" (Stange, p. 54). His pictures became a part of many exhibits, reports, folders, magazines, newspaper articles, and lantern slides of the time. (An example of his work is in Chapter Two.)

The Director of the National Child Labor Committee described Hine in 1929 as "the first person to focus the camera intelligently, sympathetically, and effectively on social work problems" (Stange, p. 66). The Director was adamant that before Hine, there was no emotional response or emotional recognition (Stange, p. 66).

**Jacob Riis.** Jacob Riis (1849–1914), the second economic-sociological photographer that Stryker recognized, was the author and photographer of *Official Images*. Riis's favorite way of presenting his documentary photographs was through a narrative to accompany his lantern show. Stryker studied both Riis and Hine in detail (Hurley, p. 13).

Stryker found that social problems were prominent in the 1920s but the camera was not often being used to depict them. Stryker and Tugwell finally ended up using Hine's work for almost a fourth of the more than 200 illustrations in *American Economic Life* (Hurley, p.13).

**From Columbia to Washington and back again.** In the 1930s Stryker served as an instructor in economics with Tugwell. Tugwell, however, soon became a member of Roosevelt's "Brain Trust"; he left Columbia University for Washington in 1933 when he received the appointment as Assistant Secretary of Agriculture. Tugwell drew many Columbia students with him to the nation's capital. During the summer of 1934, in fact, Stryker took a part-time job with the Information Division of the Agricultural Adjustment Administration (AAA). Here Stryker found a wealth of photographs maintained by the Department of Agriculture. Stryker was intrigued.

In the fall of 1934 Stryker returned to his teaching job at Columbia, but he also began compiling a picture book on agriculture of the period. He hired former student Arthur Rothstein to help him with the work (Hurley, pp. 26–27).

**Tugwell and the Resettlement Administration.** Tugwell believed that the emergency relief measures prior to 1934 had not helped America's rural residents—the poorest residents in the nation. Tugwell and others helped convince Roosevelt to form the Resettlement Administration (RA), an independent agency with Tugwell as administrator. Because Tugwell had served previously as United States Assistant Secretary of Agriculture, the Resettlement Administration had a tie with the Department of Agriculture.

The Resettlement Administration offered grants and loans to small farmers and tenants for "rehabilitation purposes"; also, as the name implies, the Resettlement Administration resettled and assisted the poorest farmers. In addition, the RA organized rural cooperatives and constructed greenbelt towns, which were actually three communities in the suburbs meant to serve as models for the rest of the nation (Fleischhauer, pp. 2–3).

**Stryker and the Resettlement Administration.** Tugwell called on Stryker again, and in July of 1935 Roy Stryker took the position as Chief of the Information Division of the Resettlement Administration. The purpose of this division was "to prepare finished reports by a battery of economists, sociologists, statisticians, photographers, and other specialists. In fact, it produced and maintained a file of still photographs and supplied copies of the pictures for news releases, put out a variety of internal and external publications, and prepared a wide range of exhibits" (Fleischhauer, p. 3).

**The Department of Agriculture and the Farm Security Administration.** In December of 1936 the Resettlement Administration became a part of the Department of Agriculture. At this point Tugwell resigned, but his hopes of help for the tenant farmers soon came into being. The Bankhead-Jones Farm Tenant Act became law about six months later. The purpose of the Bankhead-Jones Farm Tenant Act was to aid the tenant farmers about whom Tugwell had long been concerned. Those farmers who participated had their average annual income increased to $538 from $375 (or less).

After its change to the Department of Agriculture, the Resettlement Administration became the Farm Security Administration (FSA). Stryker continued in his section which was now called the Historical Section, not the Information Division. While Stryker headed the division, he had varying numbers—depending on the budget—of photographers working for him. (Interestingly enough, however, Stryker would never hire Hine.) Stryker often gave the photographers (who totaled about 20 over an 8-year period) specific instructions, but he also told them to "photograph what caught their interest, even if it had no direct connection to the agency or its mandate." Stryker "envisioned a pictorial record of America" (Fleischhauer, p. 5). During a five-month period in 1936 Stryker distributed 965 pictures for publication. They were used in *Time, Fortune, Today, Literary Digest,* and *Business Week.* Two of his exhibits appeared at the Democratic National Convention of 1936 and the Museum of Modern Art. By 1940 the Historical Section was distributing 1,406 photographs per month (Stange, p. 108).

**Organizing the photographs.** Organizing and filing the tremendous number of photographs required much planning. John Vachon, a federal employee who would later photograph North Carolina, had worked hard to organize the photographs. The system he used was to try to keep the files in a series as the photographs were taken; for instance, he placed together all of a photographer's pictures done at one time on one subject (for instance, all photos done on Hall County, Texas). Stryker's section began to provide more guidance by increasing the descriptive phrases on the file. In 1942 Paul Vanderbilt became a part of the organization. He began to reorganize the file so that one could locate the photographs also by subject. There is one collection for the original lots; there are 1,580 lots by states with about 49 photographs in each lot. Then Vanderbilt developed a vertical file classification system with 88,000 prints. On the back of each print is a lot number which Vanderbilt called the "bridge" between the files (Fleischhauer, p. 53). The collection of 130,000 photographs was in good hands with Paul Vanderbilt, but there was another danger (Hurley, pp. 166–168). Would the government destroy the files?

**The Office of War Information.** With the coming of World War II, the government tried to change the direction of Stryker's section. A budget reduction occurred in 1942. The Farm Security Administration struggled. Stryker and Will Alexander, head of the Farm Security Administration, decided that this was no longer the best place for photographic documentation. A logical location would be the Office of War Information (OWI). Associate Director Milton Eisenhower established within the OWI a Bureau of Publications and Graphics, directed by Stryker. With him, Stryker brought his files and his photographers.

At the OWI Stryker did not have a great deal of administrative freedom. Stryker wrote Lange that his position was not "editorial director" but "administrative operator"; he saw the organization now as a service where he hunted photographs, ran the lab, and maintained files (Stange, p. 133).

**Protecting the photograph collection.** Stryker did manage, however, to incorporate the News Bureau file, formerly the Division of Information, into his own files. In July of 1943 Stryker made plans to protect these files by writing directly to Jonathan Daniels, administrative assistant to the President.

The 130,000 photographs in this office contained the record of the war's impact on the domestic scene—the small town, the farm and the people—and the Administration's record during the 1930s of the land, the efforts of the RA and the FSA, and other valuable pictographic information. These images were in one place.

Stryker considered the oldest pictures to be as valuable as the most recent to the Office of War Information—if the Office were to tell completely both here and abroad the story of America at war. Stryker feared that this coverage, conceived and produced as an unbroken continuity, was in danger of being dispersed to various locations.

The nation's preoccupation with the war, in Stryker's opinion, threatened the preservation of current and past materials. To Stryker, the dismemberment of the files would be fatal for a live, active record. He believed that out of America at peace grew the strength of America at war. He viewed the nation's prewar soil and people as the same soil and people that were helping to fight the war.

Stryker believed it was possible to preserve the record intact and still make it available to the OWI and other war agencies for current use. He believed by transferring the custody of the file to the Library of Congress with instructions to place it on loan to the OWI for the duration of the war, the records could be kept intact and safe. This transfer would not mean additional expense to the Library, would preserve the whole record, and would not hinder proper use by the Office of War Information (Hurley, p. 170).

Daniels agreed with Stryker. Stryker began to prepare to change his place of employment and to ensure the transfer of the federal images.

**A summary of Stryker's work with the federal government.** Between 1935 and 1943 Roy Emerson Stryker directed the photographic section of the federal government. Through these eight years the purpose of the photographic section remained the same: to document the nation through photography. The section moved through three government agencies during its existence. First, Stryker's section worked as a part of the Resettlement Administration in 1935. In 1937 the section (still headed by Stryker) became a part of a second agency: the Farm Security Administration; during the winter of 1937–1938 only Russell Lee, Arthur Rothstein, and Stryker worked in the photographic section of the RA. In 1942 Stryker and his section became a part of the third agency: the Domestic Operations Branch of the Office of War Information.

In July of 1943 Stryker began to make arrangements for the preservation of the photographic files and to prepare for his future and that of his staff. The Library of Congress agreed to Stryker's request that the Library assume custody of his files. In September Stryker—along with several of the section's photographers—left the federal government but continued their photographic documentation of the nation through a new source: Standard Oil Company.

Fewer than twenty photographers were involved with Stryker and his dreams through the years. Some worked with him only a few months, but some stayed for five or six years. Women like the renowned Dorothea Lange and Marion Post Wolcott worked with Stryker, as did such noted photographers as Walker Evans, Arthur Rothstein, Jack Delano, Carl Mydans, John Vachon, and Ben Shahn. (All of these photographers recorded images from North Carolina.)

Whoever worked with him, Stryker directed their work to make sure the documentation was historically and sociologically sound, yet Stryker also gave them the freedom to photograph that which they found aesthetically pleasing. Stryker never wanted to compromise the standards of these camera artists. For these historical, sociological, and aesthetic reasons the immense collection is priceless today (Fleischhauer, p. vii–xi, 1–14).

**Stryker and Standard Oil.** In September of 1943 Stryker resigned from the OWI. Stryker (and those photographers he took with him) continued the American photographic survey at Standard Oil Company (Fleischhauer, pp. 5–7). At Standard Oil, Stryker had much more administrative control over the documentary photographs than at the OWI. Stryker planned on a group of 25,000 photographs, but by the time the end of the project in 1949, he had amassed 68,000 photographs. (Stange, p. 142). This collection "was the largest photographic documentation project ever undertaken in America by anyone other than the federal government" ("The Photographers: Roy E. Stryker").

**From Standard Oil to Pittsburgh Photographic Library to Jones & McLaughlin Steel.** Stryker left Standard Oil in 1950—after seven years—to become Director of the Pittsburgh Photographic Library (Stange, p. 145). Stryker resigned from there in 1952, but he was involved in the transfer of the materials. In 1960 the collection moved from Pittsburgh to the Carnegie Library of Pittsburgh.

Stryker served Jones & McLaughlin Steel Corporation on a documentation project. He continued to accept consulting jobs and conduct seminars at the University of Missouri. In the 1960s he returned to the West. Stryker died on September 27, 1975 ("The Photographers: Roy E. Stryker").

**Stryker and his federal photographs.** After Stryker's death, the irreplaceable federal photographic files became a part of the Library of Congress in 1944 and 1946. They remain there even today for the use of patrons interested in reconstructing this time in history.

**The federal images.** Tugwell in 1965 described the federal photographs as an "art form." By using documentary photographs, the FSA helped make reform "legitimate" (Stange, p. 130).

Jack F. Hurley, a photography historian, states that

> ...[t]he photographs that his [Stryker's] staff had taken had begun a new trend in American aesthetics. They had taught that a picture could be beautiful and still possess a social conscience. The pictures had helped to galvanize public opinion behind programs to aid the rural poor

(at least for awhile), and they had recorded the texture and "feel" of life in the 1930s in a way that no other project had done [Hurley, p. 173].

Walker Evans referred to the collection to which he had contributed as

> ...[a] pure record and not propaganda. The value and, if you like, even the propaganda value for the government lies in the record itself which in the long run will prove an intelligent and far-sighted thing to have done. NO POLITICS whatever [Fleischhauer, p. 61].

Maren Stange — whose work Daniel and others call a "revolutionist analysis" (Daniel, *Official Images*, p. xi) — claims the files are lacking the

> ...resolution of art and the particularity of documentary. The project stands today as a compelling and enduring monument to the cultural prestige of liberal reformers, but the acclaim it is granted reveals the extent to which central institutions and communications modes have diminished the authority of artistic and political perceptions and installed in their place the devalued currency of instrumental discourse [Stange, pp. 130–131].

In 1973 Stryker referred to his files as a "serious tool of communication" (Fleischhauer, p. 9). Lawrence Levine seems to agree. He reminds the "reader" of the photographs to remember that human beings adapt to forces and frequently rise above them by actively participating. In other words, an individual can be both reactive and proactive. Statistics alone may not tell the reader enough. Photographs can help to tell the whole story (Fleischhauer, p. 15).

**Federal photographs in *North Carolina During the Great Depression: A Documentary Portrait of a Decade*.** The photographs collected and included in *North Carolina During the Great Depression: A Documentary Portrait of a Decade* can also help to tell the whole story — the story of the wreck of people's life as well as their recreation; their pleasures and their pains; their despair and their dignity; their victories and their victims. Because Stryker included many kinds of photographs, the serious student has evidence of the soundness of his collection and of the complexity of the subjects — especially the North Carolinians who were poor but proud.

One can interpret the photographs, then, and supplement them with other evidence. The photographs are the "creators" and the "creation" of the Great Depression. They — like the recreational movies of the time — are not a means of escapism but a way of reaffirming traditional values (Fleischhauer, p. 24).

# *Bibliography*

"1930s Bestsellers." (No author) http://www.caderbooks.com/best30.html

"About the NAACP." http://www.naacp.org/about.asp

"Automotive History 101." http://www.autoshop-online.com/auto101/histtext.html

Badger, Anthony. *Prosperity Road.* Chapel Hill, North Carolina: University of North Carolina Press, 1980.

Bamberger, Bill and Cathy N. Davidson. *Closing: The Life and Death of an American Factory.* New York: W. W. Norton and the Center for Documentary Studies, 1998.

Barabba, Vincent P., Director of Census. *Historical Statistics of the United States: 1785–1945.* Washington, D.C.: U.S. Government Printing Office, 1975.

Barefoot, Pamela. *Mules and Memories.* Winston-Salem, North Carolina: John F. Blair, 1978.

Barnwell, Mildred Gwin. *Faces We See.* Gastonia, North Carolina: Southern Combed Yarn Spinners Association, 1939.

Beer, George Louis. *The Origins of the British Colonial System.* Gloucester, Mass: Peter Smith, 1959.

Bell, John L., Jr. *Hard Times: Beginnings of the Great Depression in North Carolina, 1929–1933.* Raleigh: North Carolina Department of Cultural Resources, Division of Archives and History, 1982.

"Ben Shahn." *Encyclopedia of World Biography.* 2nd edition. Gale Research, 1998. www.galenet.com

Berolzheimer, Ruth. *The Quick Dinners for the Woman in a Hurry Cook Book.* Chicago: Consolidated Book Publishers, 1942.

Best, Selma Philbeck. Oral Interview on February 26, 2001.

Biggerstaff, Frances. Oral Interview on February 26, 2001.

Biggerstaff, Virginia. "Retirement of Miss Cleo Burns as Teacher: Ends Life Time of Service in Local Schools." *Forest City Courier*, May 28, 1953.

Biles, Roger. *The South and the New Deal.* Lexington, Kentucky: University of Kentucky Press, 1994.

Billings, Henry. *All Down the Valley.* New York: The Viking Press, 1952.

Bishir, Catherine W., Michael T. Southern, and Jennifer F. Martin. *A Guide to the Architecture of Western North Carolina.* Chapel Hill: University of North Carolina, 1999.

Bishop, Mary. *Billy Graham: The Man and His Ministry.* New York: Grosset and Dunlap, 1978.

Blanton, Mae (Mrs. Ed). Oral Interview, March 12, 2001.

Botkin, B. A. *A Treasury of Southern Folklore.* New York: Bonanza Books, 1949.

*Boxcar Bertha.* Hollywood, California: Metro Goldwyn Mayer and United Artists Studio, 1972. (Starring Barbara Hershey and David Carradine).

Boyd, Rosamonde Ramsey. Oral Interview, August 15, 1988.

Brandon, Kitty. "White Closing Doors February 15 after 112 Years." *Mebane Enterprise.* (February 3, 1993), pp. 1–2.

Brewster, Paul G. and others. *North Carolina Folklore*, Vol. I. Durham, North Carolina: Duke University Press, 1961.

"Briarhoppers Publicity Sheet." Courtesy of Dwight Moody.

Brokaw, Tom. *Greatest Generation.* New York: Random House, 1998.

Brooks, John. Oral Interview on March 13, 2001.

Bryon (No first name). "The New Deal Program." http://web54.sd54.k12.il.us/schools/keller/newdeal/chats.htm

Burns, Nell. Oral Interview, September 1, 1996.

Burns, Robert Ewart. "My Trip to the Fair." A journal entry.

Burns, Robert Ewart. Oral Interview, 1983.

Byerly, Victoria. *Hard Times Cotton Mill Girls*. Ithaca, New York: Cornell University, 1986.

Bynum, William B. and others. *The Heritage of Rutherford County, North Carolina, Volume I, 1984*. Winston-Salem, North Carolina: Genealogical Society of Old Tryon County, 1984.

Caldwell, Erskine. *Tobacco Road*. New York: Grosset and Dunlap, 1937.

Campbell, Carlos. *Birth of a National Park in the Great Smoky Mountains*. Knoxville, Tennessee: University of Tennessee Press, 1960.

Carpenter, Lucille. Oral Interview, February 24, 2001.

Carpenter, Walda. Oral Interview, February 23, 2001.

Center for Disease Control and Prevention, "Fact Sheet: Hookworm Infection." http://www.cdc.gov/ncidod/dpd/parasites/hookworm/factsht_hookworm.htm

Chase, R. (1943). *The Jack Tales*. Boston: Houghton-Mifflin.

"Chick Hatchery." *Forest City Courier*, A-1, February 6, 1930.

Chitwood, Oliver Perry, Frank Lawrence Owsley, and H. C. Nixon. *The United States from Colony to World Power*. New York: D. Van Nostrand Company, 1953.

"Cioppino, Chicken Divan, Fake Food Were Big in '30's." http://www.dispatch.com/news/newsfea99/century/food/rec15fod.html

"The Clarence Hamilton Poe Papers." Collection Number: MC 177. www.lib.ncsu.edu/archives/collections/html/MC0177.html

Clark, Thomas D. *Pills, Petticoats, and Plows*. Norman: University of Oklahoma Press, 1944.

*Cleveland Star*. Newspapers of the 1920's and 1930's. Cleveland Memorial Library, Shelby, North Carolina

*Cliffside Station: Duke Power Company*. Charlotte, North Carolina: Duke Power, 1947.

Coffin, Tristram P. and Hennig Cohen. *Folklore in America*. Garden City, New York: Doubleday and Company, Inc., 1966.

"Colfax Free Fair Rated Best in State." *Forest City Courier*, September 3, 1936.

Collins, Helen. Family recipe.

Colquitt, Harriet Ross. *The Savannah Cook Book*. Charleston: Colonial Publishers, 1933.

Cooper, George M., Frances Roberta Pratt, and Margaret Jarman Hagood. "Four Years of Contraception as a Public Health Service in North Carolina," *American Journal of Public Health* (December, 1941), 1248–1252.

Corbitt, David Leroy. *Addresses, Letters and Papers of John Christoph Blucher Ehringhaus, Governor of North Carolina, 1933–1937*. Raleigh: Council of State, 1950.

Corbitt, David Leroy. *Addresses, Letters and Papers of Clyde Roark Hoey, Governor of North Carolina, 1937–1941*. Raleigh: Council of State, 1944.

Cornwell, Patricia Daniels. *A Time for Remembering*. San Francisco: Harper and Row, 1985.

Curtis, Donnis. Oral Interview, February 26, 2001.

Curtis, James. *Mind's Eye, Mind's Truth*. Philadelphia: Temple University Press, 1989.

Cyber Palate LLC. "Soul Food." http://www.cuisinenet.com/glossary/soul.html

Daniel, Pete. *Breaking the Land: The Transformation of Cotton, Tobacco, and Rice Cultures Since 1880*. Urbana: University of Illinois Press, 1985.

Daniel, Pete, Merry Foresta, Maren Stange, and Sally Stein. *Official Images: New Deal Photography*. Washington, D.C.: Smithsonian, 1987.

Davis, Anita Price. *Children's Literature Essentials*. Boston: American Press, 2000.

Davis, Anita Price and Marla J. Selvidge. *Focus on Women*. Huntington Beach, California: Teacher Created Materials, 1995.

Davis, Buren. Oral Interview, September 1, 1996.

Davis, Getty Mrs. Oral Interview, September, 28, 1996.

Davis, Robert. Oral Interview, September 1, 1996.

Dawson, Sue. "Depression Forced Cooks to Economize Creatively." http.//www.dispatch.com/food0915/rec30.html

Dodd, Donald B. *Historical Statistics of the States of the United States*. Westport, Connecticut: Greenwood Press, 1993.

Dodd, Donald B. and Wynelle S. Dodd. *Historical Statistics of the South: 1790–1970*. University of Alabama Press, 1973.

Donnermeyer, Joseph F. "Crime and Violence in Rural Communities." www.ncrel.org/sdrs/areas/issues/envrnmnt/drugfree/v1donner.htm

Donovan, Frank Robert. *Wheels for a Nation*. New York: Crowell, 1965.

Draper, Theodore. "Gastonia Revisited," *Social Research*, Volume 38 (Spring, 1971), pp. 3–29.

"Editorial." *The Forest City Courier*. November 7, 1929, editorial page.

"Ellenboro Center of State's Potato Producing Area," *Forest City Courier*, September 3, 1936, C 1–4.

"Employment and the Construction of the Greenbelt" http://otal.umd.edu/~vg/mssp96/ms09/project3.html

*Encyclopedia of Photography.* New York: Crown Publishers, Inc. (A Pound Press Book), 1984.

Evans, Sid. The State Center for Health Statistics, North Carolina Department of Health and Human Services, Raleigh, North Carolina (#919-433-4728)

Evory, Ann. *Contemporary Authors.* Vol. 6, New Revision Series. Detroit: Gale Research Company, 1995.

*Farm Journal.* December, 1931, p. 15.

Federal Writer's Project, Works Progress Administration. *North Carolina: A Guide to the Old North State.* Chapel Hill: University of North Carolina Press, 1939.

Federal Writer's Project, Works Progress Administration. *These Are Our Lives.* Chapel Hill: University of North Carolina Press, 1939.

"Fiddler's Grove: Home of the Oldest Continuous Ole Time Fiddler's Contest in North America" http://www.fiddlersgrove.com

Finch, Christopher. *The Art of Walt Disney From Mickey Mouse to the Magic Kingdom.* New York: Abradale Press and Harry A. Abrams, Inc., 1973.

"Fireside Chats of Franklin D. Roosevelt." http://www.mhree.org/fdr/fdr.html

Fisher, Andrea. *Let Us Now Praise Famous Women.* New York: Pandora, 1987.

"Five Star Library Series: Engel van Wiseman Publishing." (A series of Big Little Books).

Fleischhauer, Carl and Beverly W. Brannan. *Documenting America, 1935–1943.* Berkeley: University of California Press, 1988.

Foner, Eric and John A. Garraty. (Editors) "Model T Ford." http://www.myhistory.org/ history_files/articles/model_t_ford.html

Frady, Marshall. *Billy Graham: A Parable of American Righteousness.* Boston: Little, Brown and Company, 1979.

"Franklin Delano Roosevelt" ("Chief New Deal Agencies During Roosevelt's Administrations 1933–1945"), *Compton's Encyclopedia,* 01-01-1994. http://www.nscds.pvt.k12.il.us/ncds/us/apushit/roosevelt/newdeal.html

Gheen, Stephen Thompson. *Governor O. Max Gardner's Role in the Gastonia Labor Strike and Related Occurrences: 1929–1930.* A Thesis Presented to the Faculty of the Graduate School of Western Carolina University, August 16, 1974.

Gibbs, Jessie. Oral Interview, February 24, 2001.

Gilbreth, Frank B., Jr. and Ernestine Gilbreth Carey. *Cheaper by the Dozen.* New York: Watts, 1948.

Ginns, Patsy Moore. *Rough Weather Makes Good Timber: Carolinians Recall.* Chapel Hill: University of North Carolina Press, 1977.

Glass, Brent D. *The Textile Industry in North Carolina* Raleigh: Division of Archives and History, 1992.

Goldston, Robert. *The Great Depression.* New York: Ballantine Books, 1968.

"Great Depression: Road to Rock Bottom." Alexandria, Va: PBS Video, 1993.

Griffin, Clarence. *Essays on North Carolina History.* Forest City, North Carolina: *The Forest City Courier,* 1951.

Griffin, Clarence. *The History of Old Tryon and Rutherford Counties.* Spartanburg, S.C.: Reprint Company, Publishers, 1977.

Grim, Valerie. Oral Presentation, March 2, 1999, at Converse College, Spartanburg, SC.

Grosvenor, Vertamae. "USA Rice Recipes." http://www.ricecafe.com/scshrimp.htm

Hamel, Paul B. and Mary U. Chiltoskey. *Cherokee Plants: Their Uses — A 400 Year History.* Sylva, North Carolina: Herald Publishing, 1975.

Hamrick, Reba. Oral Interview, February 24, 2001.

Hapke, Laura. *Daughters of the Great Depression: Women, Work and Fiction in the American 1930s.* Athens, Georgia: University of Georgia Press, 1995.

Harris, Bill. "Radio Reaches Rural America: The Early Days of REA." http://www.radioremembered.org/

Heimann, Robert K. *Tobacco and Americans.* New York: McGraw-Hill, 1960.

Hemminger, Graham. "Tobacco." Penn State *Froth,* November 1915, p. 19 as quoted in Burton Stevenson's *Home Book of Quotations.* New York: Dodd, Mead and Company, 1967, and Hobbs, S. Huntington, Jr. *N.C: An Economic and Social Profile.* Chapel Hill, North Carolina: University of North Carolina Press, 1958.

Henderson, Gary. "Disease of the Poor," *Spartanburg Herald-Journal,* April 8, 2001, pp. A-1, A-6.

Henry, Philip N. and Carol M. Speas. *The Heritage of Blacks in North Carolina: Volume I, 1990.* Charlotte, North Carolina: North Carolina African-American Heritage Foundation in cooperation with the Delmar Company, 1990.

Herring, Harriet L. *Passing of the Mill Village.* Chapel Hill: University of North Carolina Press, 1949.

Herring, Harriet L. *Welfare Work in Mill Villages.* Chapel Hill: University of North Carolina Press, 1929.

High, Stanley. *Billy Graham: The Personal Story*

*of the Man, His Message, and His Mission.* New York: McGraw Hill, 1956.

Hillman, Bill. "Big Little Books." http://www.geocities.com/Hollywood/Boulevard/6643erbmot44.html

"History: The Monopoly Story" http://www.monopoly.com/history/history.htm

Hobbs, S. Huntington, Jr. *North Carolina: An Economic and Social Profile.* Chapel Hill, North Carolina: University of North Carolina Press, 1958.

Hood, Charles Newton. "How the La Rue Stakes Were Lost," in Shoemaker, J. W., Mrs., *Shoemaker's Best Selections for Reading and Recitations.* Philadelphia: The Penn Publishing Company, 1906.

Horton, W. P. (Chairman) and others on State School Commission. *Report of the State School Commission for the Scholastic Years 1938–1939 and 1939–1940.* Raleigh, North Carolina: The State School Commission, 1940.

Hunt, Louise. Oral Interview, May 25, 2001.

Hurley, F. Jack. *Portrait of a Decade: Roy Stryker and the Development of Documentary Photography in the Thirties.* Baton Rouge: Louisiana State University Press, 1972.

Ickes, Harold. *PWA: A Four-year Record of the Construction of Permnent and Useful Public Works.* Washington, D.C.: Federal Emergency Administration of Public Works, 1937.

International Center of Photography. *Encyclopedia of Photography.* New York: Crown Publishers, Inc., 1984.

"It's a Fake." *Fargo Forum,* Thursday Evening, 27 August 1936, p. 6.

James, Mertice M. and Dorothy Brown. *The Book Review Digest* (41st Annual Collection). New York: H. W. Wilson Company, 1945.

Jennings, Peter and Todd Brewster. *The Century.* New York: Doubleday, 1998.

"Joe Louis" http://www.duboislc.com/ShadesOfBlack/JoeLouis.html

"John Vachon." *Contemporary Photographers.* 3rd edition. St. James Press, 1996. www.galenet.com/servlet/BioRC/hits

Johnson, Bruce. *A History of the Grove Park Inn.* Asheville: Grove Park Inn, 1991.

Johnson, Thomas H. *The Oxford Companion to American History.* New York: Oxford University Press, 1966.

Jones, H. G., Professor Emeritus at University of North Carolina Interview/letters, 1996.

Jones, H, G. *North Carolina Illustrated: 1524–1984.* Chapel Hill: University of North Carolina Press, 1983.

Jones, T. W. Oral Interview, March 2, 2001.

Jones, Weimar. "Southern Labor and the Law," *Nation,* Volume CXXI, 1930, page 16 as cited by Tindall, George Brown. *The Emergence of the New South, 1913–1945.* No place given: Louisiana State University Press and the Littlefield Fund for Southern History of the University of Texas, 1967.

"Kay Kyser," *Compton's Encyclopedia Online,* v. 3.0. The Learning Company, 1998. http://www.comptons.com/encyclopedia/ARTICLES/0575/05764864_Q.html

"Kay Kyser, the Ol' Professor of Swing!" http://www.kaykyser.net/hits.html

Kindred, Davis. "Joe Louis' Biggest Knockout." http://www.sportingnews.com/archives/sports2000/moments/140271.html

Kirby, Jack Temple. *Rural Worlds Lost: The American South, 1920–1960.* Baton Rouge: Louisiana State University Press, 1987.

Koster, Kim. "True Blue." *Duke Magazine.* Volume 87. January–February 2001, pp. 2–7, 60.

Kraut, Alan. "Dr. Joseph Goldberger and the War on Pellagra." http://www.nih.gov/od/museum/exhibits/goldberger/full-text.html

Kronenberger, Louis. *Atlantic Brief Lives: A Biographical Companion to the Arts.* Boston: Little, Brown and Company, 1971.

Kuralt, Charles. *American Moments.* New York: Simon and Schuster, 1998.

Kuralt, Charles and Loonis McGlohon. *North Carolina Is My Home.* Charlotte, North Carolina: The East Woods Press, 1986.

Kurian, George Thomas. *Datapedia of the United States: 1790–2000.* Lanham, Maryland: Bernan Press, 1994.

Langley, Joan and Wright. *Yesterday's Asheville.* Miami, Florida: E. A. Seemann, 1975.

Lanier, Ruby J. *Blanford Barnard Dougherty, Mountain Educator.* Durham: Duke University Press, 1974.

Larkin, Margaret. "Ella May's Songs," *The Nation.* Vol. 129. October 9, 1929, pp. 382–383.

Lefler, Hugh Talmage and Albert Ray Newsome. *North Carolina: The History of a Southern State.* Chapel Hill: The University of North Carolina Press, 1954.

Lefler, Hugh Talmage and Albert Ray Newsome. *North Carolina: The History of a Southern State.* Chapel Hill: The University of North Carolina Press, 1963.

Lefler, Hugh Talmage and Albert Ray Newsome. *North Carolina: The History of a Southern State.* Chapel Hill: The University of North Carolina Press, 1973.

Le Gloahec, John. Benjamin E. Washburn Papers, 1905–(1913–1939)–1960. http://www.rockefeller.edu/archive.ctr/rf_bew.html

Leviticus 17: 10–14; 11: 4, 7–8.

Lewis, Jone Johnson. "Comstock Law." http://womenshistory.about.com/homework/tory/library/ency/blwh_comstock.htm

Lewis, Sinclair. *Cheap and Contented Labor: The Picture of a Southern Mill Town in 1929*, New York: United Textile Workers of America and Women's Trade Union League, 1929 as cited by Tindall, George Brown. *The Emergence of the New South, 1913–1945*. No place given: Louisiana State University Press and the Littlefield Fund for Southern History of the University of Texas, 1967.

"Listen, Mr. Easterner." *Fargo Forum*. Thursday Evening, August 27, 1936, p. 6.

London, H. M. *North Carolina Manual: 1939*. Raleigh: Publication of the Legislative Reference Library, 1939.

Ludlum, David M. *The American Weather Book*. Boston: Houghton Mifflin, 1982.

McArthur, W. H. Photographer, historian, architect, and retired owner of McArthur's Metal, Forest City, North Carolina, Oral Interview, August 2–4, 6, 7, 1999.

McCutcheon, Marc. *Everyday Life from Prohibition through World War II*. Cincinnati, Ohio: Writer's Digest Books, 1995.

McElvaine, Robert S. *Down and Out in the Great Depression*. Chapel Hill: The University of North Carolina Press, 1983.

McElvaine, Robert S. *The Great Depression: America, 1929–1941*. New York: Times Books, 1984.

McGlohon, Joe. "The Penderlea Homesteads" http://www.euonymus.com/index2.html

"Marion Post Wolcott." *Contemporary Photographers*. 3rd edition. St. James Press, 1996. www.galenet.com/servlet/BioRC/hits

Martin, Annette. Oral Interview, April 6, 2001.

Martin, Dan. Oral Interview, April 6, 2001.

Martin, T. W. Oral Interview, March 2, 2001.

"May," *Life*. (May, 1997), 40–46.

Maynor, Joe. (1979) *Duke Power: The First Seventy-five Years*. Charlotte, North Carolina: Delmar.

Merrill, Perry. *Roosevelt's Forest Army: A History of the Civilian Conservation Corps, 1933–1942*. Montpelier, Vermont: Perry H. Merrill, Publisher, 1981.

Mills, Kara. "History 3124: Ch. 7 — Troubled Times." http://mckenna.cses.vt.edu/hist3124/ch7.html

Mitchell, Curtis. *The Making of a Crusader*. Philadelphia: Chilton Books, 1966.

"Model T Photographs." http://www.hfmgv:org/histories/showroom/1908/photos.html. Copyright 1995–1999, Henry Ford Museum and Greenfield Village.

Monopoly Companion. "History: The Monopoly Story." http://www.monopoly.com/history/history.htm

"Mountain Dew" in "A Portrait of the Artist as a Young Man." http://www.members.nbci.com/elstongunn/good.html

"Name Bushong South's Leading Farm Teacher," *Forest City Courier*, September 3, 1936, C 1–4.

National Emergency Council. *Report on Economic Conditions of the South*. Washington, D.C.: U.S. Government Printing Office, 1938.

ncstuff. "People: Paul Eliot Green (1894–1981)." http://www.ncstu›.com/people/greenp.htm

Neely, Sharlotte. *Snowbird Cherokees*. Athens, Georgia: University of Georgia Press, 1991.

*New York Times* on the Web. "Oscars 2001: 1930–1931" http://www.nytimes.com/events/oscars/1930.html

Niven, David. *Bring on the Horses*. Downsville, Ontario, Canada: Listen for Pleasure Limited, 1975, 1980.

*North Carolina Yearbook for Home Demonstration Clubs*. Raleigh: North Carolina Home Demonstration Clubs, 1955.

Olson, Susan. "Birth Control," *The Guide to American Law*. St. Paul: West Publishing, 1983.

Opie, Iona and Peter. *The Oxford Dictionary of Nursery Rhymes*. London: Oxford University Press, 1966.

Orr, Oliver H., Jr., J. Sullivan Gibson, and Hugh T. Lefler. "North Carolina." Volume 13. *Merit Students Encyclopedia*. Old Tappan, New Jersey: Crowell-Collier Encyclopedia Corporation, 1969, pp. 458–480.

Pacher, Sara and Constance Elizabeth Richard. "Insider's Guide to the North Carolina Mountains" http://www.insiders. com/ncmths/main-annual4.htm

Parramore, Thomas C. *Carolina Quest*. Englewood Cliffs, New Jersey: Prentice-Hall, Inc., 1978.

Parramore, Thomas C. *Express Lanes and Country Roads: The Way We lived in North Carolina, 1920–1970*. Chapel Hill: University of North Carolina Press, 1983.

Parramore, Thomas C. Oral Interview, April 30, 2001.

Parsons, Benny. *Inside Track: A Photo Documentary of NASCAR Stock Car Racing*. New York: Artisan Press, 1996.

Patterson, Jim. "Grand Ole Opry Celebrates 75th birthday." http://www.cnn.com/2000/SHOWBIZ/Music/10/15/grandoleopry.ap/

Pendleton, Deborah. "The Great Depression." http://www2.ncsu/cep/ligon/am/ag/depression.

Perdue, Theda. *North Carolinians: The Indians of North Carolina*. Raleigh, North Carolina: Division of Archives and History, 1985.

"The Photographers: Roy E. Stryker" www.clpgh.org/exhibit/photog14.html
"Poe Hall." www.ncsu.edu/facilities/buildings/poe.html
"Polio History Timeline" www.pbs.org
Pollock, John. *To All Nations: The Billy Graham Story*. New York: Harper and Row, 1985.
*Portraits of the FSA Photographers*. http://leweb2.loc.gov/ammem/fsahtml/fsap3.html
Powell, William S. *North Carolina through Four Centuries*. Chapel Hill, North Carolina: University of North Carolina Press, 1989.
Pratt, Frances R. "Programs for Public Health Nurses in Birth Control Work," *American Journal of Public Health*, Volume 30 (September, 1940), pp. 1096–1098.
President's Organization on Unemployment Relief and the Committee on the Mobilization of Relief Resources. "Certainly We Will Lend a Hand." *Farm Journal*, December 1931, p. 15.
Price, Edward Rollins. Oral Interview, April 8, 2001.
Price, Plato Rollins. Resident of Spruce Pine, North Carolina; Hollis, North Carolina; and Cleveland County, North Carolina (1887–1976).
"Prize Winning Colfax Community Exhibit." *Forest City Courier*, September 3, 1936, C 1–4.
Raper, Arthur Franklin and Ira DeA. Reid. *Sharecroppers All*. Chapel Hill: The University of North Carolina Press, 1941.
"Records of the Farmers Home Administration." http://www.nara.gov/guide/rg096.html
Redhawk, William. "Cooking with Acorns." http://siouxme.com/acorn.html
Reed, James. *From Private Vice to Public Virtue*. New York: Basic Books, 1978.
Reitman, Ben. *Boxcar Bertha*. Los Angeles: Amok Publishing Company, 1988.
Retro. "Old Maid: Retro Style." http://www.retroactive.com/hawaii/oldmaid1.html
"Rhema: Wilderness Breads." http://home.aol.com/keninga/wildwheat/wildwhea.htm
Rittner, D. "Great Depression Decal." http:/egi.ebay.com/aw-cgi/Ebay[SAPI.dll/View Item&item.
Robbins, Wanda. Oral Interview, April 1, 2001.
Roosevelt, Franklin. *The Public Papers and Addresses of Franklin D. Roosevelt*. Volumes 1–5. New York: Random House, 1938.
"Roosevelt's New Deal." http:// www.libarts.sfasu.edu/history/134-Unit%207B.html
Rosenblum, Naomi. *A History of Women Photographers*. New York: Abbeville Press, 1994.
Rutherford County Cooperative Extension Office, Public Records, March 12, 2001.
Salmond, John A. *Gastonia 1929: The Story of the Loray Mill Strike*. Chapel Hill: The University of North Carolina Press, 1995.
*Sears Roebuck Catalog of the Thirties*. Franklin Square, New Yorki: Nostalgia, Incorporated, 1978.
"Shelby Gets Jolt in Market Stampede," *Cleveland Star*, October 15, 1929, p. 1.
"Short History of the Model T Automobile." Ford Media Site. http://media.ford.com/article_display.cfm?article_id+860
"Six Banks of This County Closed Their Doors Tuesday." *The Rutherford County News*, February 6, 1930, p. 1.
"Six Rutherford Banks Close Their Doors This Week." *The Forest City Courier*, November 7, 1929, p. 1.
Skelton, Nancy. Oral Interview on December 1, 1996.
*Smoky Mountains Magazine* at http://smokymtns.com/dew2.htm
Stange, Maren. "Symbols of Ideal Life: Technology, Mass Media, and the FSA Photography Project," *Prospects*, 11 (1986): 81–104.
Stick, David. *The Outer Banks of North Carolina*. Chapel Hill, North Carolina: University of North Carolina Press, 1958.
Stoney, George and Judith Helfand (producer and director). *Uprising of '34*. New York: First Run/Icarrus Films, 1995.
Stryker (Roy) Papers. Series I: Correspondence, 1924–1972. Louisville, Ky.: University of Louisville Photographic Archives.
Stryker (Roy) Papers. Series II: Professional Activities, 1912–1971. Part A. Personal Papers and Awards, 1912–1969. Part B. Writings by Stryker, 1936–1963. Louisville, Ky.: University of Louisville Photographic Archives.
Tarrow, Davis. *Field to Factory*. Washington, DC: Smithsonian Institution, 1994.
Taylor, Mildred. *Let the Circle Be Unbroken*. New York: Dial, 1981.
Thomas, Katharine Elwes. *The Real Personages of Mother Goose*. New York: Lothrop, Lee and Shepard Company, 1930.
Thompson, Bertha as told to Dr. Ben L. Reitman. *Boxcar Bertha: An Autobiography*. New York: Amok Press, 1988.
Time-Life Editors. *This Fabulous Century: 1930–1940*. New York: Time-Life Books, 1969.
Tindall, George Brown. *The Emergence of the New South, 1913–1945*. No place given: Louisiana State University Press and the Littlefield Fund for Southern History of the University of Texas, 1967.
Trachtenberg, Alan. *Reading American Photographs*. New York: Hill and Wang, 1989.
Trachtenberg, Alan. "Walker Evans." *Dictionary of American Biography*. Supplement 9: 1971–1975. New York: Charles Scribner's Sons, 1994. http://galenet.com/serlet/BioRC/hits

Trelease, Jim. *Reading Aloud*. (Video) Springfield, Mass.: Reading Tree Productions, 1993.

Tsisghwanai (Traveller Bird), *The Path to Snowbird Mountain: Cherokee Legends*. New York: Farrar, Straus and Giroux, 1972, p. 4 as quoted in Sharlotte Neely, *Snowbird Cherokees*. Athens, Georgia: University of Georgia Press, 1991.

Tugwell, Rexford, Thomas Munro, and Roy E. Stryker. *American Economic Life*. New York: Harcourt, Brace, 1925.

Turner, C. E. *Personal and Community Health*. St. Louis: C. V. Mosby, 1956.

Ullman, Morris B. *Statistical Abstract of the United States: 1940*. Washington, D.C.: US Department of Commerce, 1940.

*United States Constitution, Eighteenth Amendment*.

*U.S. News and World Report*, October 19, 1992, p. 60.

Uys, Errol Lincoln. *Riding the Rails: Teenagers on the Move During the Great Depression*. New York: TV Books, 1999.

Van Noppen, Ina Woestemeyer and John J. Van Noppen. *Western North Carolina Since the Civil War*. Boone, North Carolina: Appalachian Consortium Press, 1973.

van Wiseman, Jerome; Wallace West; and President Roosevelt's Inaugural Address. *The Fighting President: The Story of Franklin D. Roosevelt*. New York: Engel van Wiseman, 1934.

Wagner, Aubrey. "Tennessee Valley Authority," Volume 18. *Merit Students Encyclopedia*. Old Tappan, New Jersey: Crowell-Collier Encyclopedia Corporation, 1969, pp. 103–104.

Waldrep, G. C., III. *Southern Workers and the Search for Community*. Urbana and Chicago: University of Illinois Press, 2000.

Walker, Melissa. *All We Knew Was to Farm*. Baltimore, Maryland: Johns Hopkins University Press, 2000.

Walker, Melissa. *Southern Women in the Twentieth Century South: A Paper Presented at the Southern Women in the Twenty-First Century Symposium*. Spartanburg, S.C.: Converse College, March 6, 2001.

Walsh, George and others. *Contemporary Photographers*. New York: St. Martin's Press, 1982.

Washburn, B. E. *As I Recall*. New York: The Rockefeller Foundation, 1960.

Washburn, Benjamin Earle. *A Country Doctor in the South Mountains*. Spindale: Spindale Press, 1944 (Third printing, 1974).

Watkins, T. H. *The Great Depression: America in the 1930s*. Boston: Little, Brown and Company, 1993.

"WBT History." http://www.wbt.com/History20.cfm

Weathers, Henry L. *Our Heritage: A History of Cleveland County*. Shelby, North Carolina: The Shelby Daily Star, 1976.

Weathers, Lee. *History of Cleveland County*. Spartanburg, South Carolina: The Reprint Company, 1980.

Wecter, Dixon. *The Age of the Great Depression: 1929–1941*. New York: Macmillan, 1948.

Wharton, Don. "Birth Control: The Case for the State," *Atlantic Monthly*, October 1939, pp. 463–465.

White, E. B. *Charlotte's Web*. New York: Harper and Row, 1957.

Whitley, Peggy. "American Cultural History, 1930–1939." http://www.nhmccd.edu/contracts/lrc/kc/decade30.html

Wilcox, Glenn C. "Introduction to the 4th edition of *The Southern Harmony and Musical Composition*." http://www.apadrecordings.com/southarm.htm

Wilson, Mildred and Nora Workman. *Chair Caning*. Raleigh, North Carolina: North Carolina Agricultural Extension Service, 1935.

Witty, Paul A. and Charles E. Skinner. *Mental Hygiene in Modern Education*. New York: Farrar and Rinehart, Inc., 1939.

Wolfe, Margaret Ripley. *Daughters of Canaan*. Lexington, Kentucky: University of Kentucky Press, 1995.

Womack, Jim. Rutherford County Farm Museum, Forest City, North Carolina, August 4, 1999.

Wormser, Richard. *Growing Up in the Great Depression*. New York: Atheneum, 1994.

Yandle, Lois Moore. *The Spirit of a Proud People*. Columbia, SC: Wentworth Printing Corporation, 1997.

"Yesterdayland: Toys." http://www.yesterdayland.com/popopedia/shows/decades/toys1930s.php

# *Index*

AAA  8, 9, 15, 45, 46, 49, 50, 225, 238
Academy Award  114, 199
Adams, Ola Mae Shockley  151
Aderholt, O. F.  180, 182
adult education  130, 133
Adult Educational Group  133
AFL  179
African American women  98, 99, 100, 101
African Americans  34, 81, 82, 100, 101, 128, 130; North Carolina  79, 100, 101
Agricultural Adjustment Administration  8, 15, 45, 46, 49, 50, 225, 238
Alcohol  54, 55, 56, 154, 155,
American Farm Bureau Foundation  37
American Federation of Labor  179
American Tobacco Company  57
*Amos 'n' Andy*  194
Asheville  19, 42, 43, 198, 215, 217, 218, 219, 221
Austin, Woodrow "Woody"  213
Automobiles  3, 6
Avery County  67
Avondale Methodist Church  204

Bailey, Linnie  47
Bankhead Cotton Act  50
Bankhead-Jones Act of 1937, 50, 51
baptismal services  203
Barbee, Carolyn, vii  96
Barnwell, Mildred Gwin  123
baseball  212, 213
Beal, Fred  179, 180, 181
Beaufort  21
Belcross  172, 235
Bessemer City  180

Best, Selma Philbeck  67, 70, 98, 207
Bethel Baptist Church  192, 205
Bickett, Thomas W.  176
Big Apple  209
Big Little Books  197
Biggerstaff, Frances  184
Biggerstaff, Virginia (Rucker)  149
birth rate (NC)  77
Black, Gertrude  136
Black Tuesday (October 29, 1929)  5
Blackwood, Wayne  vii
Blanton, Mae, vii  108, 110
blood  104
Bluegrass Festival  220
Boiling Springs  218
Boney, Dan C.  81
Bonus Army  8
Bonus Expeditionary Force  8
books  198
bootlegging  56
Bostic  72
*Boxcar Bertha*  88
boxcar children  86
Boyd, Rosamonde Ramsey  204, 206
Brain Trust  8, 238
brewing  54
Briarhoppers  195
Brokaw, Tom  116
Brooks, B. B.  65
Brooks, John, vii  65, 67
bums  88
Burke County  19
Burns, Cleo  108, 114, 138
Burns, Nell, v  1, 42, 67, 84, 118, 119, 120, 121, 128, 132, 135, 136, 137, 148, 149, 150, 153, 154, 157, 158, 164, 189, 190, 197, 201, 203, 204, 218
Burns, Robert Ewart  69, 120, 151, 201, 215, 222, 224
Bushong, A. B.  48, 74, 75, 103, 105, 138, 143, 216, 217

Cadets of Temperance  54
Café society  210
Caldecott Award  120
Camels  57, 58
campaign buttons  93
Cannon, Charles A.  163
Cannon Mill  185
Cape Fear River  18
card games  188
Caroleen  96
Carolina food  159, 160, 208, 209
Carolina Power and Light Company  165
Carpenter, Dewey S. Jr.  97, 97
Carpenter, Dewey S. Sr.  96, 97
Carpenter, Lucille, vii  109
Carpenter, Walda, vii  6, 40, 97, 113, 114, 128, 138, 139, 143
Carrboro  120, 155, 158
Cash, W.J.  218
Caswell County  34, 109, 110, 169
CCC  8, 15, 26, 38, 40, 41, 113
chain gang  94
Chapel Hill  76, 77, 124, 125, 129, 136, 137, 138, 182, 183, 214, 219, 233
Charleston (dance)  209
Charlotte  42, 44, 179, 180, 206, 212, 213
*Charlotte's Web*  120, 121
Chatham County  20
Cherokee  84, 85, 86, 107, 108, 128, 129, 156, 158, 159, 213, 214
Cherokee County  84
Cherokee Indian Reservation  84, 85, 86
Cherryville  217
Chesterfield  57
chestnut tree  44
Chicago World's Fair  24
child labor  95, 115, 116, 117, 118, 119, 123, 175
children  115, 116
Chimney Rock  9

chitlins 106
churches 201
CIO 186, 228
circuses 213
civic groups 208
Civil Works Administration 25
Civilian Conservation Corps 8, 15, 26, 38, 40, 41, 113
class structure 177
Cleveland County 212, 217
Cliffside 126, 200
Cliffside Mills 16, 17, 53
Cliffside School 126
Cliffside Steam Station 167, 168
clothing for women 109
Cole, Grady 195, 213
Colfax Free Fair 74, 216, 217
Colfax Gin 52
college sports 213
Collins, Helen vii
Committee on Industrial Organization 186
Communism 179, 180, 181, 182
compensation (unemployment) 90
Compton, Billy 120
Comstock Law 77
Concord 177
conserving food 102
consolidation 129, 136, 137
construction toys 189
contraception 77, 150
Coolidge, Calvin 63
cottage industries 100
Cotton Acreage REduction Week 46
county agent 38
Cramer, Stuart W. 161
Cramerton Mills 161
crime rate 94
Croatan National Forest 64
Curtis, Donnis, vii 103, 104, 105, 106, 107, 118, 128, 150, 169, 193, 194, 207

dance marathon 209, 210
dances 209
Dare County 133
Darrow, Charles 187
Daughters of Temperance 54
Daves, Fay 192
Daves, Zeb 192
Davis, Archie K. Fellowship vii
Davis, Betty Toney 33
Davis, Buren Lee 104, 105, 106, 107
Davis, Getty 1, 35, 36, 37, 99, 102, 156, 157, 168, 169, 170, 217
Davis, John 23, 24, 35, 156, 157, 168, 169, 170
Davis, John Ed 168, 169
Davis, Pitt 24
Davis, Robert 44
Davis, Tracy 108
Delano, Jack 16, 172, 173, 235, 236, 240
Department of Agriculture 238
Dewey, Thomas E. 93

Dillon, Imogene, viii 7, 33
Director of Negro Welfare 80
Dismal Swamp 18
Disney, Walt 199, 201
domestic workers 100
Dorn, Etol 23
dropout rate 95, 125, 126, 130
drought 13, 15
Duke, James B. 51
Duke Power Company 150, 151, 165, 166, 167, 168
Duke University 214
Duncan, A. C. 84
Dunn, Joe vii
Durham 57, 81, 165, 174, 186, 214
Durham County 100

Eagle Roller Mill 67
Education 95, 96; African American 138; males 95, 96
Ehringhaus, John Christoph Blucher 46, 128, 130, 132, 133, 166
Eisenhower, Dwight 8
election results of 1932 90
election results of 1936 90
election results of 1940 90
electrification 164, 165, 166, 167
Elevjhem, Conrad 141
Ellenboro 52, 53, 63, 60, 71, 74, 89, 103, 105, 111, 138, 192, 202, 205, 217
Ellenboro School 202
Ellenboro School Chick Hatchery 48
Emergency Relief Appropriation 170
Employment: children 95; men 94
employment statistics: North Carolina 92; United States 92
*Endothia parasitica* 44
Engel van Wiseman Book Corporation 197
Evans, Walker 51, 230, 231, 234, 236, 240, 241
exhibit trains 4

fairs 213, 215, 216, 217, 224, 225
"fake food" 209
fall line 16
Farm Bureau 208
Farm Security Administration 9, 105, 110, 170, 225, 238
Farmers Home Administration 168, 169
farms 30
Fayetteville 174
Federal Emergency Relief Administration 122, 123, 130, 131, 169, 228
Federal Farm Board 46
federal photographs 1, 2, 15, 16, 219, 225, 226, 227, 228, 229, 230, 231, 232, 233, 234, 235, 236, 240
federal relief (1932) 81
Federal Wages and Hours Act of 1938 123

Federal Writer's Project 1, 21, 157, 158, 159
feldspar 67, 96
FERA 122, 123, 130, 131, 228
*Fighting President* 197, 198
Fireside Chats 195, 196
fireside industries 100
fishing 18, 21
flood of 1940 17,19
FmHA 168, 169
food (African American) 159, 160, food (Carolina) 159, 160, 208, 209
food companies 109
foodstuffs 67
Force Act of 1870 83
Forest City 84
forests 60
Foster, E. O. 49
Freeman, Martha vii
freight rates 72, 73
Frogboro 134
FSA 9, 105, 110, 170, 225
FSA–OWI Collection, iv 8, 9, 18, 19, 20, 29, 30, 31, 34, 36, 37, 47, 49, 51, 59, 60, 63, 77, 78, 81, 87, 82, 88. 101, 105, 109, 110, 115, 116, 119, 120, 134, 141, 152, 153, 155, 158, 164, 169, 170, 171, 173, 211, 214
Fuquay Springs 18
furniture 67

Gallup Poll 50
Gamble, Clarence J. 77
Gardner, O. Max 48, 108, 124, 127, 128, 130, 133, 136, 149, 182
Garner 55, 57
Garner, John N. 92, 93
Gaston County 112, 127, 161, 162, 163, 178, 179, 180, 181, 182, 217
Gastonia 112, 127, 161, 162, 163, 178, 179, 180, 181, 182, 184, 185
Gehrig, Lou 196
general store 210, 211
Gibbs, Jessie, vii 104, 152, 153, 211, 212, 218
Gibson Mill 185
Gibsonville 174
Gilbreth, Frank 176
Gilbreth, Lillian Evelyn 176
Goldberger, Joseph 36, 141, 142, 143
Gosnell, Lisa vii
government housing 82
government stills 56
Graham 47
Graham, Billy 206, 207
Graham, Frank Porter 2, 76, 137, 138, 182, 183
Graham County 84
Grandfather Mountain 220
granite 67, 68
Grant, C. D. 105
Granville County 16, 20, 101, 211
Great Smoky Mountains National Park 21, 40, 42, 64, 65, 66, 85, 91

# Index

"Greatest Generation" 116, 117
Green, Paul 26, 219, 220
Green, William 179
Green Pastures Rally 42
Greene, Dorothy vii
Griffin, Charles 9
Grindstaff, Ervin 96
gristmills 70
Grove, Edwin 61, 147, 148, 149, 221, 223, 224,
Grove Park Inn 42, 43, 61, 147, 148, 149, 221, 223, 224
Guilford County 170

Halifax County 82, 235
Ham, Mordecai 204, 205, 206
"Ham and Ram" 204
Hamrick, Fannie Lou 80
Hamrick, Reba, vii 32
Hamrick's Lumber Yard 62, 63
Harnett County 219
Hatcheries: chick 74; fish 21
Haw River 20
Haynes, Charles H. 126
Haynes, Raleigh Rutherford 17, 53
Haynes Mills 126
health: African American 155, 156; Native American 156
health departments 149, 150, 151
Hearst, Wiliam Randolph 90
Henderson, Gary 142
high school sports 213
higher education 138
Hine, Lewis 117, 237
Hinson, A. W. 185
Hitler, Adolf 196
Hiwassee Dam 28, 29
hoboes (unattached, penniless people looking for work) 80
Hoey, Clyde R. 57, 72, 73, 75, 77, 111, 123, 124, 132, 133
hog killings 105, 106, 107
holidays 215, 216, 217, 218
Hollis 131
Hollis School 136, 137, 150
Home Demonstration Clubs 107, 108, 109, 111, 138, 208
Hood, Charles Newton 135
hookworm 143, 145, 146, 147
Hoover, Herbert 7, 90, 93
Hoover carts 6
Hooverville 8
Hopewell Methodist Church 201
Hopkins, Harry 130
"How the La Rue Stakes Were Lost" 135
hurricanes 13

"I Gave My Love an Apple" 190, 191
illiteracy 125, 126
images of women 114, 115
income (per capita for NC and US) 89, 90
industries: cottage 100; fireside 100
infant mortality 79
Inland Waterway 23

insurance commissioner (NC) 81
Interstate Commerce Commission 86

Jackson County 84
Johnson, Hugh 90
Johnson, J.A. 31, 119
Johnston County 172
Johnstone, G. A. 178, 179
Jolly, Mack, vii 22
Jones, H. G. vii 1, 115, 116
Jones, Sarah vii
Jones, T. W. vii 6

Kannapolis 163, 177
kaolin 65
Kelley, Kenneth vii
Kelley, Norma vii
*Kitty Foyle* 114, 199
KKK *see* Ku Klux Klan
Knights of Labor 174
Ku Klux Klan 83, 84
Ku Klux Klan Act (1871) 83
Kuralt, Charles 9, 157
Kyser, Kay 193

Labor Day strike of 1934 184
labor movement before 1880s 174
Lake Junaluska 201, 218
Lake Lure 9, 10, 11, 42
Lake Lure Inn 9, 10, 11
Landon, Alfred M. 90, 93
Lange, Dorothea 29, 30, 31, 36, 51, 59, 88, 229, 230, 236, 240
Leakesville 180
Ledbetter Mill 72
*Let Us Now Praise Famous Men* 231
letters to President Franklin Delano Roosevelt 91, 121, 122
Leviticus 104, 105, 106
Lewis, John L. 186
Lexington 180
Liggett and Myers 57
*Little Orphan Annie* 193, 194, 187, 188, 197
"Live at Home" 48, 108
livermush 106
Lodge 7 of the Grand United Order of Odd Fellows 82
Logan, Frances 203
Long, Will West 214
Loray Mill 178, 179, 180
*Lost Colony* 26, 27, 219, 220
Louis, Joe 196, 197
Lovelace, T. B. 17
Lowry, Fuller 88
Lucky Strike 57, 58
Lumbee tribe 88

MacArthur, Douglas 8
malaria 147
Manteo 22, 26, 27
manufacturing 67
Manville-Jenckes Company 178, 179
marble 68

Marion 161, 180
marriage rate 94
Martin, Annette, vii 5, 23, 107, 144, 151
Martin, Dan, vii 104, 105, 106, 107
Martin, Jo Ann vii
Martin, Sarah Harrill 102
Martin, T. W. vii 7, 8, 10, 87, 89, 133, 138
McArthur, W. H. vii 4, 5, 11, 144, 208
McArthur Will 4, 5, 11, 208
McCann Erickson Company 63, 95
McDaniel, Thomas R. vii
McGee, Susan, vii 192
McGowan Community Cannery 104
McKinney Mill 70, 71
Mebane 63, 64
Methodist Youth Fellowship 201, 218
men 96
mica 65, 66, 67
migrant workers 88, 172,
migration of African Americans 79
mill village 126, 127, 161, 162, 163, 165
mill village school 126, 127
mills 16
mining 65
Mitchell County 67
Model T 3, 4,
molasses 157
Monopoly 187
moonshining 54, 55, 56,
Mooresboro 96
Morley, Christopher 114
Morrill Act 37
Morse, Locus B. 9
Mount Olive 81
mules 31, 32, 33, 49
music 191, 192
Mydans, Carl 171, 227, 228, 236, 240
MYF 201, 218

National Emergency Council 2, 29, 72, 73, 76, 77
national forests 64
National Industrial Recovery Act 90, 186
national purchase units 64
National Recovery Administration 83, 90, 91, 92
National Textile Workers Union 179
National Youth Administration 121, 131, 138
Native Americans (NC) 85, 107, 128, 129, 213
NEC 2, 29, 72, 73, 76, 77
New York World's Fair 224
NIRA 90, 186
Niven, David 199
Norfolk Southern Depot 73
North Carolina Art Society 218

North Carolina Department of Labor 186
North Carolina Erosion Control Project 26
North Carolina Industrial Commission 186
North Carolina Labor Law of 1937 123
North Carolina Militia 177
North Carolina State Department of Conservation of Development 21
North Carolina State Salary Commission 133
North Carolina Symphony 218
NRA 83, 90, 91, 92
NTWU 179
NYA 121, 131, 138

Oakley, Titus 101
Office of War Information 25, 225, 235, 239
Old Maid 188
Ole Time Fiddlers Festival 220
one-room schoolhouses 128
outdoor games 197
Outer Banks 96, 219, 220
OWI 25, 225, 235, 239
Oxford 134, 135
Oxley, Lawrence Augustus 80
oysters 21, 24, 25

parades 208
Parkdale Mill 185
parlor games 187
Parramore, Thomas vii
pellagra 36, 140, 141, 142, 143
Pembroke Farms 87
Penderlea Homesteads 105, 116, 170, 171
perlew 160
perloo 160
perlou 160
Pershing, George 180, 181
Person County 29, 59
photographers, federal 219, 225, 226, 227, 228, 229, 230, 231, 232, 233, 234, 235, 236
Piedmont Organizing Council 177, 178
Pineville 180
pirlou 160
Pisgah National Forest 64
Plum Tree 96
Plymouth Box and Panel Company 63, 95
POC 177, 178
Poe, Clarence Hamilton 40
poliomyelitis 139, 147
population statistics of North Carolina 78, 92
pork 159, 160
potatoes (sweet) 74, 103, 104, 105
POUR 7
preserving food 102, 103
Price, Arthur Fred 66, 67

Price, Edward Rollins, vii 96
Price, Falls vii
Price, Paul 89
Price, Plato Rollins 44, 96, 189, 190, 211, 212
Price, Roy 96
Proctor and Gamble 77
*Progressive Farmer* 39, 40
Prohibition 3, 51, 52, 54
Pruette, Beulah 32, 62, 69, 70, 97, 103
public schools 124, 125, 126, 127, 128, 132
publications of the 1930s for children 198
Pythian Order of Greensboro 82

Qualla Reserve 84, 85, 86, 107, 213
quarries 68
Queen Ann Mill 53

RA 9, 50, 160, 169, 170, 171, 172, 225, 229, 238, 239
radio 191, 192, 193
railroad trespasser 86
Raleigh 81, 174
Ramsey, Rosamonde 204, 206
REA 166
recreation parks 213, 217
registration (African American) 83
Reidsville 57, 186
relief agencies (NC) 80
remedies 152, 153, 154
*Report on Economic Conditions of the South* 2, 76, 140
*Report to the President* 77
Resettlement Administration 9, 50, 160, 169, 170, 171, 172, 225, 229, 238, 239
revivals 203, 204
Reynolds, R. J. 57, 58
Rhodes Manufacturing Company 117
rickets 141
Riis, Jacob 237
Roanoke Island Amphitheatre 26, 219
Robertson's Cotton Gin 47
Rocky Broad River 9
Rocky Mount 104
Rogers, Ginger 114
Roosevelt, Eleanor 61, 121, 122
Roosevelt, Franklin Delano 1, 2, 8, 38, 40, 42, 45, 46, 48, 51, 61, 65, 66, 77, 90, 91, 92, 93, 121, 122, 130, 147, 148, 149, 195, 196, 197, 198
Rothstein, Arthur 18, 51, 60, 81, 115, 225, 226, 227, 234, 236, 240
Rural Electrification Administration 166
Rural Rehabilitation Division of the Federal Emergency Relief Administration 169
rural-urban profile (NC) 89
rural women 101, 102

rural youth 128
Rutherford County 40, 69, 96, 146, 205, 208, 212
Rutherfordton 4

SAL 89, 111
Schenck-Warlick Textile Mill 16
Schmeling, Max 196
school dropouts 120, 125, 126
school events 261
school law of 1933 125
school transportation 132
Scotland County 8
scrapple 106
Seaboard Airline Railway 89, 111
Seeley, Fred 61
segregation 83, 85, 86
serial 199
Shahn, Ben 51, 116, 228, 229, 236, 240
shape note singing 191, 192
sharecroppers 31, 34, 35
Shelby 42, 43, 67, 124
Shiloh Church 205
Shockley, Ola Mae 5, 7
Shoofly 16
Singing on the Mountain 220
*Sister of the Road* 88
Skelton, Nancy vii
skull controversy 225, 226
Smith, Alfred E. 83
*Snow White* 132, 199, 201
snuff 155
Social Security Act of 1935, 123
softball 212, 213
soil 29, 30
Soil Conservation and Domestic Allotment Act 50
Sons of Temperance 54
soul food 159
South Dakota 225, 226
Southern Combed Yarn Industry 112
*Southern Harmony* 191
Southern Power Company 150, 151, 165
Southport 21
Spindale 67, 70, 96
Spindale Mills 96
sports 213
Spruce Pine 67, 96
square dance 210
Statesville 31, 119
Stem 211
stills 55, 56, 57
storing food 103
Stryker, Roy 6, 8, 9, 15, 16, 50, 114, 172, 225, 229, 230, 231, 232, 233, 234, 235, 236, 237, 238, 239, 240
subsistence farming 156, 157
Subsistence Homesteads Division of the Department of the Interior 169
Swain County 84, 133
sweet potatoes 74, 103, 104, 105

Taft, William Howard 61
tariff 72, 73
teacherage 133
teachers 130, 131; African American 133
temperance 54
Tenant Purchase Program 170
tenants 34, 35, 132
Tennessee Valley Authority 28, 29
textbooks 133
textile unions 174, 175, 176, 177, 178
textile wages 174, 175, 176, 177, 178
textile workers (women) 183
textiles 67
theater 199
Thompson, Bertha 87, 88
Tidewater Power Company 165
tobacco 46, 56, 57, 58, 59, 60, 67, 154, 155
*Tobacco Road* 88
Toney, Fay 33
tourist attractions 220
tourist industry 74, 75
tractors 31, 32, 33
tramps 88
traveling entertainment 213
Tri-State Growers' Cooperative 46
Truman, Harry 93
Tugwell, Rexford 8, 15, 92, 172, 225, 227, 238
TVA 28, 29, 50

unemployment (African American) 82
unemployment compensation 90
Unemployment Compensation Commission 90
Union Grove 220
Unionization: from 1900 until end of World War I 174; in early 1920s 176; from 1927 through 1929 177, 178, 179, 180; in the 1930s 183
United Textile Workers 175, 176
University of North Carolina (Chapel Hill) 76, 77, 124, 125, 129, 136, 137, 138, 182, 183, 214, 219
UTW 175, 176
Uwharrie 64

vaccinations 150
Vachon, John 51, 82, 164, 169, 170, 234, 236, 240
Vanderbilt, Paul 239
View Master 188
Virginia Electric and Power Company 165

Wadesboro 37
wages 175, 176, 177
Walker, James, vii 17, 52, 52, 53, 71, 72, 74, 89, 105, 111, 126, 200, 202, 204, 205
Walker, Melissa vii
Wallace, Henry A. 50, 92, 93
War Relocation Authorities 290
Washburn, Benjamin E. 146, 147, 151, 152
Waters, Nell 136, 137
Watkins, Robert 32, 62, 69, 70, 72, 103, 120
Watkins Products 96
WBT 191, 195, 213
Weathers, Lee 42
Welfare Department 114
Wellmon, Carolyn, vii 23
whiskey running 56
Whistler, Anna McNeill 218
Whistler, James McNeill 218
White, E. B. 120, 121
White, Sam 63

White, Will 63
White Furniture 60, 61, 63, 64, 176
Whitesides, Elyas 6
Whitesides, Laura 6
whitewash 164
Wiggins, Ella May 180, 181, 182
Wilkie, Wendell 90
Willard, North Carolina 105, 116
Williams, Walker 191
Willis, Jeff vii
Wilson, Woodrow 61
Wilson Mills 129
Wilson, North Carolina 99
Winston-Salem 57, 88, 186
Wolcott, Marion Post 19, 20, 31, 34, 37, 47, 49, 51, 87, 101, 105, 109, 110, 119, 120, 134, 141, 152, 153, 155, 158, 169, 231, 232, 233, 234, 236, 240
Wolfe, Thomas 198, 218, 219
Women: 96, 98, 99, 100; African American 98, 99, 100, 183; textile workers 183
women in the work force 111, 112, 113, 114
women's clothing 109
Women's Clubs 107, 108
women's images 114, 115
Woodmen of the World 208
work force (women) 111, 112, 113, 114
Workmen's Compensation Act 186
Works Progress Administration 21, 26, 130, 131
World War I 3
WPA 21, 26, 130, 131, 191

Yancey County 67
Yanceyville 49, 109
Yandle, Lois Moore 212, 213
Yarborough, Sarah vii
Yelton Milling Company 67, 70

www.ingramcontent.com/pod-product-compliance
Lightning Source LLC
Chambersburg PA
CBHW081548300426
44116CB00015B/2796